# Cooking Yankee
# with a
# French Accent

# Cooking
# Yankee
## with a
# French Accent

## By Monique A. Belisle

Down East Books / Camden, Maine

ISBN 0-89272-207-X
Library of Congress Catalog Card Number 85-72751
Cover design by Karen Moody
Composition by Typeworks, Belfast, Me.
Printed by Capital City Press, Montpelier, Vt.
Manufactured in the United States of America

5   4   3   2   1

Down East Books / Camden, Maine

*Affectionately dedicated to my mother and teacher,*
*Rita Fournier Belisle,*
*whose love, encouragement, and confidence*
*have meant more to me than words can express.*

# Contents

Introduction                                          9

Nine Weeks of Menus                                  11

Meal Planning Ideas                                  14

A Note About Seasoned Salt                           17

Appetizers & Dips                                    19

Soups & Chowders                                     28

Beef                                                 36

Pork, Lamb, Veal (and Moose)                         46

Poultry                                              57

Fish & Seafood                                       69

Luncheon & Dinner Salads                             79

Salads & Salad Dressings                             82

Egg, Cheese & Vegetable Dinners                      90

Desserts                                             95

Vegetables                                          107

Biscuits & Breads, Noodles & Rice                   122

Butters & Sauces                                    128

Fruit                                               130

Beverages                                           132

Index                                               135

# Introduction

AMONG MY EARLIEST MEMORIES I cherish the look of pride on my father's face as dinner guests in our home showered my mother with praise for the daily feasts and French-Canadian specialties she prepared for our family and friends. I was eager to follow her example, to learn how to concoct meals that "pleased the eye as well as the palate," and I drank in everything she could teach me. By the time I was in high school I knew that I wanted to earn my living as a cook, and I spent summer vacations at the Oakledge Resort in Burlington, Vermont, studying the methods of the chef.

From those earliest days I yearned to own my own restaurant, and in 1965, with my friend and partner, Patricia Salters, opened the first full-service restaurant in Sanford, Maine. However, I still had a dream – of a fully equipped kitchen of my own design, surrounded by a fine restaurant. That dream came true in 1975, when Pat and I opened our highly successful Ogunquit establishment. Pat, an industrious soul, managed the front, business end of the restaurant, while I indulged myself in the kitchen, cooking – such joy!

We decided to operate the restaurant on a seasonal schedule, and each year in the off-season we traveled abroad, gathering new recipes and learning new skills. Armed with these, we began to feature an International Night at the restaurant, presenting foods of Europe and the Orient as well as our traditional New England cuisine touched with a dash of spice *à la Canadienne*. As a result, more and more often came the query from our patrons: "Could we have the recipe?" My standard reply was, "When I retire, I'll write a cookbook." And now, I have.

Pat and I have worked on this book for over three years (in the time not devoted to our second love, golf!): me, devising, refining, testing recipes; Pat, employing her organizational skills in arranging my efforts in manuscript form, as well as serving as amanuensis, guinea pig, and friend. Without her help, this book might never have come to be.

So, here they are: treasured family recipes, reflecting my French-Canadian heritage; traditional Yankee staples; the most requested favorites from my restaurant days; and classic European cuisine. I have also included many menu suggestions, for family meals as well as for entertaining, to help the busy cook wondering *what goes best with what?*

I hope that you will enjoy preparing the dishes in this book as much as I have enjoyed preparing the book for you. Bon appêtit!

*Monique A. Delisle*

# Nine Weeks of Menus

(In my family, Saturday is traditionally the cook's day off, a time to go out for dinner or to let another family member do the cooking. Along with these suggested menus, then, I'd also encourage you to adopt that pleasant tradition. Saturday's menu suggestion is: enjoy an evening out!)

## WEEK #1

Sunday: *Teriyaki Rib Roast of Beef*
Chawan-Mushi (Shrimp Custard Soup); Baked Bananas; Almond Rice; Stir-Fried Broccoli; Pineapple Snow; Lapa Lapa

Monday: *Fresh Vegetable Casserole*
Wedge of lettuce with Slavic Dressing; Bacon-Cheese Biscuits

Tuesday: *Beef in Oyster Sauce*
Chow Mein Noodles, Hot Spicy Peaches, fortune cookies

Wednesday: *Chicken Cacciatora alla Romana*
Egg Noodles, Cheesy-Crouton Salad, Mocha-Ricotta Custard

Thursday: *Country Style Pork Ribs*
*in Tangy Sauce*
Quick Baked Chili-Cheese Potatoes,

Green Beans Almondine

Friday: *Baked Haddock au Gratin*
Noodles and Cashew Toss, Spinach and Grapefruit Sauté

## WEEK #2

Sunday: *Roast Duckling in Brandied*
*Orange-Raspberry Sauce*
Almond Rice; Maman's Golden Salad; Broccoli in Lemon; Peppermint Patty Crêpes

Monday: *Mussels with Linguine*
Gabrielle's Green Salad; French Garlic Toast

Tuesday: *Wok Pepper Steak*
Oriental Steamed Rice; Avocado Sunshine Salad with Orange Mayonnaise

Wednesday: *Olé Molé Chocolate Chicken*
Egg noodles; mixed greens with Celery-Seed Dressing

Thursday: *Baked Stuffed Pork Chops*
Maple Baked Apples; Bacon-Fried Corn

Friday: *Applejack Filet of Sole*
Whipped Chantilly Potatoes, Onion and Fruit Sauté

11

## WEEK #3

Sunday: *Pork Loin Roast Lyonnaise*
Whipped Potatoes; Onion-Buttered Broccoli; Jellied Waldorf Salad; White Russian Pie

Monday: *Baked Chicken Breast Yvette*
Egg noodles; salad greens with Herbal Vinaigrette Dressing

Tuesday: *Pork Chow Mein*
Spinach-Mandarin Salad; Hot Orange Pudding

Wednesday: *Delmonico Steaks Roquefort*
Blue-Cheese Stuffed Potatoes; Zucchini in Anisette

Thursday: *Sautéed Calf's Liver with Bacon Rolls and Broiled Bananas*
Oriental Steamed Rice; Green Beans Almondine

Friday: *Tuna Patricia*
Eggplant Parmigiana

## WEEK #4

Sunday: *Halibut Trois Rivières*
Lyonnaise Potatoes; Tomatoes Dijon; Cheesy-Crouton Salad; Cheese-It Biscuits; Banana Split Ice Cream Pie; Café Royale

Monday: *Pain de Boeuf Fromager (Beef and Cheese Loaf)*
Baked Stuffed Potatoes; Hot Spicy Peaches

Tuesday: *Soy Sauced Chicken Bake*
Oriental Steamed Rice; celery sticks; Banana Split Salad

Wednesday: *Pork Chops alla Parmigiana on Toasted Garlic Bread*
Pasta; Cheesy-Crouton Salad; chianti

Thursday: *Rich Man–Poor Man Steak au Poivre*
Cheese-Chive Potatoes; French Style Peas

Friday: *White Fish Piquant*
New Potatoes in Lemon Sauce; Creamy Green Beans

## WEEK #5

Sunday: *Roast Chicken with Fruit and Nut Stuffing*
Canadian Cheese Soup; Whipped Potatoes; giblet gravy; Acorn Squash Bake; Cranberry Salad; Flamed Coffee Ice Cream Sipper

Monday: *Chili by Rhum*
Cheese-It Biscuits; garden salad with Parisienne Dressing

Tuesday: *Filet of Sole Oriental*
Oriental Steamed Rice; Stir-Fried Broccoli

Wednesday: *Fettuccine Armando*
Easy and Grand Caesar Salad; Baked French Bread and Cheese

Thursday: *Pork in Apple Cider*
Whipped Potatoes; Onion and Fruit Sauté

Friday: *Baked Stuffed Jumbo Shrimp*
Rice au Gratin; Spinach Elegante

## WEEK #6

Sunday: *Sirloin Steak with Béarnaise Sauce*
Baked Stuffed Potato; Broiled Tomato Slices; Athenian Salad; Bacon-Cheese Biscuits; Mud Pie; Johnny's Amazing Hot Apple Pie

Monday: *Stir-Fried Chicken and Cashews*
Oriental Steamed Rice; Spinach Mandarin Salad

Tuesday: *Sweet and Sour Pork*
Oriental Steamed Rice; Almond Float

Wednesday: *Poulet Suisse*
French bread toast; carrot sticks; broccoli; cauliflowerets

Thursday: *Beef Stroganoff*
Buttered egg noodles; Onion-Buttered Broccoli

Friday: *Broiled Scallops in Garlic Butter*
Bordeaux Potatoes; Broccoli in Lemon


## WEEK #7

Sunday: *Roti D'Agneau*
*(Roast Leg of Lamb Provençal)*
Minted Grapefruit; Skewers of Baked French Bread and Cheese; Potatoes au Gratin; hearts of lettuce with Roquefort Dressing; Orangey-Orange Parfait

Monday: *Quiche Lorraine with Pistachios*
Banana Split Salad; Onion-Buttered Green Beans

Tuesday: *Chicken Cantonese with*
*Soft Fried Noodles*
Fortune cookies

Wednesday: *Baked Sirloin Steak*
Quick-Baked Cheese-Garlic Potato; Spinach-Mandarin Salad

Thursday: *Choucroute Garnie*
*(Pork Meats over Sauerkraut)*
Small boiled potatoes; Dijon mustard

Friday: *Haddock à l'Orange*
Baked Potato; Green Beans Almondine


## WEEK #8

Sunday: *Champagne Ham*
Sweet Potatoes à la Sugar Shack; Baked Stuffed Oranges; Cheese-Custard Broccoli; Gabrielle's Green Salad; Apple Fritters

Monday: *Asparagus au Gratin Casserole*
Cucumber and Onion Slices in Sour Cream; Bacon-Cheese Biscuits

Tuesday: *Stuffed Chicken Breasts Polynesian*
Steamed Rice; Buttered Peas; Almond Float

Wednesday: *Fruit and Calf's Liver Flambé*
Egg noodles; Green Beans Almondine

Thursday: *Steak Diane*
Shoestring Potatoes; Mushroom Caps; Broiled Tomato Slices

Friday: *Maman's Salmon Pie*
Creamed Green Beans; Jellied Waldorf Salad


## WEEK #9

Sunday: *Baked Stuffed Filet of Sole Bertrand*
Baked Potato, Roman Style; Carrots Vichy; Strawberries Belle-Isle Parfait; Café Royale

Monday: *Boeuf Poitou*
Hearts of lettuce with Slavic Dressing

Tuesday: *Sesame Chicken with*
*Cumberland Sauce*
Oriental Steamed Rice; Spinach-Mandarin Salad

Wednesday: *Pork Chops in a Jiffy*
Whipped potato; mushroom gravy; Orange-Glazed Carrots

Thursday: *Coq au Vin*
Baked Potato "Stuffies"; Frozen Cheese-Strawberry Salad

Friday: *Rainbow Trout Italiano*
Easy and Grand Caesar Salad; Cheese-It Biscuits

# Meal Planning Ideas

*Fettucine Armando*
Easy and Grand Caesar Salad; Baked French Bread and Cheese; vintage Petit Sirah

*Baked Sirloin Steak*
Quick-Baked Cheddar-Garlic Potatoes; Spinach Mandarin Salad; Cheese-It Biscuits; Orangey-Orange Parfait; black tea

*Chicken Cantonese with Soft Fried Noodles*
Fortune cookies; Chinese tea

*Stuffed Chicken Breasts in Supreme Sauce*
Oriental Steamed Rice; Broiled Tomato Slices; Café Royale

*Beef Stroganoff*
Buttered egg noodles; Broccoli with Fresh Lemon; hot rolls; rosé wine; Strawberries Belle Isle; tea

*Turkey Parmigiana*
Pasta; Easy and Grand Caesar Salad; Mocha-Ricotta Custard; coffee

*Veal Jeannine*
Chantilly Potatoes; Fresh Asparagus with Lemon; Instant Strawberry Ice; mint tea

*Pork Chops in a Jiffy*
Whipped potatoes; mushroom gravy; Onion and Fruit Sauté; Hot Apple Fritters; coffee

*Soy-Glazed Scallops*
Oriental Steamed Rice; Fresh Vegetable Stir-Fry; Chocolate-Cinnamon Fudge Parfait; almond tea

*Broiled Ham Slices in Brandied Raspberry Sauce*
Sweet Potatoes; Broiled Pineapple Slices; Fresh Rolls; salad greens with Herbal Vinaigrette Dressing; raspberry sherbet; chilled ginger ale

*Asparagus au Gratin Casserole*
Spiced Hot Peaches; Bacon and Cheese Biscuits; Petits Pôts de Chocolat; coffee

*Haddock Macadamia*
Egg noodles; Spinach and Grapefruit Sauté; Stuffed French Bread; Hurry-up Elegant Glazed Cake; lemon spiced tea

*Wok Pepper Steak*
Oriental Steamed Rice; Stir-Fried Broccoli; Avocado Sunshine Salad with

Orange Mayonnaise; Lemon Cookies; herbal tea

**Lobster Stew**
Oyster crackers; fresh tossed salad with Celery Seed Dressing; light Beaujolais wine; lemon sherbet; tea

## SPECIAL DINNERS

**Standing Rib Roast of Beef, au Jus**
Cream of Carrot Soup; Yorkshire Pudding; Lyonnaise Potatoes; Cauliflower Mornay; Jellied Waldorf Salad; Cherries Jubilee; a pony of Benedictine

**Flamed Tenderloin Steak, Dijon**
Tomato-Cheese Soup; Haddock à l'Orange; Lemon Sorbet; Baked Stuffed Roman Potatoes; Fresh asparagus tossed with toasted almonds; hot rolls; fresh fruit with Ice Cream Dressing; Marinated Strawberries and Kiwi; coffee

**Chicken Breasts in Apricot Sauce**
Cold Maine Blueberry Soup; egg noodles; Cheese-Custard Broccoli; Frozen Cheese and Strawberry Salad; Petits Pôts de Chocolat; Café Cointreau

**Apricot-Almond Glazed Pork**
Brandied Pumpkin Soup; Chantilly Potatoes; French Style Peas; hot rolls; Rita's Cinnamon Apple Roll; Café Royale

## LUNCHEONS

**Quiche Lorraine with Pistachios**
Banana Split Salad; Green Beans Almondine; Petits Pôts de Chocolat; coffee and tea. (Serves 6)

**Camille's Vegetable Dinner Salad**
Pâté Maison with little toast rounds; Brandied Macaroons; coffee and tea. (Serves 6)

**Mini Crabmeat Puffs**
Parmesan Mousse with pretzels; Fresh Asparagus with Lemon; Cheddar Cheese Broccoli Bake; Cranberry and Fruit Salad; relishes; Brandied Banana Bread; Galette des Rois; coffee and tea. (Serves 12)

## SUNDAY BRUNCH

**Eggs Monique**
Fresh Fruit à la Grand Marnier; Sticky Caramel Buns; coffee; milk

**Eggs Oscar, Dijon**
Spring Greens Soup; Fruit Scones with Strawberry Butter; orange-spice tea

## "PARENTS' NIGHT OUT" MEALS
### (Prepare ahead or cook the day before, heat and serve)

**Steak Roast Wrap with Vegetables**
Wedge of lettuce with Slavic Dressing; rewarmed Bacon and Cheese Biscuits; Mint Surprise Cookies; milk

**Ragoût de Poule aux Boulettes**
Egg noodles (added at cooking time); French Bread; Gabrielle's Green Salad; Mud Pie; milk

**Pain de Boeuf Fromager**
Baked Potatoes; Frozen Cheese and Strawberry Salad; Chewy Peanut Butter and Chocolate Bars; milk

**Brother Paul's Italian Sauce Parmigiana with Spaghetti and Meatballs**
French Garlic Bread; salad greens with Italian Cheese Dressing; grapes; chocolate mints; milk

## SUMMERTIME DINING

*Hickory Smoked Turkey*
> Foil-Baked Potatoes; tossed salad; Roasted Corn; French Garlic Bread; Instant Strawberry Ice; minted iced tea

*Steak and Mushroom Dinner Salad*
> Canadian Potato Salad; Maman's Golden Salad; Stuffed French Bread; Frozen Chocolate Chip Cheesecake; iced lemonade

*Charcoal Grilled Chicken with Peach Glaze*
> New England "Stuffies"; Broccoli with Lemon in Foil; Cucumber and Onion Slices in Sour Cream; Peaches and Cream Parfait; iced coffee

*Teriyaki Sirloin Steak*
> Cook-Out Potatoes; Foil-Baked Bananas; Spinach Mandarin Salad; Chocolate-Cherry Mint Ice Cream Pie; coffee

# A Note About Seasoned Salt

I have developed this savory blend of herbs and spices to enhance the natural flavors of many foods. You'll find it listed as an ingredient in recipes throughout this book — about 100 of them! — so it's a good idea to make up a batch to have on hand as you cook. If you run out, regular salt will do, though with a certain amount of flavor lost. Also, when cooking for those on a low-sodium diet (or for anyone conscious of salt intake) you will probably want to reduce the amount of Seasoned Salt or regular salt used, but do include at least a dash, if allowed, to bring out the best in these dishes.

A jar of this Seasoned Salt also makes a delightful gift for a budding chef.

## Seasoned Salt

*Makes 1¼ cups*

1 cup table salt
1 teaspoon dried thyme leaves
1½ tablespoons garlic salt
2 teaspoons dried oregano
½ teaspoon dried dill
2 teaspoons paprika
1 teaspoon curry powder
1 tablespoon dry mustard
1 teaspoon onion powder

Combine all ingredients in a blender bowl and process until all the spices are completely mixed. Store in a jar with a tight lid.

# Appetizers & Dips

## Apricot Steak Bites

*The brandied marinade makes the difference.*

*Makes 10 to 12     Cooking time: 10 to 15 minutes*

1 pound lean, tender beef
½ cup apricot brandy
20 to 24 small whole mushrooms

Trim all fat from meat. Discard fat. Cut meat into 1-inch cubes. Pour apricot brandy over meat cubes, turning to coat. Cover and marinate at room temperature 2 to 3 hours. Drain and reserve marinade. Preheat oven to broil. Using 4- to 5-inch skewers, alternate 2 steak cubes and 2 mushrooms on each skewer. Broil 5 inches from heat source 10 to 15 minutes, or until desired doneness, turning occasionally and basting with the marinade.

## Gourmet Avocado Dip

*Serve with taco chips, with a seafood cocktail, or as stuffing for a tomato.*

*Makes 2½ cups     Cooking time: 15 minutes*

1 cup potatoes, mashed and cooled

1 medium avocado, peeled and
  seeded
2 tablespoons lemon juice
½ teaspoon Seasoned Salt (page 17)
¼ teaspoon pepper
1 clove garlic, pressed
¼ cup heavy cream
2 tablespoons olive oil
¼ teaspoon chili powder
⅛ teaspoon hot pepper sauce

Cut avocado into large chunks, place in blender with lemon juice, blend. Add mashed potatoes and remaining ingredients; blend until smooth. Chill at least one hour before serving to allow flavors to blend.

## Baked Clams

*Simply delicious.*

*Serves 4     Cooking time: 5 to 10 minutes*

2 pounds (about 24 medium) fresh
  clams
3 tablespoons salt
¼ cup butter or margarine, softened
1 garlic clove, minced
dash of Seasoned Salt (page 17)

19

2 slices of bacon
beer
¼ cup fresh Parmesan cheese, finely
  grated

Place clams with salt in a sink half full of cold water and let soak. Meanwhile, combine the softened butter with the garlic and Seasoned Salt, mix well. Partially cook the bacon, cool it slightly, and cut into ½-inch pieces. Set aside.

Drain the clams, rinse thoroughly. Discard any with opened or cracked shells. Pour ¼ inch of beer into a Dutch oven. Add the clams. Cover and cook one minute after steaming begins. Drain. (The strained cooking liquid makes a delicious drink.) Discard top half of shells. Remove the neck membrane and replace clams in the half shells.

Preheat oven to broil. Top each clam with a dab of garlic butter, a pinch of cheese, and a piece of bacon. Place under the broiler, 5 inches from the heat source, and cook until the bacon is crisp. Serve very hot.

## Barbecued Chicken Wings

*Feature these tasty morsels as the first course in your Oriental dinner.*

*Makes 24 pieces*            *Marinate overnight*
                        *Cooking time: 30 minutes*

  12 chicken wings
  1 teaspoon salt
  3 garlic cloves, chopped
  ½ teaspoon ginger
  ¼ cup hoisin sauce
  2 tablespoons sherry

Remove tips from chicken wings and discard. Cut wings in two at the joint. Rinse and pat dry. Run a sharp knife around one end of joint to cut tendons, push meat toward other end, making a handle of one end. Sprinkle salt over chicken pieces and rub in well. Place in a casserole dish. Combine remaining ingredients in blender bowl,

process until smooth, pour over chicken. Cover and chill overnight or at least 8 hours, turning once. Preheat oven to 375°. Lay pieces on rack in a shallow baking pan. Bake 15 minutes, turn, baste with marinade, and bake until tender, about 15 minutes more.

## Cheese-Onion Tidbits

*Makes 15 to 20 pieces      Cooking time: 5 minutes*

  ¼ cup mayonnaise
  ½ cup fresh Parmesan cheese, finely
    grated
  2 dashes hot pepper sauce
  dash of Seasoned Salt (page 17)
  1 loaf small party rye bread
  1 medium, sweet Bermuda onion,
    sliced thin

Combine mayonnaise, cheese, hot pepper sauce, and salt. Blend well. Spread mixture on slices of the party bread. Top each with enough of the center of the onion slice to cover the bread (save outer rings for another dish), and cover with additional mayonnaise mixture.

Preheat oven to broil. Broil until tops are bubbly. Serve at once.

## Christmas Wreath of Vegetables

*An attractive and nourishing platter. Herbs and lemon rind add a distinctive flavor.*

*Serves 12            Cooking time: 15 minutes*

  1 medium head cauliflower
  1 medium bunch broccoli
  1 lemon
  2 cloves garlic
  1 bay leaf
  3 tablespoons Seasoned Salt
    (page 17)
  1 pint cherry tomatoes

Cut stems from cauliflower and broccoli and trim into florets. Cut the rind from the lemon, using the yellow part only – no white (save lemon for the dressing). Place rind in a large pot of boiling water with the garlic, bay leaf, and salt. Boil for 5 minutes. Add vegetables, return to a boil, and cook 4 minutes.

Drain immediately and rinse in cold water. Shake dry. Discard seasonings. Arrange on a large platter, broccoli outside, cauliflower inside, mound the tomatoes in the center. Serve with Gourmet Avocado Dip (see index) or with lemon-flavored mayonnaise (below).

## Lemon-Flavored Mayonnaise

*Makes about 2 cups*

  strained juice of 1 lemon
    (used above)
  1 teaspoon dry mustard
  1¾ cups mayonnaise

Combine lemon juice and dry mustard, stirring until well blended. Fold mixture into the mayonnaise. Scrape the fruit from the squeezed lemon and fold into the mayonnaise. Chill and serve with Christmas wreath of vegetables.

## Clams Gourmet

*A Maine appetizer.*

*Makes 24 pieces*          *Cooking time: 3 minutes*

  ½ pound sharp cheddar cheese,
    shredded
  2 6½-ounce cans chopped clams,
    drained
  1 tablespoon parsley, finely chopped
  1 tablespoon chives, finely chopped
  1 clove garlic, finely minced
  dash of hot pepper sauce
  dash of pepper
  6 slices pumpernickel bread, cut in
    quarters, or half of "party size"
    loaf

Preheat oven to broil. Combine cheese, clams, parsley, chives, garlic, hot pepper sauce, and pepper and mix well. Spread mixture on bread squares and place on broiler pan. Broil until bubbly.

## Creton

*A delicious French-Canadian pâté de maison.*

*Makes 3 cups*          *Cooking time: 1 hour*

  1 medium onion, coarsely chopped
  1 clove garlic, coarsely chopped
  1 cup milk
  1 pound ground pork, regular grind,
    not too lean
  1 cup coarse bread crumbs
  1 teaspoon Seasoned Salt (page 17)
  ½ teaspoon pepper
  ½ teaspoon celery salt
  ⅛ teaspoon cinnamon
  ⅛ teaspoon nutmeg
  dash of sage

Process onion, garlic, and milk in blender until smooth. Combine with remaining ingredients in a heavy Dutch oven. Mix well. Cover and simmer on very low heat for an hour; stir and break up chunks occasionally. Cool slightly. Pour into blender and process until smooth.   Pour into a very lightly oiled 3-cup mold and cover. Chill until firm. To unmold: invert on a serving platter. Serve with little toast rounds.

## Flamed Hickory-Smoked Mussels

*Toasted French bread and a good Beaujolais make this a delightful snack. Use fresh or canned smoked mussels; this recipe illustrates both.*

*Serves 2*          *Cooking time: 3 to 10 minutes*

*Using fresh mussels:*
  2 pounds fresh mussels
  2 tablespoons butter or margarine
  ½ cup onions, chopped

2 cloves garlic, minced
1 cup Chablis
liquid hickory smoke
1 tablespoon peanut oil
2 tablespoons brandy
½ lemon cut in 2 wedges

Scrub mussels with a brush, debeard, discard any with opened or cracked shells. Melt the butter in a 6-quart Dutch oven. Add ¼ cup onions and 1 garlic clove. Cook until onions are transparent. Add the wine and the mussels. Cover and steam until mussel shells open, about 7 minutes. Drain (the strained cooking liquid makes a delightful drink). Discard any mussels with unopened shells. Remove the meat from the shells and place single layer in a casserole dish. Lightly spray with liquid hickory smoke. Marinate at room temperature for 30 minutes, drain.

*Using canned mussels:*
  2 3- to 4-ounce cans smoked mussels
  ¼ cup onions, chopped
  1 clove garlic, minced
  1 tablespoon peanut oil
  2 tablespoons brandy
  ½ lemon, cut in 2 wedges

*To cook either version:* Heat the peanut oil in a wok or a flambé pan. Gently sauté ¼ cup onions and 1 clove of garlic until golden. Add the mussels and toss together to heat through. Remove from heat. Warm the brandy carefully, *never* boil it. Pour warmed brandy over the mussels. Tilt the pan and use a long match to ignite the brandy. Serve as soon as the flames die out, along with the lemon wedges.

## Beignets au Fromage

*Fried cheese pieces.*

*Serves 4 to 6*     *Cooking time: 3 to 4 minutes*

  oil for deep frying
  6 2-inch wedges of Brie or
    Camembert Cheese

1 egg
½ cup milk
½ teaspoon Seasoned Salt (page 17)
¼ teaspoon pepper
3 cups fresh bread crumbs
1 large bunch green grapes
2 apples
¼ cup lemon juice

Pour 2 inches of oil into a large skillet, heat to 350°. Cut each wedge of cheese in half lengthwise, then crosswise. (If using Camembert, shape the crust around the soft center so it covers as much of center as possible.) Combine the egg, milk, salt, and pepper. Dip each piece of cheese into egg mixture, then coat thoroughly with crumbs. Fry a few at a time until crisp and brown on both sides.

Cut apples into 8 wedges each, and dip wedges in the lemon juice. Serve immediately with the grapes and the fried cheese. Makes 24 pieces.

## Frogs' Legs Nuggets with Hot Pepper Sauce

*A most unusual taste teaser.*

*Serves 6 to 8*     *Frogs' legs soak overnight*
            *Cooking time: 25 minutes*

  1 pound frogs' legs, fresh or frozen
  ½ cup milk
  ½ cup green pepper, chopped and
    seeded (about half a pepper)
  ¼ cup hot peppers, chopped and
    seeded
  ¾ cup apple cider vinegar
  3 cups sugar
  ½ cup flour
  1 stick butter or margarine
  ¼ cup arrowroot (cornstarch may
    be substituted)
  1 or 2 drops green food coloring
    (optional)
  2 teaspoons orange rind, freshly
    grated

Thaw frozen frogs' legs. Cut into 1-inch nuggets. Soak the nuggets in milk overnight to remove fishy taste.

Make the sauce: place the chopped peppers in a blender bowl with 1 tablespoon of the vinegar. Blend until smooth. Pour pepper mixture into a 3-quart saucepan, add the sugar and remaining vinegar, stir to mix. Bring to a boil, stirring constantly until the sugar dissolves. Simmer 5 minutes, removing scum if it forms. Dissolve the arrowroot in ¼ cup cold water. Gradually add to pepper mixture, stirring constantly until sauce thickens. Remove from heat.

Drain frogs' legs nuggets. Roll in flour. Melt butter in a large skillet and sauté the breaded nuggets for about 10 minutes or until tender. Add food coloring, if desired, and orange rind to warm pepper sauce and stir to mix. Dip cooked nuggets into the spicy sauce.

## Miniature Crab Puffs

*Make ahead, pack in an airtight container, and store in your freezer.*

*Makes 4 dozen     Cooking time: 30 to 45 minutes*

⅓ cup butter or margarine
½ teaspoon salt
¾ cup flour
3 eggs
6 ounces fresh or frozen crabmeat
3-ounce package cream cheese, softened
⅓ cup sour cream
2 tablespoons salad olives with pimento, chopped
1 scallion, minced
¼ cup Parmesan cheese, freshly grated
¼ teaspoon Seasoned Salt (page 17)

Preheat oven to 325°. In a small saucepan bring ¾ cup water, the butter, and salt to a rapid boil. Add flour all at once, stirring until a ball is formed and leaves the sides of the saucepan. Remove from heat and add the eggs, one at a time, beating until mixture thickens and gets creamy. Drop by teaspoonfuls onto a greased cookie sheet. Bake 25 to 30 minutes. Cool on rack.

Drain the crabmeat and slice thinly. Combine with remaining ingredients and mix very well. Fill tiny puffs (filled puffs may be frozen at this point). Replace on cookie sheet, return to oven and bake for 10 minutes. (To heat frozen puffs, place on a cookie sheet and bake at 400° for 15 to 17 minutes.)

## Parmesan Mousse

*A refreshing appetizer.*

*Makes 4 cups*

¾ cup milk
2 eggs, separated (keep whites cold)
6 ounces fresh Parmesan cheese
⅓ cup ricotta cheese
finely grated rind and juice of 1 medium lemon
1 tablespoon Italian-Cheese Salad Dressing (see index)
2 drops hot pepper sauce
½ cup heavy cream
1 envelope unflavored gelatin
¼ teaspoon Seasoned Salt (page 17)
dash each of nutmeg and paprika

Heat milk to lukewarm. With a wire whisk, beat egg yolks slightly in a large bowl. Add warm milk gradually to egg yolks and whisk until blended. Add cheeses and blend. Add lemon juice and rind, salad dressing, and hot pepper sauce and mix well.

Beat cream to stiff peaks. Fold into egg/milk/cheese mixture. In a small saucepan, soften the gelatin in ⅓ cup cold water, then dissolve over low heat. Add to mixture in bowl gradually and stir until well mixed.

Beat egg whites until stiff, fold into mixture. Pour into a lightly oiled 1-quart ring mold. Chill until set.

To serve: dip mold in warm water to the depth of the gelatin for 15 seconds. Place your serving dish on top of the mold and carefully turn it over. Serve with pretzel sticks and crackers.

## Mini Seafood Quiche

*Delicious, and takes only minutes to prepare.*

*Makes 2 dozen*      *Cooking time: 20 minutes*

  package of 12 refrigerated
    butterflake rolls
  5-ounce can small shrimp or
    crabmeat, drained
  1 egg, beaten
  ¼ cup whipped cream or non-dairy
    whipped topping
  ¼ cup milk
  1 tablespoon brandy
  ¼ teaspoon Seasoned Salt (page 17)
  dash of pepper
  2 ounces of Gruyère cheese,
    cut into 24 slices

Preheat oven to 375°. Lightly grease 2 dozen miniature muffin tins. Divide each roll in two and press one section into each cup of the muffin tins. Place 2 shrimp or one small chunk of crabmeat into each shell. Combine remaining ingredients except the cheese and pour an equal amount into each shell. Top each with a slice of cheese. Bake for 20 minutes.

## Moules Marinière

*Mussels on the half shell.*

*Serves 4 to 6*      *Cooking time: 20 to 25 minutes*

  24 mussels
  3 tablespoons butter or margarine
  3 tablespoons onions, minced
  1 clove garlic, minced
  ½ cup Chablis
  1 recipe Herb Butter (see index)

Scrub mussels with a brush to remove sand. Debeard. Discard those with opened or cracked shells.

Melt the butter, add the onions and garlic, and sauté until onions are clear. Add the wine and mussels, cover, and steam until the shells open (5 to 6 minutes). Discard any with unopened shells. Drain.

Preheat oven to 400°. Remove mussels from shells, saving one shell per mussel. Put a small amount of herb butter in the shell, top with a mussel, add more herb butter on top. Place in single layer in a baking dish and bake for 10 minutes. Serve sizzling hot.

## Porky Melons

*Sweet and sour bites.*

*Serves 6 to 8*      *Cooking time: 15 to 20 minutes*

  24 one-inch pieces of watermelon
    rind preserves
  12 bacon slices, cut in half

Preheat oven to 375°. Drain watermelon pieces. Wrap bacon around each piece and secure with toothpicks. Place on a rack of a baking pan and bake 15 to 20 minutes or until bacon is crisp. Serve hot.

## Potted Cheese

*A nutty, tangy spread.*

*Makes 2½ cups*      *Prepare the day before*
                 *Cooking time: 5 minutes*

  2 tablespoons sesame seeds
  1 cup cheddar cheese, grated
  ¾ cup bleu cheese, crumbled
  ¾ cup butter or margarine
  3 tablespoons brandy
  1 teaspoon Dijon mustard
  ½ teaspoon Worcestershire sauce
  ⅛ teaspoon ground nutmeg
  dash of hot pepper sauce

Preheat oven to 375°. Spread sesame seeds on a cookie sheet and toast in the oven until golden brown, about 3 minutes. Allow the cheeses and butter to soften at room temperature. Mix together. Blend toasted seeds and remaining ingredients into cheese mixture and stir until smooth. Pack into a 2½-cup crock and cover. Refrigerate overnight to allow flavors to blend. Serve with crackers, toast, or celery sticks.

## Pâté de Trois Foies

*A blend of various livers creates this tasty spread.*

*Makes 3 cups*         *Cooking time: 30 minutes*

½ pound calf's liver, cut in pieces
½ pound pork liver, cut in pieces
½ pound chicken livers, cut in pieces
½ pound slab bacon, rind removed, diced
¾ cup cold water
2 garlic cloves, diced
1 medium onion, chopped
1 bay leaf
1 teaspoon Seasoned Salt (page 17)
½ teaspoon celery salt
½ teaspoon pepper
pinch each of thyme and savory

Combine all ingredients in a Dutch oven and bring to a boil, stirring frequently. Reduce heat and allow to simmer gently for 30 minutes. Cool slightly. Pour ingredients into a blender bowl. Turn blender to "purée" setting and blend until completely smooth. Pour into a lightly oiled 3-cup mold and cool. Cover and chill until firm.

To serve: turn onto a sectioned platter, garnish with fresh parsley sprigs. Serve with sweet gherkin pickles, cocktail onions, and wheat crackers.

## Shrimp in Beer Batter

*Great nibbles while watching a football game.*

*Serves 4*         *Cooking time: 20 minutes*

20 medium raw shrimp, peeled and deveined

2 cups flour
½ cup light beer
1 teaspoon paprika
½ teaspoon salt
⅛ teaspoon garlic powder
oil for frying
spicy-hot mustard or cocktail sauce

Dredge the shrimp in 1½ cups of the flour. Pour beer into a mixing bowl. Sift remaining ½ cup flour (with the paprika, salt, and garlic powder) into beer and mix thoroughly until batter is frothy. Heat oil to 375°. Dip floured shrimp into the beer batter and fry, a few at a time, for 4 minutes. Drain on absorbent paper toweling. Serve with mustard or sauce.

## Tangy Cheddar Spread

*A speedy appetizer.*

*Makes 1½ cups*

8 ounces cheddar cheese spread (Wispride)
¼ to ½ cup milk
2 teaspoons fresh parsley, chopped
⅛ teaspoon garlic powder

Combine all ingredients in a blender and blend until smooth. Add milk to desired consistency. Serve with crackers.

## Champignon Farci de Noix

*Walnut-stuffed mushrooms.*

*Serves 4 to 6*         *Cooking time: 25 minutes*

1 pound large fresh mushrooms (approximately 15)
3 tablespoons butter or margarine
¼ cup onions, minced
½ cup soft bread crumbs
½ cup walnuts, finely chopped
¼ cup parsley, finely chopped

½ teaspoon Seasoned Salt (page 17)
dash of pepper

Preheat oven to 350°. Wipe mushrooms with a damp cloth and remove stems. Finely chop the stems and reserve caps. Melt butter in a skillet. Brush mushroom caps with some of the melted butter and place in a greased baking dish, set aside. To remaining butter in the skillet add the onions and chopped mushroom stems and sauté 5 minutes. Add other ingredients and mix well. Spoon mixture into mushroom caps and bake 20 minutes.

## Rita's Mystery Canapés

*An easily prepared, delicious hors d'oeuvre.*

*Serves 15 to 20*     *Cooking time: 2 to 3 minutes*

  1 loaf white bread, thinly sliced
  ½ cup butter or margarine
  1 envelope dried onion soup mix

Remove the crust from the bread slices. Melt the butter in a medium saucepan, add the onion soup mix, and stir to dissolve and blend. Preheat oven to broil. Using a pastry brush, brush one side of each trimmed bread slice with onion-butter mixture, spreading the onion bits evenly over the bread. Cut each slice into 3 strips and place on a cookie sheet. Broil six inches from the heat source until golden brown. Serve immediately.

These canapés may be prepared ahead of time, covered tightly, and frozen. Broil when ready to serve.

## Smoked Oyster Spread

*A flavorful appetizer.*

*Makes 2 cups*

  8-ounce package cream cheese,
    softened
  ¼ cup half & half

3 tablespoons mayonnaise
2 tablespoons onions, minced
2 tablespoons pimento, finely
  chopped
¼ teaspoon Seasoned Salt (page 17)
3- or 4-ounce can smoked oysters,
  drained and chopped

Combine all ingredients. Mix well and chill at least 2 hours to allow flavors to blend. Serve with crackers.

## Skewers of Baked French Bread and Cheese

*Outstanding as an appetizer or a light meal with wine and salad.*

*Serves 6 to 8*     *Cooking time: 3 to 4 minutes*

  1 loaf of French bread
  1 recipe Herb Butter, softened
    (see index)
  8-ounce chunk of mozzarella cheese

Preheat oven to 450°. Remove the crust from the bread. Cut bread into ½-inch slices. Toast the bread slices and spread herb butter on one side. Cut the cheese into ⅓-inch thick slices the same diameter as the bread slices. Using 4- to 5-inch skewers, thread 1 slice of bread, one slice of cheese, another slice of bread, another slice of cheese, ending with a slice of bread. Place on a cookie sheet and bake just long enough to soften the cheese. Dab with additional herb butter and serve immediately.

## *Saucisson en Croute*

*Garlic sausage wrapped in cream cheese pastry.*

*Serves 4*     *Cooking time: 1 hour*

  1 pound garlic, kielbasa, or
    knackwurst sausage
  ½ cup Dijon mustard
  1 garlic clove, puréed
  1 teaspoon pepper, freshly grated

½ pound cream cheese, softened
½ pound butter or margarine,
  softened
¼ cup heavy cream
½ teaspoon Seasoned Salt (page 17)
2½ cups flour
1 egg, beaten

Slice kielbasa in two pieces, if large. Place selected sausage in a skillet with ¼ cup water. Cover and simmer 5 minutes. Do not boil. Do not prick sausage skin. Drain off the water and continue cooking slowly, uncovered, turning with tongs, until the sausage is evenly browned.

Combine the mustard, garlic, and pepper in a small bowl, mix well and set aside.

Combine the cream cheese, butter, cream, and salt and mix until well blended. Gradually add the flour and form a ball. Turn onto a floured surface and roll out dough in a large rectangle (if sausage was cut, shape into two rectangles).

Preheat oven to 350°. Spread cooked sausage with the mustard mixture. Place in the center of the dough and wrap dough around the sausage to cover completely. Add 1 teaspoon cold water to the beaten egg, mix well. Seal the pastry edges with the egg mixture, then brush mixture over entire surface of dough. Carefully lift sausage *en croute* onto a Teflon-coated cookie sheet and bake 45 minutes or until golden brown. Cool slightly, slice, and arrange on a serving platter. Serve with mustard.

# Soups & Chowders

## Brandied Pumpkin Soup

*A festive start for Thanksgiving dinner.*

*Serves 4 (1½ qts.)     Cooking time: 20 minutes*

¼ cup butter or margarine
½ cup onions, finely chopped
3½ cups chicken broth
2½ cups fresh cooked pumpkin,
    mashed
¼ teaspoon ground ginger
¼ teaspoon ground nutmeg
1 teaspoon Seasoned Salt (page 17)
¼ teaspoon white pepper
2 tablespoons brandy
½ to 1 cup half-and-half

Melt the butter in a Dutch oven. Add onions and sauté until clear. Add chicken broth. Gradually stir in mashed pumpkin and simmer gently until heated through. Add spices and brandy. Use half-and-half to thin. Heat through; *do not boil*. Taste and adjust seasoning.

## Canadian Cheese Soup
## with *Grands-Pères*

*A traditional holiday soup with dumplings.*

*Serves 4 to 6          Cooking time: 45 minutes*
*(1½ qts.)                 with Dumplings: 1 hour*

Soup:
    ½ cup carrots, grated
    ½ cup celery, finely chopped
    ¼ teaspoon Seasoned Salt (page 17)
    ¼ cup butter or margarine
    2 tablespoons onions, finely chopped
    ¼ cup flour
    2 cups milk
    2½ cups sharp cheddar cheese,
        shredded
    2 cups chicken broth

Combine carrots, celery, and salt in 1 cup of boiling water. Cook until tender; do not drain. Melt butter in a Dutch oven. Add onions and sauté until clear but not brown. Add flour. Stir constantly and cook until frothy. Add milk all at once. Cook and stir constantly. As mixture starts to thicken, gradually add cheese and stir until melted. Add cooked vegetables with their liquid and chicken broth. Heat through; *do not boil*.

Grand-Pères:
    1½ cups flour
    2 teaspoons baking powder
    ¼ teaspoon Seasoned Salt

1 tablespoon parsley, finely chopped
1 egg, beaten
½ cup milk
2 tablespoons melted shortening

Sift flour, baking powder, and salt together. Add parsley. Combine egg, milk, and shortening. Add to dry ingredients all at once. Stir just to moisten flour. Drop by teaspoonfuls into the hot soup. Cover and cook over very low heat, 20 minutes. (Don't peek while dumplings are cooking, or they will deflate.)

## Chawan-Mushi

*Shrimp custard soup – an Oriental appetizer.*

*Serves 4          Cooking time: 15 to 20 minutes*

1 egg, well beaten
1 cup chicken broth
1 teaspoon soy sauce
½ teaspoon Seasoned Salt (page 17)
½ cup fresh spinach, cut bite-size
4 medium shrimp, peeled and
   deveined
½ cup fresh mushrooms, sliced
4 water chestnuts, sliced thin
4 strips of lemon peel
soy sauce

Combine egg, chicken broth, soy sauce, and salt. Soak cut spinach in hot water to soften, about 3 minutes. Drain completely.

To assemble: Place a shrimp in each of four 5-ounce custard cups. Top with equal amounts of drained spinach pieces, mushrooms, and water chestnuts. Pour egg mixture over vegetables. Cover tightly with foil.

Set cups on a rack in a Dutch oven. Pour boiling water around cups, one inch deep. Cover and steam over low heat for about 15 minutes, or until a knife inserted in the center comes out clean. Remove foil. Top each cup with ¼ teaspoon soy sauce and lemon twist.

## Cherry and Fruit Soup

*An appealing appetizer with a touch of brandy.*

*Serves 4 (1 qt.)          Cooking time: 15 minutes*
                          *Chill: 3 hours*

½ cup sugar
½ cup sweet cherries, drained, pitted
¼ cup canned peaches, drained,
   sliced
¼ cup canned mandarin orange
   sections, drained and quartered
2 tablespoons seedless raisins
2 tablespoons lemon juice
1½ cups orange juice
1 tablespoon cornstarch
1 tablespoon brandy
stemmed cherries

Combine sugar with 1 cup boiling water in a Dutch oven. Stir to dissolve. Add cherries, peaches, oranges, raisins, lemon juice, and bring to a boil. Reduce to lowest heat immediately and barely simmer while you prepare the sauce.

Pour orange juice in a small saucepan and bring to a boil. Dissolve cornstarch in 4 tablespoons very cold water. Add to the orange juice, reduce heat, and, using a wire whip, whip until smooth and thick. Remove from heat, add brandy and cooked fruit. Stir, being careful not to tear the fruit. Cool, then chill for 3 hours.

Serve in chilled, decorative soup cups. Garnish with a stemmed cherry.

## Cold Maine Blueberry Soup

*A refreshing soup to serve on a hot summer day.*

*Serves 6 (1½ qts.)          Chill: 4½ hours*

1 envelope unflavored gelatin
¼ cup cold water
4 cups orange juice
3 tablespoons fresh lemon juice
¼ cup sugar

2 cups fresh blueberries, rinsed
and drained
1 tablespoon grated orange rind
1½ teaspoons fresh mint leaves,
crushed

Soften gelatin in cold water in a small glass or stainless steel bowl. Place the bowl in a pan of hot, not boiling, water and stir to dissolve the gelatin. Combine the juices, sugar, and gelatin mixture, stir until the sugar is dissolved. Chill until mixture thickens as syrup, about 1½ hours. Fold in blueberries and chill for 3 hours more. To serve, spoon into chilled soup cups and top each cup with ½ teaspoon grated orange rind and ¼ teaspoon crushed mint.

## Corn Soup, Oriental Style

*Serve with Maman's Bacon and Cheese Biscuits for a complete meal.*

*Serves 4 (1½ qts.)*        *Cooking time: 20 minutes*

2½ cups chicken broth
1-pound can cream style corn
1 teaspoon Seasoned Salt (page 17)
¼ teaspoon pepper
¼ teaspoon garlic powder
½ cup smoked ham, diced
2 teaspoons scallions, finely chopped
1½ tablespoons cornstarch
½ cup cold water
2 eggs, well beaten

Pour chicken broth into a Dutch oven. Cover and bring to a boil. Reduce heat and add corn; stir to blend, heat through. Combine spices. Place 2 tablespoons of diced ham and ½ teaspoon scallions into each of 4 soup bowls. Dissolve cornstarch in cold water, add to hot soup and stir constantly until thickened. Gradually add beaten eggs while stirring vigorously, forming Oriental-style egg "shreds." Quickly add spices and stir to blend. Pour soup over ham and scallions.

## Cream of Carrot Soup

*Serves 6 (2½ qts.)*        *Cooking time: 45 minutes*

¼ cup butter or margarine
½ cup onions, chopped
4 cups carrots, peeled, chopped
½ teaspoon Seasoned Salt (page 17)
dash of pepper
dash of sugar
dash of thyme
½ cup flour
6 cups chicken broth
1 cup heavy cream

Melt butter in a Dutch oven. Add onions and sauté until clear. Add carrots. Sprinkle spices over carrots. Gradually stir in the flour. Mix well and cook, stirring constantly, for 2 minutes. Add broth, using a wire whip, and blend completely. Slowly bring to a boil, stirring constantly. Lower heat, cover and cook for ½ hour. Cool slightly and purée in the blender. Return to Dutch oven, add cream, and heat through.

## Cream of Cauliflower Soup

*Serves 6 (2½ qts.)*        *Cooking time: 45 minutes*

2 tablespoons vegetable oil
¼ cup onions, finely chopped
½ cup celery, finely chopped
½ cup carrots, finely grated
4 cups cauliflowerets
1 tablespoon parsley, chopped
4 cups chicken broth
2 teaspoons Seasoned Salt (page 17)
½ teaspoon pepper
small piece of bay leaf
2 tablespoons butter or margarine
3 tablespoons flour
1 cup milk
½ cup half-and-half
½ cup sour cream

Heat oil in a 6-quart Dutch oven. Add onions and sauté over medium heat until clear. Add celery, carrots, and cook 2 minutes, stirring constantly. Add cauliflower and parsley. Cook 15 minutes, covered, over low heat, stirring occasionally. Add chicken broth, salt, pepper, and bay leaf, bring to a boil, and simmer 5 minutes. Melt butter in a 1½-quart saucepan, add flour and stir to mix well. Cook until frothy, remove from heat and slowly add milk. Mix very well, scraping bottom of pan to blend thoroughly; return to heat. Bring almost to a boil, stirring constantly, until mixture thickens. Add half-and-half. Stir well and add this cream sauce to soup. Taste and adjust seasoning. Remove bay leaf and simmer. Dilute sour cream with ½ cup soup broth; mix well. Add to soup and heat through.

## Creamy Haddock Stew

*Add a fresh tossed salad for a meal.*

*Serves 4 (1½ qts.)*                     *Cooking time: 25 to 30 minutes*

1 pound haddock, rinsed, cut into
  inch chunks
1 cup potatoes, diced
½ cup onions, chopped
1 celery stalk, finely chopped
½ bay leaf
2½ teaspoons Seasoned Salt
  (page 17)
¼ teaspoon pepper
2 tablespoons butter
2 tablespoons flour
1 cup milk

Combine the first 7 ingredients (haddock to pepper) in a Dutch oven with 2½ to 3 cups of water. Bring to a boil and simmer 15 minutes. Remove bay leaf. Melt butter in a separate small saucepan and add flour. Cook and stir until mixture becomes frothy. Remove from heat and add milk all at once. Mix very well, making sure you scrape the bottom edges of the pan. Return to heat and simmer slowly, using a wire whip to stir until thick. Add to cooked fresh mixture.

## French Onion Soup, *au Gratin*

*Serves 4 to 6 (2 qts.)*        *Cooking time: 45 minutes*

½ cup butter or margarine
1 pound onions, peeled, thinly sliced
2 one-ounce packages of "au jus"
  mix, or 4 cups Basic Beef Stock
  (below)
2 cups chicken broth
6 slices French bread, ½ inch thick
2 teaspoons Seasoned Salt (page 17)
½ teaspoon pepper
3 tablespoons dry sherry
1 cup Emmentaler (Swiss) cheese,
  grated

Melt butter in a large Dutch oven. Add onions and sauté, stirring, until all are light brown. Dissolve packages of "au jus" mix in 3½ cups boiling water. Add to onions with chicken broth and stir to mix well. Bring to boil. Reduce heat and simmer 25 minutes, skimming off scum as it forms. Preheat oven to 300°. Toast French bread slices, cool, and dry on a rack. Add salt, pepper, and sherry to soup. Taste and adjust seasoning. Pour into 6 ovenproof bowls. Top each serving with a slice of toast and sprinkle about 2 tablespoons grated Emmentaler cheese on top of each. Bake 10 minutes or until the cheese is melted and bubbly. Serve with additional cheese.

## Basic Beef Stock

*Use whenever a recipe calls for beef broth.*

*Makes 3½ quarts*        *Cooking time: 5 hours*

4 pounds beef neck bones and/or
  beef shank cut in two
3 celery stalks with leaves
1 large onion peeled and studded
  with 4 whole cloves
1 cup canned tomatoes
1 medium carrot, quartered
bouquet garni (place the following
  in a cheesecloth bag and tie

securely: 1 fresh parsley stalk,
2 sprigs of fresh thyme or
1 teaspoon dried thyme, 1 bay leaf,
1 garlic clove, chopped,
½ teaspoon crushed black
peppercorns)
1½ tablespoons Seasoned Salt
(page 17)

Preheat oven to 400°. Place beef bones in a baking pan and bake for 30 minutes, turn and bake 30 minutes longer. Remove from pan and place in a large stock pot.

Drain off fat from baking pan and deglaze pan with 1 cup warm water, scraping cooked bits from bottom. Pour into stock pot. Add 4 quarts of cold water to stock pot with remaining ingredients except salt. Bring to a boil slowly, removing scum as it forms. Cover and simmer one hour.

Add the salt and simmer 3 hours longer. Remove bones, bouquet garni, and vegetables. Strain through a fine strainer or wet muslin. Chill. Remove fat before using.

If a clear stock is not essential, remove cloves from the onion and place onion, celery stalks, and carrot in a blender with 2 cups broth and purée. Add to broth after straining.

## Gazpacho Monique

*Chilled fresh vegetable soup.*

*Serves 6 (1½ qts.)*          *Chill: 6 hours*

1 cup tomaotes, peeled, diced
½ cup green peppers, seeded, diced
½ cup celery, finely chopped
½ cup firm cucumber, diced
¼ cup onions, chopped
1 small garlic clove, chopped
2 sprigs fresh parsley
1 teaspoon chives, snipped
pinch of dried tarragon
2 tablespoons red wine vinegar
2 tablespoons olive oil
1 teaspoon Seasoned Salt (page 17)
½ teaspoon Worcestershire sauce

dash of hot pepper sauce
2 cups tomato juice

In a glass or stainless steel bowl (do not use plastic or aluminum) combine tomatoes, peppers, celery, and cucumber. Carefully stir to mix. Combine remaining ingredients in blender. Purée until smooth. Pour over vegetables; cover and chill, at least 6 hours.

To serve, pour into chilled mugs. Garnish each with thin cucumber slice that is cut halfway and hooked onto rim of mug. Serve with herbed croutons or pretzels.

## Hubbard Squash Soup

*Serves 6 (2 qts.)*          *Cooking time: 45 minutes*

¼ cup butter or margarine
1 cup onions, finely chopped
½ cup celery, finely chopped
¼ cup flour
3 cups milk
2 teaspoons Seasoned Salt (page 17)
¼ teaspoon basil
½ teaspoon pepper
¼ teaspoon nutmeg
1½ cups chicken broth
3 cups hubbard squash, cooked
   and mashed
2 tablespoons parsley, finely chopped

Melt butter in a Dutch oven. Add onions and celery and sauté until tender but not brown. Add flour and cook and stir constantly until frothy. Add milk all at once and stir until mixture starts to thicken. Add salt, basil, pepper, and nutmeg, blend together. Add chicken broth, cooked squash, and parsley; stir and heat through. Cool slightly. Spoon into blender and purée. Return to Dutch oven and reheat, but do not boil.

Serve hot with a dash of nutmeg.

## Lobster Stew *à la Canadienne*

*Serves 4 (1½ qts.)*     *Cooking time: 20 minutes*

½ cup butter or margarine
1¾ cups cooked lobster meat, cut
  bite-size
1 teaspoon lemon juice, fresh
¼ teaspoon paprika
½ teaspoon salt
¼ teaspoon white pepper
3 cups hot milk
1½ cups heavy cream

Melt butter in a 3-quart saucepan. Add lobster meat and sauté gently over a low fire to heat thoroughly. Sprinkle lemon juice over the lobster. Stir constantly to prevent separation. Add paprika, salt, and pepper. Mix well. Remove pan from heat and add milk all at once. Return to heat and simmer slowly for 5 minutes. Add cream, heat through, but *do not boil.* Remove from heat and adjust seasonings. Let stand a few minutes before serving.

## Maine Shrimp Stew

*Serves 4 (1½ qts.)*     *Cooking time: 45 minutes*

3 cups chicken broth
1 teaspoon Worcestershire sauce
3 peppercorns
1 thick lemon slice
3 thick onion slices
½ bay leaf
celery stalk with leaves
1 pound fresh Maine shrimp,
  shelled and deveined
¼ cup butter or margarine
¼ cup flour
2 cups half-and-half
½ teaspoon Seasoned Salt (page 17)
½ teaspoon white pepper
dash of hot pepper sauce

Pour chicken broth in a Dutch oven and bring to a boil. Add the next 7 ingredients (Worcestershire sauce to celery stalk) and simmer 10 minutes. Add shelled shrimp. When boiling starts again, remove from heat and let stand 3 minutes.

Remove shrimp with a slotted spoon, cool, and dice. Remove and discard the bay leaf. Pour cooking liquid in blender with ½ cup of cooked shrimp. Blend until smooth.

Melt butter in Dutch oven. Add flour and cook until frothy. Remove from heat and add blended cooking liquid. Stir well, scraping the bottom edges to blend completely. Return to heat and cook, stirring constantly, until mixture thickens. Add half-and-half, remaining shrimp, spices, and heat through.

## New England Clam Chowder

*Better if made the day before, allowing the flavors to "marry."*

*Serves 4 to 6 (2 qts.)*     *Cooking time: 35 minutes*

1½ pounds small fresh clams,
  in the shell
3 tablespoons salt
1 tablespoon butter or margarine
½ cup (4 ounces) salt pork, scalded
  and diced
2 cups onions, coarsely chopped
4 ounces beer
½ cup milk crackers, finely crushed
1½ cups potatoes, diced
½ bay leaf
1 teaspoon Seasoned Salt (page 17)
½ teaspoon pepper
2 cups half-and-half

Place clams with salt in a sink half full of cold water. Swish clams around in the water and let soak. Meanwhile, melt butter in a 3-quart saucepan. Add diced salt pork and sauté over low heat until the pork turns golden. Add onions, cover, cook until onions are clear.

While onions are cooking, drain and rinse clams thoroughly. Place clams in a Dutch oven, pour beer over them, and cover. Steam until the clam shells open. Remove from heat, uncover, cool just enough to handle. Remove clams from their shells, discarding any that are broken or unopened. Strip off neck skin, swish clams in the cooking liquid, set aside.

Strain the cooking liquid several times through cheesecloth. Add enough water to make 3½ cups. Pour cooking liquid into Dutch oven.

Pour cooked onion mixture in blender, process until smooth. Add to clam liquid with milk crackers, potatoes, bay leaf, salt, and pepper and stir well. Cover; simmer 15 minutes. Remove and discard bay leaf. Add half-and-half and cooked clams. Heat through, but *do not boil*.

Float a thin pat of butter in each bowl. Serve with crackers.

## Potage Canadienne

*A creamy pea soup.*

*Serves 6 (2½ qts.)*     *Cooking time: 1¾ hours*

1 pound meaty ham bone
3½ cups water
3 cups chicken broth
1 pound yellow or grean split peas,
    sorted and rinsed
¾ cup leeks, finely chopped
½ cup carrots, finely chopped
½ cup celery, finely chopped
1 teaspoon Seasoned Salt (page 17)
½ teaspoon sugar
¼ teaspoon marjoram
½ teaspoon pepper
2½ cups milk
1 cup heavy cream

Place ham bone in a large Dutch oven. Add water, chicken broth, and peas. Bring to a boil, reduce heat, skim, and simmer 45 minutes, stirring occasionally. Add vegetables and spices and continue simmering, stirring often, until the vegetables are very soft and mixture is thick, about 40 minutes. Remove bone. When cool enough to handle, cut off meat and dice it. Gradually stir in milk and cream. Add cooked ham and sim-

mer another 10 minutes, stirring occasionally. Sprinkle with additional salt to taste.

## Spring Greens Soup

*The secret of this soup is the crisp vegetables.*

*Serves 6 (2½ qts.)*     *Cooking time: 15 minutes*

6 cups chicken broth
½ cup white wine
¼ cup soy sauce
2 teaspoons ground ginger
4 cups scallions, diced, stem included
4 cups fresh pea pods (or two
    packages frozen), sliced diagonally

Bring chicken broth to a boil in a Dutch oven. Add wine, soy sauce, and ginger. Add scallions and pea pods and barely cook, 2 to 3 minutes.

## Swiss Chard Soup

*Serves 4 to 6 (2 qts.)*     *Cooking time: 45 minutes*

1 pound Swiss chard
¼ cup butter or margarine
½ cup celery, sliced
1 garlic clove, minced
½ cup onions, chopped
1 large carrot, sliced thin
1 small leek, white part only, sliced
1 cup potatoes, peeled and diced
3 cups chicken broth
1 cup half-and-half
1 teaspoon parsley, finely chopped
1 teaspoon Seasoned Salt (page 17)
½ teaspoon pepper
dash of nutmeg
plain yogurt

Rinse, drain, and separate the leaves from the stalks of Swiss chard. Slice stalks and set aside. Chop leaves and set aside.

Heat butter in a large Dutch oven, add chard stalks, celery, garlic, onions, carrots, and leeks and sauté until vegetables are soft.

Add potatoes and chicken broth. Cover and cook until potatoes are tender, about 20 minutes. Remove from heat and cool slightly. Purée, a small amount at a time, in the blender, adding the chard leaves in the later batches. Return to the Dutch oven; add half-and-half and spices. Heat through, but *do not boil*.

To serve, float a dollop of yogurt on the soup as a garnish.

## Tomato-Cheese Soup

*Fast, easy, and elegant.*

*Serves 2 (3 cups)*     *Cooking time: 15 minutes*

10-ounce can condensed tomato soup
1½ cups milk
¼ teaspoon garlic powder
1 tablespoon parsley, finely chopped
1¼ cups sharp cheddar cheese, grated

Pour soup in a medium saucepan. Using a wire whip, stir in milk. Add garlic powder and parsley. When soup is hot, gradually add the cheese, stirring constantly. Remove from heat, cool slightly. Pour into blender and purée until creamy. Return to saucepan and warm through. *Do not boil.*

## Vichyssoise de Québec

*This classic soup may be served hot or cold.*

*Serves 8 (3 qts.)*     *Cooking time: 35 minutes*
                                  *To serve cold, chill 4 hours*

4 leeks, white part only
¼ cup butter or margarine
1 medium onion, chopped
1 garlic clove, minced
3½ cups potatoes, peeled, diced
4 cups chicken broth
1 tablespoon Seasoned Salt (page 17)

¼ teaspoon white pepper
dash of hot pepper sauce
2 cups milk
2½ cups whipping cream
1 teaspoon chives, finely snipped

Cut green tops from leeks, discard. Slice the bottoms thinly. Melt butter in a Dutch oven, add sliced leeks, onions, and garlic. Sauté until tender but not brown. Add diced potatoes, chicken broth, salt, pepper, and hot pepper sauce; simmer until the potatoes are tender, about 25 minutes. Cool slightly.

Purée the potato mixture, a small amount at a time, in a blender. Return to Dutch oven and stir in milk and cream, stirring constantly. Heat through, sprinkle with chives and serve. To serve cold: Chill soup 4 hours, then pour soup in chilled mugs and top with chives.

## Zucchini Cream Soup

*Cook and freeze your harvest of zucchini to enjoy this soup all winter long.*

*Serves 2 to 3 (1 qt.)*     *Cooking time: 25 minutes*

2 medium zucchini
3 chicken bouillon cubes
13-ounce can evaporated milk
1 teaspoon Seasoned Salt (page 17)
1 teaspoon parsley, finely chopped

Wash zucchini, cut off ends, and slice ¼-inch thick. Do not peel. Have about one inch of water boiling in a large saucepan or Dutch oven. Add the sliced zucchini. Cover and cook until tender, about 10 to 15 minutes. Drain, reserving ¼ cup of the liquid to dilute the bouillon cubes. Spoon zucchini into blender and purée. (Note: Zucchini may be frozen at this stage for winter use; cool and store in a freezer container. To serve, thaw and continue the recipe.) Return to the saucepan, add bouillon liquid, milk and spices. Stir and heat through.

# Beef

## Baked Sirloin Steak

*The spicy sauce bakes right into the meat. Suggested Menu: Quick Baked Cheddar-Garlic Potatoes, Spinach-Mandarin Salad.*

*Serves 4*　　　*Cooking time: 30 minutes*

⅓ cup butter or margarine
3-pound sirloin steak, 2 inches thick
½ teaspoon Seasoned Salt (page 17)
¼ teaspoon pepper
2 tablespoons flour
3 medium onions, thinly sliced
1 large carrot, shredded
1 cup tomato sauce
½ cup water
½ teaspoon hot pepper sauce

Preheat oven to 450°. Melt 2 tablespoons of the butter in oven-proof skillet; as butter starts to brown, add the steak. Sear quickly on both sides. Remove to warm platter and season with salt and pepper. Trim off excess fat.

Drain fat from skillet but keep crusty bits. Add and melt remaining butter, stir in flour, and cook over medium heat until frothy. Add onions, carrots, tomato sauce, ½ cup water, and hot pepper sauce. Mix well.

Cook 5 to 6 minutes. Push cooked vegetable mixture to one side of skillet, add the partially cooked steak, and cover it with vegetable mixture. Transfer skillet to the oven and bake, uncovered, for 20 minutes. (For well done, cook an additional 10 minutes.)

To serve: Cut the steak into 4 equal parts, top with the vegetable sauce.

## Beef in Oyster Sauce

*Stir-fry cooking at its best. Suggested Menu: chow mein noodles, Hot Spicy Peaches, fortune cookies.*

*Serves 4*　　　*Cooking time: 15 minutes*

1 pound London broil
1 tablespoon sherry
4 tablespoons peanut oil
1 tablespoon soy sauce
¼ teaspoon baking soda
½ teaspoon sugar
1 small sweet red pepper
1 cup fresh mushrooms, sliced
½ cup bamboo shoots
½ cup water chestnuts, thinly sliced
2 garlic cloves, crushed
dash of ginger
¼ cup oyster sauce

2 tablespoons cornstarch
¼ teaspoon sesame oil
2 scallions with stems, sliced

Cut beef into ¼-inch slices. Combine wine, 1 tablespoon of the oil, soy sauce, soda, and sugar. Mix well. Add meat; marinate 15 minutes or longer.

Seed pepper, remove membrane, and cut into thin strips. Prepare other vegetables.

Heat 2 tablespoons oil in wok or large skillet, add garlic and beef. Sauté until redness disappears from meat, about 3 to 5 minutes. Sprinkle with dash of ginger. Remove contents to warmed platter. Add final tablespoon of oil to wok or pan and heat. Add peppers, mushrooms, shoots, and chestnuts; stir-fry 2 minutes. Add oyster sauce. Dissolve cornstarch in ¾ cup cold water, add to wok and stir until thick. Add meat with juices, sesame oil, and scallions; stir.

Serve surrounded by noodles.

## Beef Stew *Maison*

*Old-fashioned goodness and flavor. Suggested Menu: hot Corn Bread, salad greens with Italian-Cheese Dressing.*

*Serves 4*　　　　　　*Cooking time: 2 hours*

1½ pounds beef chuck, cut in
　2-inch cubes
2 tablespoons shortening
2 cups canned tomatoes
½ cup onions, chopped
1 garlic clove, sliced
2 teaspoons Seasoned Salt (page 17)
1 teaspoon sugar
½ teaspoon pepper
1 teaspoon Worcestershire sauce
½ cup celery, bias cut
4 carrots, peeled, sliced thick
8 small white onions, peeled
3 small potatoes, peeled, quartered
3 tablespoons flour
½ cup cooked peas

Trim off all fat from meat. Melt shortening in Dutch oven. Add meat, brown on all sides. Drain tomatoes, set aside, and add enough water to tomato liquid to make 2 cups. Drain fat from pan. Add tomato liquid, onions, garlic, salt, sugar, pepper, and sauce. Cover and simmer, *do not boil,* for 1½ hours. Add celery, carrots, onions, and potatoes. Cook 15 to 20 minutes or until vegetables are tender. Add tomatoes and heat through. Dissolve flour thoroughly in ½ cup cold water. Add to stew, stirring constantly until stew thickens, about 5 minutes. Stir in peas and serve.

## Beef Stroganoff

*A classic: lean, tender beef in a rich sauce. Suggested Menu: buttered egg noodles, Broccoli with Lemon.*

*Serves 4*　　　　　*Cooking time: 30 minutes*

1 pound beef sirloin or leftover
　roast beef
¼ cup butter or margarine
salt and freshly ground pepper
½ cup onions, chopped
1 garlic clove, crushed
1 cup mushrooms, thinly sliced
3 tablespoons flour
½ teaspoon Seasoned Salt (page 17)
1 tablespoon tomato paste
¾ cup beef broth
1 cup dairy sour cream
2 tablespoons sherry

Preheat oven to 200°. Cut meat into ½-inch strips, 2 inches long. Melt 2 tablespoons butter in skillet. Add meat and sear quickly on both sides. Remove to warmed platter, season with salt and pepper. Place in oven and turn oven off. Add remaining butter to skillet; sauté onions, garlic, and mushrooms until onions are tender but not brown. Combine flour, salt, and dash of pepper. Sprinkle over vegetables in skillet, toss, stir and cook 1 minute. Blend tomato paste with broth, add to skillet, cook and stir until thickened. Return meat to skillet. Stir in sour cream and wine. Heat through, but *do not allow to boil.*

## Boeuf Poitou
## (Bean-Pot Beef with Vegetables)

*Set oven timer or start your crock pot, and this slow-cooked dinner is ready when you come home. Suggested Menu: hearts of lettuce with Slavic Dressing.*

*Serves 4*        *Cooking time: 4 hours*

2-pound beef round roast
1 pound fresh green beans
8 carrots, peeled, cut in half
2 medium potatoes, peeled, quartered
4 small whole onions, peeled
1 bay leaf
½ teaspoon ground savory
1 tablespoon Seasoned Salt (page 17)
1 teaspoon pepper
1 tablespoon honey

Preheat oven to 300°. Remove all fat from roast. Place meat on bottom of bean pot. Rinse beans, snip off ends and scatter over meat. Top with carrots, potatoes, onions, spices, and honey. Cover with cold water. Cover and bake 4 hours. (Do not open oven door during cooking process.)

If prepared in a crock pot, add less water (to within ¼ inch of top of contents) and cook at simmer setting for 3½ to 4 hours.

## Brother Paul's "Italian Sauce Parmigiana" with Meatballs

*A Frenchman's touch to a family favorite. Suggested Menu: spaghetti, garlic toast, Caesar Salad.*

*Serves 4*        *Cooking time: 4 hours*

*Sauce:*
2 tablespoons olive oil
¼ cup (2 ounces) salt pork, minced
½ cup Spanish onions, chopped
1 garlic clove, minced
3½ cups canned Italian tomatoes
3 cans tomato paste
4 cups water
¼ cup fresh parsley, chopped
2 teaspoons Seasoned Salt (page 17)
½ teaspoon pepper
2 teaspoons sugar
½ teaspoon oregano
1 bay leaf, crushed
¼ cup Romano cheese, grated

*Meatballs:*
1½ pounds ground beef
2 eggs, beaten
1 teaspoon Seasoned Salt (page 17)
¼ teaspoon pepper
¼ teaspoon oregano
¼ teaspoon garlic powder
½ cup grated Romano cheese
2 tablespoons fresh parsley, chopped
2 teaspoons grated lemon rind
¼ cup fine dry bread crumbs

Heat oil in Dutch oven, add pork, sauté 3 minutes. Add onions and garlic. Sauté until onions are clear. Add tomatoes, tomato paste, water and seasonings, except cheese. Cover and simmer for 1 hour, stirring occasionally. Remove from heat and cool slightly. Process in blender until smooth. Return to heat and bring to a simmer.

Combine all ingredients for meatballs in large bowl. Mix thoroughly with hands, and shape into golfball-sized meatballs. Add to sauce, cover, and simmer another 1½ hours, stirring frequently. Stir in the reserved ¼ cup of cheese just before serving. Serve over spaghetti with extra Romano cheese.

## Chili by Rhum

*Hearty, rib-sticking fare with a touch of rum. Suggested Menu: Cheese-It Biscuits, garden salad with Parisienne Dressing.*

*Serves 4*          *Cooking time: 2 hours*

1 tablespoon salad oil
1 large onion, chopped
1 garlic clove, finely chopped
1 medium green pepper, chopped
1 pound lean beef chuck, ground
2 cups tomatoes
6-ounce can tomato paste
2 tablespoons chili powder
½ teaspoon dried oregano
1 teaspoon salt
¼ teaspoon black pepper
dash of cayenne pepper
dash of paprika
½ cup dark rum
16-ounce can kidney beans, drained

Heat oil in Dutch oven. Add onions, garlic and green pepper, sauté for 5 minutes. Add meat, break up any chunks. Cook and stir until redness of meat disappears. Drain off fat. Add tomatoes, tomato paste, spices, and rum. Cover and simmer over very low heat for 1½ hours, stirring frequently. Add beans, stir gently. Cover and cook an additional half-hour. Check seasonings and adjust to taste.

## Delmonico Steaks, Roquefort

*A blend of anisette and cheese makes this meal unusual. Suggested Menu: Baked Stuffed Potatoes, Fresh Broccoli with Lemon.*

*Serves 4*          *Cooking time: 10 to 20 minutes*

4 ounces Roquefort cheese, softened
¼ cup butter or margarine, softened
1 tablespoon anisette liqueur
4 8-ounce Delmonico steaks,
    1- to 1½-inch thick

salt and pepper, to taste

Steaks should be at room temperature before cooking. Cream together cheese and butter. Add anisette and blend well. Place steaks on cold rack of broiler pan, 3 inches from heat source. Broil 3 to 4 minutes on each side for rare, 5 to 6 minutes on each side for medium, and 6 to 8 minutes on each side for well done. Salt and pepper both sides. Spread each steak with cheese-butter mixture. Serve immediately.

## Flamed Tenderloin Steak, Dijon

*Suggested Menu: Baked Stuffed Roman Potatoes, Asparagus with Almonds.*

*Serves 4*          *Cooking time: 30 minutes*

4 tablespoons butter or margarine
4 6-ounce beef tenderloin steaks
salt and freshly ground pepper
⅓ cup brandy
1 cup heavy cream
1 tablespoon Dijon mustard
1 tablespoon fresh lemon juice
dash of Seasoned Salt (page 17)
dash of pepper
4 large mushroom caps

Preheat oven to 200°. Melt 3 tablespoons of the butter in skillet. As it starts to brown, add steaks. Sauté over medium high heat 5 minutes. Turn with tongs, season with salt and pepper, sauté 5 minutes more or until meat juices ooze out. Remove from heat, add brandy, and flame. When flame dies, place steaks on warmed platter in the oven. Turn oven off.

Combine remaining ingredients in bowl and blend. Add to pan juices. Stir and simmer until sauce thickens and reduces by one-third. Score mushroom tops, sauté in remaining tablespoon of butter until tops are golden. Pour sauce over steaks, top each with mushroom cap.

## Marinated London Broil Cookout

*A great barbeque meal. Suggested Menu: Cookout Potatoes, Roasted Corn, Garlic Toast.*

*Serves 4*          *Marinate 6 to 8 hours*
          *Cooking time: 8 to 10 minutes*

2-pound London broil steak,
    2 inches thick
1 bottle Italian salad dressing
1 small piece suet

Prick steak all over with fork. Place in casserole dish, pour dressing over steak, turn to coat. Cover and chill 6 to 8 hours, turning occasionally.

To cook: Remove from marinade, slash fat edge to prevent curling during cooking process. When coals are hot, tap off ash with fire tongs. Place grid over heat, grease with suet. Broil steak for 3 or 4 minutes; turn and broil 4 minutes more. Steak must be rare. (Check doneness by inserting knife tip; juices should ooze red.) Place on carving board and slice at an angle against the grain, ¼ inch thick. (Be sure to catch all the meat juices for "French-dipping.")

## Pain de Boeuf Fromager

*A crusty beef and cheese loaf. Suggested Menu: Baked Stuffed Potatoes, Hot Spicy Peaches.*

*Serves 4*          *Cooking time: 1½ hours*

2 tablespoons butter or margarine
½ cup onions, chopped
¼ cup green pepper, chopped
1 cup soft bread crumbs (1½ slices)
2 eggs, well beaten
1 cup tomato sauce
1½ pounds lean ground beef
½ pound lean ground pork
½ teaspoon Seasoned Salt (page 17)
½ teaspoon pepper
¼ teaspoon thyme, dried
¼ teaspoon garlic salt

1¼ cups sharp cheese, diced

Preheat oven to 350°. Melt butter in saucepan. Add onions and green pepper, cover, and steam over medium-low heat until onions are clear. Tear bread into blender and process, turning blender on/off ("pulse" on food processor) until crumbly. Beat eggs in mixing bowl. Add cooked vegetables with butter, tomato sauce, bread crumbs, meats, and spices. Mix well. Add cheese and mix. Press mixture into loaf pan, rounding top. Bake for 1½ hours. (For a crunchier top, broil for a few minutes before serving.)

## Pâté Chinois

*An old Canadian recipe, in spite of its name. Suggested Menu: Cheesy-Crouton Salad with Italian-Cheese Dressing.*

*Serves 4*          *Cooking time: 40 minutes*

4 medium potatoes, peeled,
    quartered
¼ teaspoon salt
¼ cup butter or margarine
¾ cup onions, chopped
1 pound lean ground beef
1 teaspoon Seasoned Salt (page 17)
½ teaspoon pepper
½ teaspoon celery salt
¼ teaspoon garlic powder
2 1-pound cans cream-style corn
¼ cup milk
½ cup sharp cheese, shredded
paprika

Preheat oven to 350°. Put potatoes in cold water with ¼ teaspoon salt, bring to a boil, and cook until fork tender, about 15 to 20 minutes. Meanwhile, melt 2 tablespoons of the butter in skillet. Add onions and sauté until clear, about 5 minutes. Add beef and cook until redness of meat disappears. Add ¾ teaspoon of the seasoned salt, pepper, celery salt, and garlic powder; mix well. Drain off excess fat. Pour into casserole dish. Pour corn evenly over meat. Mash cooked potatoes with milk, 2 tablespoons butter, ¼ teaspoon Seasoned Salt, and dash of pepper. Spread evenly atop corn. Sprinkle cheese evenly over potatoes. Sprinkle lightly with paprika. Bake for 20 minutes. Change oven setting to broil, and cook until cheese topping is bubbly and golden.

## Ragoût de Boeuf

*Made a quick way, with leftover cooked beef. Suggested Menu: hot biscuits with Tomato Butter, Gabrielle's Green Salad.*

*Serves 4*          *Cooking time: 20 minutes*

2 cans condensed onion soup
3 medium potatoes
2 cups cooked beef, cubed
½ teaspoon Seasoned Salt (page 17)
¼ teaspoon pepper
2 tablespoons flour
1 cup cooked peas

Combine onion soup with 2 soup cans cold water in Dutch oven. Bring to a boil. Peel and cube potatoes; add to boiling soup. Reduce heat and simmer 10 minutes or until potatoes are tender. Add beef, salt, and pepper. Dissolve flour in ½ cup cold water. Add to simmering liquid and stir until thickened, about 3 to 5 minutes. Stir in peas and serve.

# Rich Man – Poor Man
## Steak *au Poivre*

*Tenderloin steaks or ground beef smothered in black pepper. Suggested Menu: Cheese-Chive Potatoes, French-Style Peas.*

*Serves 4*          *Cooking time: 20 to 30 minutes*

*Rich Man:*
4 7- to 8-ounce beef tenderloin steaks
vegetable oil

*Poor Man:*
1½ pounds lean ground beef

*Both:*
black pepper, coarsely ground
⅔ cup butter or margarine
3 tablespoons shallots or onions, minced
¼ cup brandy
1 cup beef broth

*Rich Man:* Eight hours before serving, brush steaks on both sides with vegetable oil, cover and chill 6 hours. Remove steaks from refrigerator, wipe off excess oil, let stand at room temperature 2 hours.

*Poor Man:* Divide beef into 4 portions. Shape into ovals, ¾-inch thick.

Preheat oven to 200°. Cover a 12-inch square waxed paper with freshly ground pepper. Press pepper into steaks, coating both sides thoroughly. Melt 2 tablespoons butter in skillet; as butter turns brown, add steaks. Cook over medium-high heat 3 to 5 minutes, use tongs or spatula to turn steaks, cook until meat juices begin to ooze out, about 5 minutes. Place steaks on a warmed platter in oven. Turn oven *off*.

Discard pan juices, retaining crusty bits. Add and melt 2 tablespoons butter over medium-low heat. Add shallots or onions, sauté until clear. Add brandy and broth. Stir well, scraping cooked bits into sauce. Boil sauce over high heat until reduced by half – mixture will thicken like syrup. Turn heat off and add remaining butter, 2 tablespoons at a time, stirring constantly. Pour sauce over steaks.

# Fruit and Calf's Liver *Flambé*

*A delicious way to introduce this nutritious food to finicky eaters. Suggested Menu: Oriental Steamed Rice, Green Beans Almondine.*

*Serves 4*          *Cooking time: 25 minutes*

1½ pounds calf's liver
½ cup milk
1 cup flour

½ teaspoon garlic powder
½ teaspoon salt
¼ teaspoon pepper
3 tablespoons butter or margarine
½ cup dry white wine
1 banana, sliced into mixing bowl
  with 1 tablespoon lemon juice
11-ounce can mandarin orange
  sections, drained
⅛ teaspoon ground ginger
2 tablespoons orange liqueur

Remove skin and membrane from liver, rinse, and pat dry. Cut into 1-inch cubes. Soak in milk for 15 minutes. Combine flour, garlic powder, salt, and pepper in plastic bag, shake well to mix. Heat butter in skillet. Drain liver and place a few cubes at a time in flour mixture. Shake bag to coat evenly. Sauté, turning to brown all edges. Add wine, cook 3 minutes. Add banana slices and lemon juice to pan, along with orange sections and ginger. Heat through, stirring constantly as mixture thickens.

Warm liqueur in saucepan. Transfer liver and fruit mixture to serving platter. Surround with rice, if desired. Pour the warmed liqueur over liver, and flame at the table.

## Sautéed Calf's Liver with Bacon Rolls and Broiled Bananas

*Transforms liver into an epicurean delight. Suggested Menu: buttered egg noodles, French-Style Peas.*

*Serves 4*                    *Cooking time: 35 minutes*

¾ cup soft bread crumbs, 1 slice
4 bananas
2 tablespoons butter or margarine,
  melted
8 slices bacon
1½ pounds calf's liver
garlic powder
salt and pepper
2 tablespoons flour
2 tablespoons Madeira or sherry
1½ cups beef broth

Partially cook bacon in skillet over medium heat. (Do not discard bacon fat when done.) Place on paper toweling to absorb excess fat and *immediately* curl into rolls. Keep warm. Preheat oven to broil. Tear bread into small pieces and place in a blender bowl. Process, turning blender on/off ("pulse" on food processor) until crumbly. Cut bananas in half, crosswise, brush with butter, and roll in bread crumbs. Place on broiler pan, six inches from heat. Broil until brown all around, turning, about 10 minutes. When the bananas are nearly done add bacon rolls to crisp—about one minute.

Rinse liver, pat dry. Sprinkle lightly with garlic powder. Sauté quickly in bacon fat in skillet, browning both sides. *Do not overcook.* Liver should be pink in the center. Lightly season with salt and pepper. Keep warm. Drain all but 2 tablespoons pan drippings. Add flour and cook, stirring constantly until frothy, about 1 minute. Gradually add the wine and beef broth. Stir until smooth and sauce thickens. To serve: Arrange liver on a warm platter, surround with bacon rolls and broiled bananas. Serve with sauce.

## Savory London Broil Steak

*Marinated in rum and soy sauce for tenderness and full flavor. Suggested Menu: Baked "Hand Warmer" Potatoes, Fresh Vegetable Stir-Fry.*

*Serves 4*                    *Marinate: 4 to 5 hours*
                   *Cooking time: 10 to 15 minutes*

1½-pound London broil
⅓ cup soy sauce
¼ cup dark rum
2 tablespoons salad oil

Trim excess fat from steak, wipe with a damp paper towel, and place in shallow dish. Combine soy sauce and rum in mixing bowl, blend well. Pour over steak, cover. Chill and marinate 4 to 5 hours, turning occasionally.

Preheat oven to broil. Drain steak, reserving marinade for basting. Brush both sides of steak with salad oil. Place on broiler pan and broil, six inches from heat, 4 to 5 minutes on each side or until steak is cooked medium rare. Slice steak diagonally and serve with pan juices.

## Sirloin Steak, 3 Ways: Teriyaki, Onion-Buttered, or Béarnaise

*Basic recipe for 4 servings*
4 12-ounce beef sirloin strip steaks,
    1½ to 2 inches thick
salt and pepper

Slash fat edge to keep steaks flat during cooking process. Let stand at room temperature for 1 hour before grilling. Broil or grill over coals for 5 minutes. Turn with tongs; salt and pepper. Cook to desired doneness; test by cutting a slit in the meat, note inside color: red – rare; pink – medium; grey-brown – well done.

*Teriyaki Sirloin:* Combine ½ cup soy sauce, ½ cup vegetable oil, ½ cup fresh orange juice, 2 teaspoons sugar, ½ teaspoon ground ginger, 1 garlic clove, pressed. Stir to blend. Add raw steak and marinate 3 to 4 hours. Drain and cook as directed.

*Onion-buttered Sirloin:* Combine ½ cup butter or margarine, ¼ cup minced onion, 2 tablespoons parsley, 2 teaspoons Worcestershire sauce, 1 teaspoon dry mustard, ½ teaspoon pepper in a small saucepan and sauté until onions are clear, about 3 minutes. Brush mixture over cooked steaks.

*Sirloin with Béarnaise Sauce:* Chop 3 small green onions, combine with ½ cup wine vinegar, 1 teaspoon dried tarragon in a small saucepan. Bring to a boil and cook rapidly until most of the liquid disappears. Melt ½ cup butter or margarine, do not brown. Put 3 egg yolks in a blender, add cooked mixture and a dash of salt. Turn blender on/off a few times (pulse). Turn blender to high speed and dribble hot butter into egg mixture until sauce thickens. Spread on cooked steaks.

## Standing Rib Roast of Beef, *au Jus*

*Suggested Menu: Yorkshire Pudding, Lyonnaise Potatoes, Cauliflower Mornay.*

*Serves 6 to 8*          *Cooking time: 4 to 5 hours*

4- to 5-pound standing rib roast
    of beef (backbone separated
    from ribs)
Dijon mustard
garlic salt
dried basil
pepper

Preheat oven to 200° (by roasting at low heat the meat will be rare, 140°, all the way through). Place roast in pan fat side up. (The bones will serve as a rack to keep meat off bottom of pan.) Spread mustard evenly to cover fat side. Sprinkle garlic salt, basil, and freshly ground pepper generously over mustard. Insert thermometer into center of roast without touching bone. Do not add water, baste, or cover roast. Do not open oven frequently during roasting, as this will slow the cooking process.

When internal temperature measures 140° (4 to 5 hours), remove roast from oven; let stand 15 minutes before carving. Spoon off fat from pan drippings, add water to deglaze pan, heat through, and serve with roast. If pan drippings are not brown, add a little liquid gravy coloring.

## Steak Diane

*Crowned with mushroom caps – fast and easy, exquisite flavor. Suggested Menu: Shoestring Potatoes, Broiled Tomato Slices.*

*Serves 4*          *Cooking time: 25 minutes*

4 6-ounce sirloin strip steaks,
    ½ inch thick
1 teaspoon dry mustard
salt and pepper
⅓ cup butter or margarine
2 tablespoons cooking oil

Beef   43

2 tablespoons brandy
2 teaspoons green onions, minced
¼ cup lemon juice
1 teaspoon Worcestershire sauce
½ cup beef broth
½ pound mushroom caps
1 teaspoon fresh parsley, chopped

Preheat oven to 200°. Trim all fat from steaks. Wrap loosely in plastic and pound to ⅓-inch thickness with mallet. Sprinkle with salt, pepper, and dry mustard. Pound spices into meat. Turn and season other side the same way.

Heat 2 tablespoons of the butter and the oil in skillet. As butter starts to brown, add the steaks, 2 at a time, and sear quickly, 1 to 2 minutes on each side. Place the steaks on a platter in the oven to stay warm and cook the other two steaks. Return the first two steaks to skillet. *Remove from fire,* pour brandy all over and flame. When flame is out return steaks to the warm oven. Turn oven off.

Add onions to skillet and sauté one minute. Add 3 tablespoons of the lemon juice and Worcestershire sauce and bring to a boil. Add broth and cook liquid vigorously until reduced by half.

Meanwhile, melt the remaining butter in a saucepan and sauté mushrooms. Add remaining lemon juice. Allow to stand a few minutes, then drain.

To serve: Spoon sauce over steaks, top with mushroom caps, sprinkle with parsley, surround with shoestring potatoes.

## Steak Roast Wrap with Vegetables

*A meal roasted in foil, easy to prepare. Suggested Menu: lettuce wedge with Slavic Dressing, Bacon-Cheese Biscuits.*

*Serves 4* *Cooking time: 2 to 2½ hours*

2 to 2½ pounds New York sirloin
   steak, 2 inches thick
1 envelope onion soup mix

4 small potatoes, peeled, cut in half
1 pound carrots, peeled
4 celery stalks with leaves
16-ounce can French-style green
   beans
2 medium tomatoes, peeled, cut
   into wedges
2 tablespoons butter or margarine,
   cubed

Preheat oven to 350°. Fold an 18″ by 60″ sheet of aluminum foil in two. Set on shallow pan. Trim all edge fat from steak. Place steak in center of foil, sprinkle with soup mix. Top and surround with potatoes, carrots, and celery. Drain beans and spread alongside steak. Top with tomato wedges. Dot with butter cubes. Fold foil to seal completely (be careful not to puncture wrap). Bake 2 to 2½ hours, until meat and vegetables are tender.

Place on a warm platter. Carefully open foil to release steam, cut steak into 4 equal pieces, and pass the vegetables.

## Steak Tartare *en Croûte*

*Prepare immediately after grinding beef for best flavor. Suggested Menu: Easy and Grand Caesar Salad, Shoestring Potatoes.*

*Serves 4* *Cooking time: 4 minutes*

1 pound lean sirloin *freshly* ground
   twice
¼ cup onions, finely chopped
1 teaspoon Seasoned Salt (page 17)
½ teaspoon freshly ground pepper
8 bread slices
⅓ cup butter or margarine, softened

Set oven to broil, or grill over slow fire.

Combine all ingredients but bread. Mix well. Spread evenly, ¼ inch thick, on 4 slices of bread and top with remaining slices. Brush all outside surfaces with soft butter. Broil or grill 2 minutes on each side until golden brown. Meat should be just warm, not cooked.

## Teriyaki Rib Roast of Beef

*Suggested Menu: Baked Bananas, Almond Rice, Stir-Fried Broccoli.*

*Serves 6 to 8*  *Marinate overnight*
*Cooking time: 2 to 3½ hours*

¾ cup mushroom soy sauce
¼ cup salad oil
½ teaspoon sesame oil
¼ cup molasses
2 tablespoons sherry
½ teaspoon ground ginger
1 tablespoon dry mustard
4 garlic cloves, crushed
3- to 4-pound boneless beef rib roast

Combine all ingredients except roast in blender. Process until smooth. Place roast in bowl and pour this marinade over roast. Cover and chill overnight or at least 8 hours, turning roast occasionally.

To cook: preheat oven to 325°. Drain roast, reserving marinade for basting. Place on rack in pan, insert thermometer into center. Bake to desired temperature: 140° for rare, 160° for medium, 170° for well done. Baste frequently. Remove roast from oven, cover loosely with foil, and let stand 15 minutes before carving. Warm remaining marinade and serve on the side.

(Substituting regular soy sauce for mushroom soy sauce is not recommended, as the regular version tends to be too salty.)

## Wok Pepper Steak

*Fast and easy — a great taste combination. Suggested Menu: Oriental Steamed Rice, Avocado Sunshine Salad with Orange Mayonnaise.*

*Serves 4*  *Cooking time: 10 minutes*

1 pound flank steak
2 teaspoons cornstarch
1 teaspoon sugar
4 tablespoons soy sauce
1 tablespoon sherry
4 tablespoons peanut oil
2 medium green peppers
dash of ginger

Cut steak into strips, 2 inches long by ¼ inch thick. Combine cornstarch, sugar, 3 tablespoons of the soy sauce, and sherry, mix well. Add meat, toss to coat, and marinate 15 minutes or longer. Seed peppers, remove rib membrane, and slice into ¼-inch strips.

Heat 2 tablespoons oil in wok or large skillet. Add peppers and stir-fry 3 minutes until tender. Scoop out with slotted spoon, set aside. Add remaining oil to wok, heat it, then add steak mixture, liquid included. Stir-fry over high heat until redness disappears, about 2 minutes. Sprinkle with ginger. Add peppers and remaining soy sauce. Heat through and serve surrounded with rice.

# Pork, Lamb, Veal (and Moose)

## Pork in Apple Cider

*Slow cooking is the secret to the wonderful flavor. Suggested Menu: whipped potatoes, Onion and Fruit Sauté.*

*Serves 4*      *Cooking time: 2 hours*

  1½ pounds lean pork, cubed
  ½ cup flour
  ½ teaspoon salt
  ½ teaspoon pepper
  ½ teaspoon garlic powder
  ¼ cup salad oil
  2 cups apple cider
  1 pound small carrots, sliced
  ½ cup onions, chopped
  ½ teaspoon rosemary
  ½ teaspoon Seasoned Salt (page 17)
  ½ teaspoon pepper

Preheat oven to 325°. Trim *all* fat off pork. Combine flour, salt, pepper, and garlic powder in plastic bag and shake to mix. Add meat cubes, shake to coat all over. Heat oil in skillet. Add floured cubes and brown all sides. Remove pork to paper towel to drain. Spoon into earthenware casserole.

Drain fat from skillet. Add cider, heat, and stir to remove all crusty bits on bottom of skillet. Place carrots and onions on top of the pork in casserole. Remove cider from heat and add spices. Pour over vegetables in casserole. Cover and bake 2 hours or until pork is tender.

## Apricot-Almond Glazed Pork

*Regal fare for a successful dinner party. Suggested Menu: Chantilly Potatoes, French-Style Peas.*

*Serves 6 to 8*      *Cooking time: 2½ to 3 hours*

  3- to 4-pound pork loin roast, boned and rolled
  salt and pepper
  2 10-ounce jars apricot preserves
  ¼ cup corn syrup
  ½ cup red wine vinegar
  ½ teaspoon salt
  ½ teaspoon each, cinnamon, cloves, nutmeg
  1 cup slivered almonds, toasted

Preheat oven to 325°. Place roast on rack of baking pan. Sprinkle generously with salt and pepper. Insert meat thermometer in center. Bake 2½ to 3 hours, or until thermometer reaches 185°.

Meanwhile, combine preserves, syrup, wine vinegar, salt, and spices in saucepan.

Bring to a boil over low heat, stirring frequently. Simmer 10 minutes. Add almonds. Spoon enough sauce over roast to glaze, then baste frequently during the last half-hour. Remove roast from oven, let stand 10 minutes before slicing. Serve with remaining sauce.

## Baked Stuffed Pork Chops

*Delicious family favorite. Suggested Menu: Maple-Baked Apples, Bacon-Fried Corn.*

*Serves 4*        *Cooking time: 40 minutes*

8 dried prunes, pitted
4 6-ounce pork chops
½ cup butter or margarine, melted
¼ cup onions, finely chopped
¼ cup celery, finely chopped
¼ cup walnuts, chopped
1 cup cornbread stuffing mix
salad oil
2 tablespoons flour
10-ounce can chicken broth
1 beef bouillon cube
dash each of pepper, thyme, and
   basil

Soften prunes in water to cover for 30 minutes. Drain, dice, set aside. Preheat oven to broil. Cut pockets in fatty side of chops. Sauté onions, celery, and nuts in ⅓ cup of the butter until onions are clear. Put stuffing mix, diced prunes, cooked vegetables with butter in mixing bowl and toss. Add ⅓ cup boiling water to bind. Stuff each chop with 2 to 3 tablespoons mixture; fasten opening with toothpicks.

Put remaining stuffing in casserole, cover, and bake with chops. Place chops in roasting pan. Brush tops with oil. Broil to brown top, then reduce oven heat to 375° and bake 30 minutes.

Melt remaining butter in saucepan. Add flour and cook until frothy. Add broth, bouillon cube, and spices. Cook and stir until thick and cube is dissolved. Remove chops to platter (discard toothpicks). Add ¼

cup water to roasting pan to deglaze. Stir, then strain. Spoon off fat, add to sauce, heat through. Serve sauce over chops.

## Barbecued Spareribs

*Cooked over charcoal, these pork spareribs are delectable. Suggested Menu: Cookout Potatoes, Roasted Corn, fresh tossed salad.*

*Serves 4*        *Marinate 5 hours*
       *Cooking time: 1 to 1½ hours*

4-pound rack of pork spareribs
salt
½ cup hoisin sauce
¼ cup tomato ketchup
¼ cup honey
¼ cup mushroom soy sauce
1 tablespoon whiskey or brandy
¼ teaspoon pepper
2 garlic cloves, crushed
½ teaspoon sesame oil

Rinse ribs, pat dry. Sprinkle salt lightly all over ribs and rub it in. Let stand 15 minutes. Rinse off salt, pat ribs dry and place in pan. Combine remaining ingredients in mixing bowl, blend well. Add to ribs and marinate 5 hours in refrigerator, turning occasionally. Drain, reserve marinade for basting. Weave ribs on spit and broil over a slow fire for 1 to 1½ hours, basting frequently. Cook until the meat is tender – no pink showing when you snip between bones – and the fat is crisp and glazed.

## Broiled Ham Slice in Brandied Raspberry Sauce

*Quick and elegant for the busy cook. Suggested Menu: Spinach-Mandarin Salad.*

*Serves 4*        *Cooking time: 10 minutes*

2-pound cooked ham slice, 1 inch
   thick
17-ounce can sweet potatoes,
   drained

8-ounce can pineapple slices
   (4 slices)
2 tablespoons butter or margarine,
   melted
12-ounce jar raspberry preserves
¼ cup brandy
4 small spiced crab apples

Set oven at broil. Score edge fat of ham slice with cuts one inch apart, ¼ inch deep, being careful not to cut into meat. Place in center of rack on broiler pan. Cut sweet potatoes in half, brush cut side with butter, arrange around 1 side of ham slice. Drain pineapple slices, reserve ¼ cup liquid. Brush slices with butter, arrange on other side of ham. Broil 3 inches from heat for 5 minutes.

Combine preserves, brandy, and reserved pineapple liquid and blend thoroughly. Turn ham. Place apples in centers of pineapple slices, brush potatoes with raspberry sauce, and broil 5 minutes more. Warm raspberry sauce and serve with ham.

## Champagne Ham

*Slow simmered in apple juice and champagne, then baked. Suggested Menu: Sweet Potatoes à la Sugar Shack, Cheese-Custard Broccoli.*

*Serves 4 to 6*          *Cooking time: 3 hours*

4 cups apple juice
1 bottle inexpensive champagne
5- to 6-pound picnic ham
8-ounce can pineapple slices
1 cup raisins
1 teaspoon lemon juice
whole cloves
¾ cup brown sugar
¼ teaspoon dry mustard
maple syrup

Pour juice and champagne in Dutch oven and bring to a boil. Add ham. Cover and simmer over low heat until tender, about 2 to 2½ hours. Meanwhile, drain pineapple slices, reserving the liquid. Simmer raisins in saucepan with pineapple liquid and lemon

juice until tender. Pour into blender bowl, process on medium speed 15 seconds, keep warm.

Preheat oven to 350°. Lift cooked ham from pot, remove and discard skin and fat. Score in a diamond pattern and insert a clove in alternate sections. Combine sugar and mustard with enough maple syrup to make a thick paste. Spread all over ham, top with pineapple slices. Place ham in roasting pan and bake 30 minutes. Slice and serve with raisin sauce.

## Choucroute Garni

*Savory pork meats with flavorful sauerkraut. Suggested Menu: small boiled potatoes, Dijon mustard.*

*Serves 4*          *Cooking time: 1¼ hours*

27-ounce can sauerkraut, drained
3 slices bacon
1 cup onions, chopped
2 large tart apples, pared, cored,
   chopped
4 peppercorns, wrapped in
   cheesecloth
3 tablespoons dry gin
½ cup dry white wine
10-ounce can chicken broth
4 pork chops
8 pork sausage links
4 slices cooked smoked ham
salad oil
Seasoned Salt (page 17), to taste
pepper, to taste

Soak sauerkraut in cold water to cover, for 15 minutes. Sauté bacon in Dutch oven until crisp; cool, crumble, and set aside. Sauté onions in bacon fat until clear. Drain sauerkraut, squeeze dry. Add to onions, toss, and cook 5 minutes. Add apples, peppercorns, gin, wine, and broth; stir. Cover and simmer over low heat for one hour, adding the chops and sausage as they are cooked.

Meanwhile, preheat oven to broil. Brush pork chops on both sides with oil, place on broiler pan 3 inches from heat. Brown, season lightly with salt and pepper, turn, and brown other side. Bury in simmering sauerkraut.

While chops are broiling, cook sausage over low heat in covered saucepan with ¼ cup water for 5 minutes; uncover and turn to brown evenly. Drain sausage on paper towel, lay atop sauerkraut along with ham slices, and complete the 1-hour cooking time.

To serve: discard peppercorns. Spoon sauerkraut onto platter, surround with meats, sprinkle crumbled bacon over top.

## Pork Loin Roast Lyonnaise

*Roasted with vegetables and fruit to flavor and tenderize. Suggested Menu: Whipped Potatoes, Onion-Buttered Broccoli, Waldorf Salad.*

*Serves 4, with leftovers    Cooking time: 2 hours*

2- to 3-pound boneless pork loin
   roast
salt and pepper
1 medium onion, sliced
2 celery stalks, sliced diagonally
1 carrot, sliced
1 medium apple, cored and sliced
½ cup dry white wine
1 tablespoon butter or margarine
2 tablespoons onions, finely chopped
2 tablespoons flour
¼ teaspoon salt
¼ teaspoon pepper
1 tablespoon Dijon-style mustard

Preheat oven to 500°. Rub roast with salt and pepper. Place in roasting pan, scatter sliced onions, celery, carrots, and apples over and around roast. Insert meat thermometer in center of roast. Bake 30 minutes. *Lower temperature to 300°* and continue baking for 1½ to 2 hours, until thermometer reads 185°.

Remove roast from pan (discard fruit and vegetables) and place on platter. Deglaze pan with the wine. Strain pan juices, spoon off all fat but reserve 1 tablespoon. Heat butter and tablespoon of fat in saucepan, add chopped onions, and sauté until clear. Add flour and stir until frothy. Add strained pan juices and whip until mixture thickens. Add mustard, salt, and pepper.

Slice pork and serve with sauce. Note: Use leftover pork for Pork Chow Mein (see index).

## Maman's "Canadian Style" Baked Beans

*Traditional Saturday night fare, served with cole slaw and French bread.*

*Serves 4                Soak beans overnight*
*Cooking time: 5½ hours*

1 pound pea beans
½ teaspoon baking soda
4 ounces lean salt pork
3 tablespoons molasses
1 tablespoon brown sugar
1 teaspoon dry mustard
1 teaspoon salt
¼ teaspoon pepper
3 onions the size of eggs, peeled

*The night before:* Sort and rinse beans thoroughly. Pour into a bean pot. Cover with cold water and soak overnight.

Preheat oven to 300°. Boil 5 cups of water. Drain the beans, rinse, and pour into a large Dutch oven. Cover with cold water, add baking soda, and parboil for 8 minutes, removing scum as it forms. Drain. Pour boiling water over the salt pork; drain and cut into 3 equal chunks. Cut one chunk into 4 slices and place on the bottom of the bean pot. Score the other 2, set aside. Combine the molasses, sugar, mustard, salt, and pepper in a 4-cup measure; add enough boiling water to make 4 cups. Pour beans over sliced pork. Add molasses mixture. Place the onions and remaining pork atop the beans. Cover and bake 5 to 5½ hours. Add water as necessary so that beans are barely covered during all but the last hour of cooking.

## Maman's Special *Tourtière*

*Mom's renowned pork pies are traditional holiday fare. Suggested Menu: Easy and Grand Caesar Salad, Spanish olives, Cranberry-Fruit Salad.*

*Serves 4*          *Cooking time: 1 hour*

> 1 pound lean ground pork butt
> ½ cup onions, finely chopped
> ½ teaspoon Seasoned Salt (page 17)
> ¼ teaspoon pepper
> dash each of ground allspice and
>     sage
> 1 medium potato, cooked, mashed
> pastry for 2-crust, 9-inch pie
>     (see index)
> milk

Break up ground pork in Dutch oven. Add onions, salt, pepper, and ¼ cup boiling water. Simmer over low heat, uncovered, for 20 minutes, stirring frequently to prevent lumps from forming. Add allspice and sage, cover, and simmer until onions are transparent—about 10 minutes.

Preheat oven to 400°. Skim off fat from meat mixture. Add mashed potato and stir well. Remove from heat and pour into pastry-lined pie plate. Cut slits in top crust and center on plate. Trim excess pastry; flute edges. Brush top crust, *not edges*, with milk. Bake 10 minutes, reduce oven heat to 350° and bake 20 minutes more or until pastry is golden.

## Pork Chops in a Jiffy

*With a quick and creamy mushroom sauce. Suggested Menu: Whipped Potatoes, Orange-Glazed Carrots.*

*Serves 4*          *Cooking time: 30 minutes*

> 4 center-cut pork chops, 1½ inches
>     thick *or* 8 1-inch loin chops
> Seasoned Salt (page 17)
> pepper

> 1 can condensed cream of
>     mushroom soup
> vegetable oil spray

Lightly spray skillet with oil. Place chops in skillet. Brown over medium heat, turn, season with salt and pepper, and brown other side. Combine soup with ¾ cup cold water, blend completely. Remove chops from skillet. Pour off all fat. Add soup to skillet, stirring in cooked crusty bits, and heat through. Add chops, cover, and simmer, *do not boil*, until chops are tender (about 15 to 25 minutes, depending on thickness of chops).

## Pork Chops *alla Parmigiana* on Toasted Garlic Bread

*The flavor of Italy, easy and inexpensive. Suggested Menu: your choice of pasta, Cheesy-Crouton Salad, Chianti.*

*Serves 4*          *Cooking time: 1 hour*

> 7 tablespoons butter or margarine,
>     softened
> ¼ teaspoon basil
> ½ garlic clove, pressed
> ½ cup fine dry bread crumbs
> ½ cup grated Parmesan cheese
> ¾ teaspoon salt
> ¾ teaspoon paprika
> 4 large pork chops, ¾ inch thick
>     or 4 boneless pork filets
> 1 egg, well beaten
> 4 slices mozzarella cheese
> 2 cups Brother Paul's Italian Sauce
>     Parmigiana (see index) or 2 cups
>     prepared spaghetti sauce with
>     mushrooms
> 4 1-inch-thick slices French bread

Combine ¼ cup of the softened butter, basil, and garlic in small mixing bowl, mix well to blend, set aside. Combine bread crumbs, Parmesan cheese, salt, and paprika in mixing bowl. Trim off all fat from edges of chops, keeping a 1-inch piece. Dip chops in beaten egg and roll in crumb mixture. Heat 3 tablespoons butter and piece of fat in skillet and brown chops over moderate heat on both sides. Remove from skillet and cut meat from bone in one piece.

Drain fat from skillet. Return meat to skillet, cover each filet with a slice of mozzarella cheese. Top with spaghetti sauce, cover, and simmer over low heat until pork is cooked, about 45 minutes.

Broil one side of french bread until darkly toasted. Remove from broiler, butter untoasted side with garlic butter, and broil until well toasted. To serve: Place one filet on each toasted bread slice, cover with additional sauce.

## Pork Chow Mein

*A tasty way to serve leftover pork. Suggested Menu: Spinach-Mandarin Salad, Hot Orange Pudding.*

*Serves 4*            *Cooking time: 30 minutes*

1-pound can bean sprouts
1 tablespoon salad oil
2 onions, halved top to bottom,
   sliced ⅓ inch thick
2 cups celery, bias sliced
2 cups cooked pork, diced
3 tablespoons soy sauce
1 tablespoon molasses
½ teaspoon Seasoned Salt (page 17)
3 tablespoons cornstarch
2 3-ounce cans chow mein noodles

Drain bean sprouts, pour into mixing bowl. Soak in cold water until ready for use. Heat oil in skillet. Sauté onions and celery until crisp-tender, 5 minutes or less. Add pork, soy sauce, and molasses, along with 2 cups water. Simmer 15 minutes. Stir in salt. Drain bean sprouts, add to skillet, stir to mix well, and heat through. Combine cornstarch with ¼ cup cold water, stir to dissolve. Add to skillet and cook, stirring, until mixture thickens. Serve over chow mein noodles.

## Country-Style Pork Ribs in Tangy Sauce

*Barbeque flavor perks up a family dinner. Suggested Menu: Quick Baked Chili-Cheese Potatoes, Green Beans Almondine.*

*Serves 4*            *Cooking time: 1½ hours*

2½ pounds country style pork ribs
Seasoned Salt (page 17)
pepper
1¼ cups tomato ketchup
¾ cup white vinegar
3 tablespoons salad oil
¼ cup Worcestershire sauce
1 teaspoon salt

Preheat oven to 325°. Rinse ribs, pat dry. Place bone-side down in baking pan. Sprinkle generously with salt and pepper. Bake one hour.

Meanwhile, combine remaining ingredients in saucepan. Bring to a boil over low heat, simmer 20 minutes. Remove ribs from oven and drain all fat from pan. Cover ribs with sauce and bake 30 minutes longer or until a fork twists easily when piercing meat.

## Rôti de Porc aux Patates Brunes (Pork roast, Canadian style)

*Succulent meat with a crisp crust, surrounded by golden-brown potatoes. Suggested Menu: Parsnips in Pineapple Glaze, salad greens with Herbal Vinaigrette Dressing.*

*Serves 4*            *Cooking time: 2½ to 3 hours*

4- to 5-pound fresh pork loin roast,
   bone-in
2 garlic cloves, thinly sliced
½ teaspoon Seasoned Salt (page 17)
¼ teaspoon pepper
½ teaspoon savory
1 teaspoon dry mustard
1 large onion, chopped
12 potatoes, peeled (size of eggs)
½ cup hot chicken broth
2 tablespoons flour

Preheat oven to 325°. With a sharp knife score the roast, making cuts ¼ inch apart and deep enough to cut through the outer skin and fat. Insert garlic slices in cuts. Place in roasting pan. Combine salt, pepper, savory, and mustard. Sprinkle over roast. Add 1 cup water. Insert thermometer in center of roast without touching the bone. Bake 2½ hours, or until thermometer reaches 185°. Baste occasionally. Add potatoes and onion during last 45 minutes, with hot broth. Turn vegetables often to brown. Remove roast and vegetables to platter. Skim off pan juices. Dissolve flour in ¼ cup cold water, add to pan. Cook and stir until thickened.

# Sweet and Sour Pork

*A favorite Chinese dinner. Suggested Menu: Oriental Steamed Rice, Almond Float.*

*Serves 4*        *Cooking time: 30 minutes*

1½-pound lean pork shoulder
2 tablespoons salad oil
1 garlic clove, minced
1 beef bouillon cube
16-ounce can pineapple chunks
¼ cup brown sugar
2 tablespoons cornstarch
¼ cup white vinegar
3 tablespoons soy sauce
½ teaspoon salt
1 small green pepper, cut in strips
¼ cup onions, thinly sliced

Cut pork into ½-inch strips. Heat oil in Dutch oven. Add pork and brown both sides. Add garlic and sauté with pork for one minute. Pour off fat. Dissolve bouillon cube in ½ cup boiling water. Add to pork, cover, and simmer, *do not boil,* until tender, about 25 minutes.

Combine sugar and cornstarch. Drain pineapple and add juice to cornstarch with vinegar, soy sauce, and salt; stir well to dis-

solve. Add to pork and cook until thick. Add pineapple, green pepper, and onion. Cook 3 minutes.

# Cassoulet

*This robust garlicky casserole is a slow-cooked French favorite. Suggested Menu: Salad greens, French bread, hearty red wine, chilled grapes.*

*Serves 8 to 10*       *Soak beans overnight*
                                *Cooking time: 3½ hours*

4 cups dried pea beans
1 tablespoon Seasoned Salt (page 17)
2 garlic cloves, minced
2 medium carrots, thinly sliced
2 medium onions, chopped
¼ cup salt pork, diced
Bouquet garni (a sprig of parsley,
   1 chopped celery stalk with leaves,
   1 bay leaf, 4 whole cloves, and a
   sprig of thyme tied in cheesecloth)
½ teaspoon pepper
2 tablespoons butter
1 tablespoon vegetable oil
1½ pounds lean boneless pork,
   all fat removed and cut in 2-inch
   cubes
1 pound boneless lamb, all fat
   removed and cut in 2-inch cubes
2 Bermuda onions, chopped
1 cup chopped shallots or green
   onions
1 cup celery, thinly sliced
1 cup tomato juice
1 cup red wine
2 tablespoons parsley, chopped
dash of cayenne pepper
½ pound garlic or Polish sausage,
   thinly sliced
2 tablespoons packaged bread
   crumbs

Sort, wash, and drain the dried beans. Combine beans with 2 quarts cold water and salt in a Dutch oven. Let stand overnight. Add garlic, carrots, onions, salt pork, bouquet garni, and pepper. Bring to a boil. Simmer, covered, for 1 hour, skimming surface as needed. Heat 1 tablespoon of the butter and the oil in a large skillet. Add pork and lamb cubes and brown on all sides. Add meats to bean mixture. In the same skillet, cook chopped onions, shallots, and celery until soft. Add tomato juice and wine and simmer for 5 minutes. Add to beans together with parsley, cayenne pepper, and sausage slices. Simmer, covered, over low heat for 1 hour, or until beans and meats are tender. If necessary, add a little water or additional tomato juice to prevent scorching. Skim off excess fat. Discard bouquet garni. Preheat oven to 350°. Transfer mixture to a large casserole. Sprinkle top with bread crumbs, dot with remaining butter. Bake uncovered 35 to 45 minutes. Adjust seasonings and serve.

## Rich Man-Poor Man Chops "Roquefort"

*Lamb chops with Roquefort or pork chops with bleu cheese — both delicious.*

*Serves 4*          *Marinate 7 hours*
            *Cooking time: 20 minutes*

*Rich Man:*
  8 loin lamb chops

*Poor Man:*
  4 large center-cut pork chops

*Both:*
  3 tablespoons olive oil
  1 tablespoon marjoram
  1 tablespoon butter or margarine
  1 cup onions, finely chopped
  1 garlic clove, minced
  salt and pepper
  4 ounces Roquefort cheese or
    4 ounces bleu cheese

Eight hours before serving: trim any excess fat off chops. Loosen meat a little from bone. Combine 2 tablespoons of the olive oil and the marjoram and brush both sides of chops with mixture. Place in casserole dish, cover, and chill 7 hours. Remove from refrigerator 1 hour before cooking.

Melt butter in skillet. Add remaining tablespoon of oil. Heat and sauté onions and garlic until golden brown. Preheat oven to broil. Place drained lamb chops on broiler pan 3 inches from heat. Broil both sides until well done, 5 to 7 minutes each side (or pan broil pork chops in a heavy skillet, cooking slowly until cooked and brown on both sides). Season with salt and pepper. Spread 2 tablespoons of the onion mixture on each lamb chop, 4 on pork chops. Top with Roquefort or bleu cheese slices. Return to oven and broil until cheese melts and is golden.

## Rôti d'Agneau Provençal

*Lamb smothered with garlic butter and baked on a bed of fresh vegetables. Suggested Menu: Potatoes au Gratin, hearts of lettuce with Roquefort Cheese Dressing.*

*Serves 4*          *Cooking time: 2½ to 3 hours*

  ½ cup butter or margarine, softened
  2 small garlic cloves, pressed
  1 teaspoon parsley, finely chopped
  ½ teaspoon Seasoned Salt (page 17)
  1 medium eggplant
  6 medium tomatoes, coarsely
    chopped
  1 green pepper, seeded, chopped
  2 medium onions, sliced
  2 medium zucchini, sliced
  5-pound leg of lamb

Combine first four ingredients in small bowl; blend thoroughly, set aside. Preheat oven to 325°. Scrub eggplant, cut off stem end, slice ½ inch thick. Soak in cold salted water for 15 minutes, using a plate to weigh slices down. Drain, rinse, and drain completely.

Scatter all vegetables in bottom of broiler pan. Remove fell (parchment-like covering) from lamb, wipe with a damp cloth. Using a utility knife or other sharp, sturdy knife, score lamb deep enough to cut through outer fat, making cuts ¼ inch apart. Spread roast with garlic butter and work it in between cuts. Insert thermometer in center, not touching the bone. Bake 30 minutes, loosely cover with foil, and continue baking until meat thermometer reaches 175–180°.

Remove from oven. Place roast on a warmed platter. Sprinkle with salt and freshly ground pepper, surround with cooked vegetables.

## Mint-Barbecued Leg of Lamb

*Spit-roasted, tender, and accented with mint for superb flavor. Suggested Menu: Foil-baked potatoes, Zucchini with Corn.*

*Serves 6 to 8        Cooking time: about 3 hours*

    5- to 6-pound leg of lamb
    1 tablespoon vegetable oil
    1 tablespoon Seasoned Salt (page 17)
    ½ teaspoon pepper
    ½ cup butter or margarine
    ½ cup wine vinegar
    ¼ cup sugar
    ¼ cup brown sugar, firmly packed
    1 tablespoon lemon juice
    1 teaspoon grated lemon rind
    ¼ teaspoon dry mustard
    ⅓ cup fresh mint leaves, crushed

Remove fell (parchment-like covering) from lamb; wipe with a damp cloth. Rub the lamb with oil, sprinkle with Seasoned Salt and pepper. Place lamb on a rotisserie spit, insert a meat thermometer in thickest part, not touching bone. Cook about 3 hours or until thermometer reads 180°. (To cook in oven: preheat to 325°. Roast 2½ to 3 hours, until meat thermometer reads 180°.)

Meanwhile combine butter, wine vinegar, and sugars in a small saucepan. Stir over low heat until the sugars dissolve. Add juice and rind, dry mustard, and mint. Stir well to blend. Remove from heat. Baste lamb frequently with mint sauce during last hour of

cooking. Let leg set 10 minutes before slicing. Serve with remaining sauce.

## Tarte d'Agneau

*A springtime of goodness in this cheese-crusted lamb pie. Suggested Menu: Fresh Spinach with Lemon.*

*Serves 6        Cooking time: 45 to 50 minutes*

*The pastry:*
    ½ cup butter or margarine, softened
    3-ounce package of cream cheese, softened
    ½ teaspoon Seasoned Salt (page 00)
    1¼ cups flour
    1 teaspoon fresh chives, finely chopped
    1 teaspoon fresh parsley, finely chopped
    pinch of dried dillweed

Mix butter, cream cheese, and salt until smooth. Add the flour and spices gradually and form a ball. Roll ball in a floured pastry cloth and chill.

    ¼ cup flour
    ½ teaspoon Seasoned Salt (page 17)
    ¼ teaspoon pepper
    2-pound boneless lamb shoulder, cut in 1-inch cubes
    2 slices of bacon
    1 garlic clove, pressed
    1 bay leaf
    1 sprig each parsley and thyme
    3 cups beef bouillon
    2 large potatoes, peeled and cut into ¾-inch cubes
    ½ cup Burgundy
    2 dozen medium pearl onions, parboiled 4 minutes
    2 pounds peas, shelled or 10-ounce package frozen peas
    1 cup pitted ripe olives
    1 egg beaten with 1 teaspoon water for glaze

Preheat oven to 400°.

Combine flour, Seasoned Salt and pepper in a plastic bag, shake to mix. Add the meat cubes and shake to coat. Cook bacon in a large oven-proof skillet until crisp. Cool and crumble. Discard all but 3 tablespoons of bacon fat. Add meat and garlic, and sauté until meat has browned on all sides. Combine herbs in a square of cheesecloth, tie as a bag. Add herb bag, bouillon, and diced potatoes to meat. Cook uncovered 10 minutes. Add remaining ingredients and cook an additional 10 minutes. Remove herb bag and add crumbled bacon.

Roll out chilled pastry on a floured surface into a thick 12-inch circle, cut circle into six 1-inch strips, and arrange lattice-fashion on top of the pie. Trim the ends and brush with the egg wash. Bake until crust is golden, about 15 minutes.

## Ragoût d'Agneau aux Petits Pois

*Use fresh or leftover lamb for this stew with tiny peas. Suggested Menu: egg noodles, Maman's Golden Salad.*

*Serves 4 to 6          Cooking time: almost 2 hours*

  2- to 3-pound boneless lamb
      shoulder (or 3 cups leftover
      cooked lamb)
  ¼ cup flour
  3 tablespoons butter or margarine
  2 large carrots, sliced
  2 celery stalks, sliced
  1 large onion, chopped
  2 sprigs of fresh parsley, chopped
  1 bay leaf
  ½ teaspoon Seasoned Salt (page 17)
  ¼ teaspoon dried thyme
  ¼ teaspoon pepper
  1 pound fresh peas, shelled, or
      10-ounce package tiny frozen peas

Remove and discard fat from lamb. Cut meat into 1-inch cubes. Put flour and meat in a plastic bag and shake to coat the lamb pieces. Melt the butter in a Dutch oven over moderate heat. Add the lamb cubes and brown on all sides. Add remaining flour from the plastic bag to pot and stir until golden. Add 3 cups hot water to browned lamb. Add remaining ingredients except peas. Cover and simmer 1½ hours, stirring occasionally. Add the peas and cook an additional 5 to 10 minutes or until the peas are tender. Remove the bay leaf and serve over cooked noodles.

## Veal or Chicken Fricassee

*A delicious combination of meat and vegetables slow-cooked for full flavor. Suggested Menu: boiled new potatoes, salad greens with Oriental Dressing.*

*Serves 4                    Cooking time: 2 hours*

  1½-pound boneless veal shoulder, or
      3 cups leftover cooked chicken or
      veal, cut in 1½-inch cubes
  4 tablespoons butter or margarine
  ½ cup onions, chopped
  ½ teaspoon Seasoned Salt (page 17)
  ¼ teaspoon pepper
  2 cups chicken broth
  2 carrots, peeled, sliced
  2 celery stalks, sliced
  1 cup cauliflower florets, sliced
  ¼ cup fresh mushrooms, sliced
  1 tablespoon fresh parsley, chopped
  2 tablespoons flour
  1 tablespoon fresh lemon juice

Wipe veal with a damp cloth. Melt 2 tablespoons butter in a heavy saucepan. Add veal (or leftover chicken) and brown on all sides. Add onions and cook lightly to just brown. Add salt, pepper, and broth and bring to a boil. Cover and simmer 1 hour. Add carrots, celery, and cauliflower and cook 15 minutes. Add mushrooms and parsley and cook 10 minutes longer. Remove meat and vegetables from heat.

Strain cooking liquid; add water to make 1½ cups. Melt remaining butter in a small saucepan. Add the flour and cook over low heat, stirring constantly, until light brown. Add cooking liquid and stir until liquid thickens. Add lemon juice, stir.

Add meat and vegetables. Serve over new potatoes.

## Veal Jeannine

*Tender cutlets covered with a flavorful wine and cheese sauce. Suggested Menu: Chantilly Potatoes, Asparagus with Lemon.*

*Serves 4*　　　　　*Cooking time: 25 minutes*

　1½ pounds boneless veal, sliced
　　¼ inch thick
　¼ cup butter or margarine
　1½ tablespoons flour
　1 cup milk
　½ teaspoon salt
　dash of white pepper
　2 cups Swiss cheese, grated
　1½ cups fresh mushrooms, sliced
　½ cup Burgundy wine
　salt and pepper

Loosely wrap veal in plastic film and pound to even thickness. Set aside.

Melt 1½ tablespoons of the butter in saucepan. Add flour and cook over low heat until frothy. Add milk and whip until mixture thickens (3 to 4 minutes); add salt and pepper. Add cheese and stir until melted — *do not boil.*

Meanwhile, melt 1 tablespoon butter in skillet, sauté mushrooms until butter is absorbed. Add to sauce, along with wine. Heat remaining butter in skillet over medium-high heat, sauté veal until tender (it cooks very quickly). Lightly season with salt and pepper. Pour sauce over veal to serve.

## Moose Steak with Mushroom Sauce

*Steak d'Original aux Champignons — A recipe for the selected hunters who bag this tasty trophy. Suggested Menu: Shoestring Potatoes, Fresh Kale.*

*Serves 4*　　　　　*Cooking time: 1½ hours*

　1½ pounds moose steak, 1 inch thick
　2 tablespoons butter or margarine
　½ cup beef consommé
　2 tablespoons tomato paste
　¼ cup California sherry or
　　cold water
　1 medium onion, thinly sliced
　1 garlic clove, crushed
　1 cup fresh mushrooms, thinly sliced
　2 tablespoons flour
　¼ to ½ cup heavy cream

Have steaks at room temperature. Cut into 4 portions. Melt butter in a large skillet over medium high heat. As butter begins to brown, add steaks. Sear both sides. Combine consommé, tomato paste, and sherry and mix well. Add to steaks with the onion and garlic. Cover and simmer over low heat for one hour or until steaks are very tender.

Preheat oven to 150°. Remove steaks to a warm platter and place in oven. Add mushroom slices to skillet, cover and cook 2 minutes. Combine flour with 2 tablespoons cold water, stir to dissolve flour completely, then gradually add to skillet, stirring constantly. As mixture thickens, add cream, stir, and heat through. Spoon sauce over steaks to serve.

# Poultry

## Ragoût de Poule aux Boulettes

*Slow-cooked chicken with pork meatballs in a hearty ragoût. Suggested Menu: Oriental Steamed Rice, Vichy Carrots.*

*Serves 6 to 8*        *Cooking time: 3 hours*

- 3 tablespoons butter or margarine
- 5- to 6-pound frying chicken, cut up, skin removed
- 2 teaspoons Seasoned Salt (page 17)
- ½ teaspoon pepper
- 1 large onion, thinly sliced
- 2 celery stalks with leaves, sliced
- ½ teaspoon poultry seasoning
- 1 pound lean ground pork
- 1 large onion, very finely chopped
- 1 garlic clove, pressed
- ¼ teaspoon savory
- ¼ teaspoon marjoram
- 1 egg, well beaten
- ⅓ cup flour

Melt butter in a Dutch oven; add chicken and cook until golden brown. Add 1 teaspoon of the Seasoned Salt, ¼ teaspoon of the pepper, sliced onions, celery; toss and cook until onions are lightly brown. Add 4 to 6 cups of cold water (enough water to cover chicken and fill about ⅓ of the pot). Add poultry seasoning and bring to a boil, cover and simmer for 2½ to 3 hours or until chicken is tender.

Meanwhile, combine ground pork, chopped onions, garlic, savory, marjoram, the egg, remaining teaspoon of Seasoned Salt and ¼ teaspoon pepper; mix thoroughly. Shape into 24 small meatballs. Roll meatballs in flour. Remove the cooked chicken from the pot, cool. Bring liquid to a rapid boil. Add meatballs, lower heat, and simmer 15 minutes, stirring gently. Remove chicken meat from the bones and return to stew. If the stock is not thick enough, thicken with remaining flour diluted in cold water. Serve over rice.

## Baked Chicken Breast, Yvette

*Tangy tomato sauce makes this chicken superb. Suggested Menu: egg noodles, salad greens with Herbal Vinaigrette Dressing.*

*Serves 4*        *Cooking time: 1 hour*

- 4 8-ounce boneless chicken breasts (not skinless)
- Seasoned Salt (page 17)
- ¼ cup vegetable oil
- ¾ cup onions, diced

½ cup celery, diced
½ cup green pepper, diced
¾ cup ketchup
1½ tablespoons brown sugar
¼ cup white vinegar
1½ tablespoons Worcestershire sauce
1 teaspoon salt
¼ teaspoon pepper

Preheat oven to 375°. Rinse chicken and pat dry. Shape into ovals and place skin-side up on roasting pan. Sprinkle with salt. Bake 20 minutes.

Meanwhile heat oil in skillet. Add onions, celery, and peppers and sauté until onions are clear. Combine remaining ingredients in blender with ¼ cup water, process until smooth, and add to vegetables. Stir, and simmer 15 minutes.

Remove chicken from oven. Lower oven temperature to 350°. Remove and discard skin, and place chicken in casserole dish. Pour sauce over chicken and bake, uncovered, 30 minutes. Serve over cooked noodles.

## Charcoal-Grilled Chicken with Peach Glaze

*Sweet-tart glaze on broiled chicken. Suggested Menu: Canadian Potato Salad, Broccoli in Foil.*

*Serves 4*                    *Cooking time: 1 hour*

3-pound frying chicken, quartered
salad oil
Seasoned Salt (page 17)
12-ounce jar peach preserves
¼ cup white vinegar
2 tablespoons pimento, chopped

Rinse chicken, pat dry. Brush with oil, season with salt. Place on grill, bone-side down, over medium coals. Grill 30 minutes, turn, grill 20 minutes longer.

Meanwhile, combine preserves, vinegar, pimento, stir to mix. Brush both sides of chicken with glaze. Grill until tender, about 10 minutes more, basting often for a pretty

finish. Heat remaining glaze and pass with chicken.

## Chicken *à la Pommery*

*Mustard sauce gives chicken an unusual and delicious flavor. Suggested Menu: fresh broccoli, Carrots Vichy.*

*Serves 4*                    *Cooking time: 45 minutes*

3 tablespoons butter or margarine
¼ cup flour
3 cups chicken broth
4 6-ounce skinless, boneless chicken breasts
½ cup flour
1 teaspoon Seasoned Salt (page 17)
½ teaspoon pepper
2 tablespoons olive oil
½ cup dry white wine
¼ cup light cream
3 tablespoons Pommery mustard

Melt butter in saucepan. Add ¼ cup flour. Cook and stir until frothy. Add broth, bring to a boil, reduce heat and simmer 30 minutes or until reduced by one-third.

Wrap chicken pieces in plastic and pound to an even thickness. Combine ½ cup flour, salt, and pepper in bag. Add chicken, shake to coat. Heat oil in skillet and sauté chicken until tender and golden on both sides. Remove from skillet; keep warm.

Drain oil from skillet, add wine to deglaze. Strain reduced broth, add to skillet and simmer 5 minutes. Add cream and mustard, mix well, heat through. Serve over chicken.

## Chicken Breasts in Apricot Sauce

*Fruit flavors grace this delectable dish. Suggested Menu: egg noodles, Cheese-Custard Broccoli.*

*Serves 6*                    *Cooking time: 45 minutes*

2 8-ounce cans apricots, drained
1 cup orange marmalade

½ cup orange juice
½ cup Burgundy
¼ cup red currant jelly
2 tablespoons brown sugar
2 teaspoons grated orange rind
2 tablespoons cornstarch
6 8-ounce skinless, boneless
   chicken breasts
½ cup flour in a plastic bag
2 tablespoons butter or margarine
2 tablespoons olive oil
½ cup apricot brandy

Purée 1 can of the apricots in blender. Transfer fruit to saucepan and add next 6 ingredients and ½ cup water. Simmer 10 minutes. Dissolve cornstarch in ¼ cup cold water, add to sauce, and stir until thick.

Rinse chicken, pat dry. Wrap in plastic and pound to an even thickness. Add breasts to flour in bag, shake to coat.

Heat oil and butter in skillet; sauté chicken until lightly brown on both sides. Remove chicken to paper towels to drain. Drain oil and wipe out skillet. Return chicken to skillet, add brandy, simmer 2 minutes. Stir in apricot sauce, coat chicken. Serve on noodles, surrounded by remaining apricot halves.

## Chicken *Cordon Rouge*

*Stuffed chicken breasts baked with a crunchy topping. Suggested Menu: Noodle Omelet, Cucumbers and Onions in Sour Cream.*

*Serves 4*       *Cooking time: 45 minutes*

½ cup butter or margarine, softened
1 garlic clove, pressed
4 7-ounce skinless, boneless
   chicken breasts
4 thin slices boiled ham
4 thin slices mozzarella cheese
1 medium tomato, finely chopped
½ teaspoon dried sage
14 saltine crackers, finely crumbled
3 tablespoons grated Parmesan
   cheese

dash each of garlic powder and
   pepper
2 tablespoons parsley, minced

Preheat oven to 350°. Combine ¼ cup of the butter and the garlic in mixing bowl. Mix well, set aside.

Wrap chicken in plastic and pound chicken lightly with mallet from the center out, to an even thickness.

Spread each slice of ham with the garlic butter. Place one slice on each chicken breast, top with a mozzarella cheese slice and ¼ of the chopped tomato. Sprinkle with a dash of sage. Tuck in sides, roll up "jelly roll" style, pressing to seal well.

Melt remaining butter in skillet. Combine cracker crumbs, Parmesan cheese, garlic powder, freshly ground pepper, and parsley in a soup bowl and mix well. Dip rolled breasts first in butter, then in crumb mix. Place in baking dish, carefully pour remaining butter atop, and bake 40 to 45 minutes.

## Chicken Divan

*Breast of chicken and tender broccoli in a rich cream sauce. Suggested Menu: egg noodles, Hot Spiced Peaches.*

*Serves 4*       *Cooking time: 1 hour*

2 10-ounce skinless, boneless
   chicken breasts
1 small onion, sliced
1 tablespoon parsley
1 small garlic clove, sliced
¼ cup butter or margarine
⅓ cup flour
2 cups chicken broth
½ cup heavy cream
3 tablespoons sherry
½ teaspoon Seasoned Salt (page 17)
¼ teaspoon dried basil
2 bunches fresh broccoli
½ cup Parmesan cheese, freshly
   grated

Place chicken breasts in saucepan with

onion, parsley and garlic, cover with cold water. Bring to a boil, then reduce heat and simmer 30 minutes, removing scum as it forms. Drain chicken, strain liquid (use to boil egg noodles). Cool chicken, then chill. Cut chilled meat into ¼-inch-thick slices.

Preheat oven to 350°. Melt butter in saucepan. Add flour, cook and stir until frothy. Add broth, stir constantly until mixture thickens. Add cream, sherry, Seasoned Salt, and basil.

While sauce simmers, place steam rack in another saucepan. Pour in cold water to just below steamer base. Add broccoli. Cover and steam 5 minutes, until just tender but still firm. Drain spears and place crosswise in baking dish. Pour half the sauce over broccoli. Arrange chicken slices on top. Add ¼ cup of the cheese to remaining sauce, stir until cheese melts. Pour over chicken. Sprinkle remaining cheese on top. Bake 20 minutes, then broil until top is golden brown.

## Chicken Cantonese with Soft Fried Noodles

*A favorite stir-fried entrée, quick and easy to prepare. Suggested Menu: fortune cookies and Chinese tea.*

*Serves 4*          *Cooking time: 10 minutes*

1 pound See-Sun noodles (available in most supermarkets)
vegetable oil spray
4 tablespoons peanut oil
Seasoned Salt (page 17)
2 garlic cloves, minced
¼ teaspoon ground ginger
2 8-ounce skinless, boneless chicken breasts, thinly sliced
2½ cups chicken broth
1½ cups celery or bok choy (Chinese cabbage), sliced diagonally
1 cup canned mushrooms, sliced
6-ounce package frozen Chinese pea pods, thawed, or 1 cup fresh snow pea pods
1 tablespoon mushroom soy sauce

3 tablespoons cornstarch
1 medium tomato, cut into 8 wedges
½ teaspoon sesame oil

Prepare all ingredients, place in separate dishes and have at hand before beginning to cook.

Put noodles in a Dutch oven, cover with cold water, stir. Bring to a boil and immediately remove from heat, strain, and run under cold water to stop the cooking action. Drain. Spread on paper toweling to absorb all moisture. Heat a large griddle, spray with vegetable oil. Spread noodles evenly over griddle; fry over medium high heat. Pour 1 tablespoon of the peanut oil over the noodles, toss to mix. Sprinkle with Seasoned Salt. When noodles are golden, turn, fry other side with another tablespoon oil, sprinkle with additional Seasoned Salt. Cook until crisp and golden.

Heat remaining 2 tablespoons of peanut oil in a wok or large skillet. Add garlic and stir-fry, over medium-high heat, for 30 seconds. Add ginger and chicken, toss and stir-fry 3 to 5 minutes. Add celery or bok choy, toss to coat with oil. Add 1½ cups of the chicken broth, stir and cook 3 minutes. Add mushrooms, pea pods, and soy sauce; stir. Dissolve cornstarch in remaining broth, add to wok, and stir until mixture thickens. Add tomato wedges and sesame oil, stir. Serve over the golden soft fried noodles. Pass the soy sauce.

## Chicken Cacciatora *alla Romana*

*Suggested Menu: egg noodles, Cheesy-Crouton Salad, Mocha-Ricotta Custard.*

*Serves 4*          *Cooking time: 1 hour*

3-pound frying chicken, cut up
½ cup flour
½ teaspoon garlic salt
½ teaspoon pepper
4 tablespoons olive oil
1 cup onions, sliced
2 garlic cloves, minced

2 cups canned Italian tomatoes
1 cup tomato sauce
1 teaspoon Seasoned Salt (page 17)
1 teaspoon celery seeds
1 teaspoon each of basil and
  oregano
2 whole bay leaves

Remove and discard skin from chicken. Rinse pieces and pat dry. Combine flour, garlic salt, and ¼ teaspoon of the pepper in bag; mix. Sauté onions and garlic in Dutch oven with 2 tablespoons of the oil until onions are clear. Remove from pan with slotted spoon and set aside. Add remaining 2 tablespoons of oil to Dutch oven, heat. Shake chicken pieces in flour bag to coat. Brown all sides in hot oil. Remove from pan, keep warm. Drain and discard all oil from pan, but leave the crusty bits. Add remaining ingredients to pan with cooked onions and garlic and simmer 5 minutes. Sink chicken pieces into sauce, cover, and simmer 45 minutes, stirring occasionally.

## Coq au Vin

*Chicken in rich brown gravy, subtly flavored with wine. Suggested Menu: Chantilly Potatoes, Frozen Cheese and Strawberry Salad.*

*Serves 4*                    *Cooking time: 1 hour*

3-pound frying chicken, cut up
2 tablespoons butter or margarine
2 tablespoons salad oil
1 teaspoon Seasoned Salt (page 17)
¼ teaspoon each of thyme and
  pepper
¼ cup brandy
12 small pearl onions
8 small carrots, pared, halved
1 garlic clove, minced
1½ cups fresh mushrooms, sliced
2 tablespoons flour
2 cups dry red wine, good quality
1 small bay leaf
1 tablespoon parsley
½ cup chicken broth

1 tablespoon tomato paste

Remove skin from chicken. Cut off and discard wing tips. Rinse, pat dry. Melt butter and heat oil in skillet. Brown chicken on all sides over medium heat, season with salt, thyme, pepper. *Remove from heat,* pour brandy over chicken, ignite. When fire dies, remove chicken to platter.

Add onions, carrots, garlic, and mushrooms to skillet, cook 5 minutes. Sprinkle flour over vegetables, stir to blend. Stir in wine. Add bay leaf, parsley, broth, and tomato paste, simmer 3 minutes. Add chicken, cover, and simmer slowly 35 to 40 minutes or until chicken and vegetables are tender. Remove bay leaf before serving.

## Lemon-Herb Chicken in a Roman Pot

*Slow cooking retains vitamins and natural flavor. Suggested Menu: Acorn Squash Bake with Fruit, hot rolls.*

*Serves 4*                    *Cooking time: 1¼ hours*

3-pound roasting chicken
1 lemon, cut in half
2 tablespoons parsley, chopped
1 tablespoon chives, snipped
1 teaspoon tarragon
½ teaspoon Seasoned Salt (page 17)
1 celery stalk with leaves
2 large potatoes, pared, quartered
8 carrots, pared, quartered

Soak Romertopf (covered clay cooking pot) under hot water for 10 minutes. Squeeze juice from lemon, retain one squeezed half. Combine juice with parsley, chives, tarragon and salt. Clean chicken cavity, rinse, and pat dry. Brush a little of the lemon mixture inside cavity. Put celery stalk and lemon half in cavity; skewer shut. Place chicken in drained Romertopf. Pour remaining lemon sauce over top of chicken. Cover, place in *cold* oven, turn oven to 400°. Bake 30 minutes. Add vegetables, cover, and bake another 45 minutes, or until chicken is tender. Remove chicken and vegetables to platter. Skim off fat from pot juices and serve with chicken.

## Olé Molé Chocolate Chicken

*South-of-the-border flavors abound in this spicy dish. Suggested Menu: Oriental Steamed Rice, mixed greens with Celery Seed Dressing.*

*Serves 4*         *Cooking time: 1½ hours*

3½-pound chicken, cut up
2 tablespoons olive oil
¼ cup unsalted peanuts
1 tablespoon toasted sesame seeds
1-ounce square unsweetened
  chocolate
1 slice bread, toasted
3 cups canned tomatoes in purée
4 teaspoons chili powder
½ teaspoon Seasoned Salt (page 17)
½ teaspoon ground cumin
¼ teaspoon cinnamon
¼ teaspoon pepper
1 garlic clove, pressed
¼ cup dark Crême de Cacao

Remove and discard skin from chicken, rinse, pat dry. Heat oil in Dutch oven. Brown chicken pieces on all sides. Remove from pan, keep warm. Pour off fat, leaving the crusty bits.

Combine peanuts, sesame seeds, chocolate, and toast in blender and process until finely chopped. Add to Dutch oven with tomatoes, seasonings, and garlic, stirring to loosen crusty bits. Bring to a boil, stirring constantly. Reduce heat and simmer 15 minutes; stir frequently.

Meanwhile, preheat oven to 350°. Sink chicken into sauce, cover, transfer to oven and bake 45 minutes or until chicken is tender. Add cacao liqueur, stir, and bake 5 minutes more. Serve with rice and plenty of ice water or chilled beer to cool palate.

## Drumsticks Parmesan

*Youngsters love this one. Suggested Menu: Bacon Fried Corn, Rice au Gratin, Banana Split Salad.*

*Serves 4*         *Cooking time: 1 to 1½ hours*

½ cup butter or margarine, melted
2 cups fresh bread crumbs (4 slices)
½ cup grated Parmesan cheese
¼ teaspoon paprika
¼ teaspoon ground savory
½ teaspoon garlic powder
1 teaspoon salt
dash of black pepper
8 to 12 chicken drumsticks

Preheat oven to 350°. Melt butter in skillet over very low heat, do not brown. Tear bread slices into chunks and place in blender bowl. Turn blender on/off (pulse) until crumbs are uniform. Combine crumbs, Parmesan cheese, paprika, savory, garlic powder, salt, and pepper in mixing bowl. Mix well.

Rinse drumsticks, pat dry. (Optional – remove skin from drumsticks.) Dip drumsticks in melted butter, then roll in crumb mixture to coat very well. Place on foil-lined baking dish, sprinkle with any remaining butter. Bake 1 to 1½ hours, depending on size of drumsticks, until golden brown. Test for doneness by inserting a fork; if it twists easily, chicken is done.

## Poulet à l'Ail Chablis

*For garlic lovers only: chicken breasts in garlic and wine. Suggested Menu: Bordeaux Potatoes, Green Beans Almondine, Chablis.*

*Serves 4*         *Cooking time: 1 hour*

4 8-ounce skinless, boneless
  chicken breasts
salt and pepper
1 to 2 tablespoons olive oil
½ cup parsley, freshly chopped

8 garlic cloves, thinly sliced
½ cup Chablis or similar dry
  white wine
4 slices provolone cheese
1 tablespoon cornstarch
4 thick slices French bread

Preheat oven to 375°. Place chicken on waxed paper and sprinkle both sides lightly with salt and pepper. Pour olive oil in casserole dish. Roll chicken breasts in oil to coat thoroughly. Shape into ovals and line in bottom of casserole, adding remaining oil. Sprinkle with parsley, spread evenly with garlic slices to cover. Pour wine around chicken. Cover with foil and bake 1 hour, or until chicken is tender. Move chicken to broiler pan, brushing any garlic and parsley back into casserole, top with cheese, and broil until bubbly.

Meanwhile, strain pan juices into saucepan. Toast bread. Mash the strained garlic and parsley and spread on toast. Dissolve cornstarch in ¼ cup cold water. Add to pan juices, cook and stir until thick. Adjust salt and pepper. Place chicken on toast, cover with sauce to serve.


## Poulet Suisse

*Roast chicken with apples, smothered in cheese fondue. Suggested Menu: French bread toast, carrot sticks, broccoli, cauliflowerets.*

*Serves 4*       *Cooking time: 2½ hours*

3-pound roasting chicken
1 large apple, cored, cut in
  12 wedges
1 medium onion, pared, quartered
¼ teaspoon garlic salt
3 tablespoons butter or margarine,
  melted
⅛ teaspoon paprika
⅛ teaspoon pepper
1 garlic clove, cut in half
2 cups dry white wine
1½ pounds Swiss cheese, diced
¼ cup Kirsch brandy

1½ tablespoons cornstarch
¼ teaspoon baking soda
dash each of salt, pepper, nutmeg
4 slices French bread, toasted, cubed
fresh chives, chopped

Preheat oven to 350°. Clean chicken cavities, remove excess fat, rinse, and drain. Slide apple wedges between skin and flesh of breast and thighs. Place onion in large cavity, sprinkle with half the garlic salt; truss. Rub chicken with butter, sprinkle with remaining garlic salt, paprika and pepper. Place in roasting pan, cover loosely with foil tent. Roast until golden brown, 2½ hours.

Use half the garlic clove to rub inside of fondue pot, discard. Press remaining half into pot, discard pulp. Add wine, heat until bubbles start to rise. Add cheese, by thirds, stir until melted. Dissolve cornstarch in Kirsch. Add to pot, stir until thick. Reduce heat, add soda and spices, and mix well. Pour enough sauce over chicken to coat. Place toasted cubes all around, sprinkle with chives. Keep remaining fondue warm as a dip for fresh vegetables.


## Roast Chicken with Fruit and Nut Stuffing

*Sunday dinner at home — my mother's family feast. Suggested Menu: Canadian Cheese Soup, whipped potatoes, giblet gravy, Acorn Squash Bake, Cranberry and Fruit Salad, Flamed Coffee Ice Cream Sipper.*

*Serves 4*       *Cooking time: 2½ hours*

¼ cup seedless raisins
2 tablespoons brandy
2 cups herb-seasoned stuffing mix
½ cup butter or margarine, melted
¼ cup celery, finely chopped
½ cup apples, pared, diced
¼ cup walnuts, coarsely chopped
3- to 4-pound roasting chicken
salt
paprika
1 small onion, quartered

2 celery heart stalks with leaves,
  chopped
6 peppercorns
2 chicken bouillon cubes
1 teaspoon Kitchen Bouquet
2 tablespoons flour

Preheat oven to 325°. Soak raisins in brandy for 15 minutes. Combine stuffing mix, ⅓ cup of the butter, ¼ cup celery, apples, walnuts, and ⅔ cup boiling water in mixing bowl; mix well. Add raisins with brandy, mix again.

Rinse chicken, clean cavity, rinse again, drain. Salt cavity and loosely spoon in stuffing. Skewer and lace shut. Brush with remaining butter, sprinkle with salt and paprika. Place on rack, breast-side down. Bake 2 hours, turn breast-side up, increase oven temperature to 425°, and roast 30 minutes longer.

Meanwhile, place onion, chopped celery stalks, peppercorns, and bouillon cubes in saucepan; add neck, skin removed, gizzard, 1 teaspoon salt, and 3 cups water. Bring to a boil, and simmer while chicken roasts. Remove chicken to warm platter. Spoon off all but 2 tablespoons fat, heat, then add flour, stirring until frothy. Strain simmered broth into flour mix, cook and stir until thick. Dice gizzard and neck meat, add to gravy with Kitchen Bouquet. Adjust seasonings.

## Sesame Chicken with Cumberland Sauce

*An intriguing combination of nutty, sweet, and sour flavors. Suggested Menu: Oriental Steamed Rice, Spinach-Mandarin Salad.*

*Serves 4*          *Cooking time: 30 minutes*

1 cup fresh bread crumbs
⅓ cup sesame seeds
2 tablespoons grated Parmesan
  cheese
1 tablespoon parsley, chopped
¼ teaspoon pepper

4 6-ounce skinless, boneless
  chicken breasts
2 tablespoons butter or margarine,
  melted
1 orange
1 lemon
12-ounce jar red currant jelly
½ teaspoon Dijon mustard
¼ teaspoon ginger
¼ teaspoon cayenne pepper
¼ cup port wine

Preheat oven to 425°. Combine first 5 ingredients, crumbs to pepper, in mixing bowl; mix well. Wrap chicken in plastic and pound to ¼-inch thickness. Dip in butter, then crumb mix. Place on cookie sheet. Bake 20 minutes.

Grate peel from orange and lemon, avoiding the bitter white layer. Place in saucepan, cover with water, bring to a boil, drain, repeat process twice. Spoon jelly into saucepan, heat until melted. Add drained fruit peels, juice of lemon and orange, mustard, ginger, and pepper, simmer 10 minutes. Stir in port and heat through. Serve sauce over chicken.

## Soy-Sauced Chicken Bake

*A succulent, easily prepared Oriental dinner. Suggested Menu: Oriental Steamed Rice, celery sticks, Banana Split Salad.*

*Serves 4*          *Cooking time: 1¼ hours*

½ cup mushroom soy sauce
2 tablespoons onions, chopped
2 garlic cloves, chopped
2 tablespoons sugar
dash of Seasoned Salt (page 17)
dash of freshly ground pepper
½ teaspoon sesame oil
4- to 5-pound roasting chicken
2 tablespoons cornstarch
4 celery stalks for garnish, cut into
  3-inch sticks

Combine first 7 ingredients in blender bowl. Process until smooth, about 30 seconds. Pour this marinade into a large mixing bowl and set aside. Rinse chicken. Place rinsed gizzard and liver in marinade. Cut chicken in half, remove excess fat, clean cavity, rinse again, and pat dry. Add halves to marinade, cover and chill 2–3 hours, turning occasionally. Preheat oven to 375°. Place chicken halves, breast side down, on rack of pan, reserve marinade for basting. Bake 30 minutes, baste, turn. Place gizzard and liver alongside chicken and bake 30 to 45 minutes longer or until tender, basting frequently. Remove chicken from oven, cool slightly and cut halves into smaller serving pieces with cleaver. Skim off fat from pan juices. Deglaze pan with ¼ cup water, strain into a small saucepan, and add remaining marinade. Dissolve cornstarch in ¼ cup cold water, add to marinade, cook and stir until thickened. Place chicken portions over rice in warm plates. Top with gravy, surround with celery sticks.

## Stir-fried Chicken and Cashews

*Chicken complemented with nuts and peapods, in a delicate orange sauce. Suggested Menu: Oriental Steamed Rice, Spinach-Mandarin Salad.*

*Serves 4              Cooking time: 15 minutes*

3 6-ounce skinless, boneless
  chicken breasts
2 tablespoons mushroom soy sauce
2 teaspoons cornstarch
1 teaspoon grated orange peel
½ cup orange juice
2 tablespoons peanut oil
1 cup salted cashew halves
¼ teaspoon ground ginger
6-ounce package Chinese pea pods,
  thawed
11-ounce can Mandarin oranges,
  drained

Cut chicken into 1-inch pieces, set aside. Blend soy sauce into cornstarch, stir in orange peel and juice, set aside. Heat oil in wok or large skillet. Add cashews and stir-fry for 2 minutes, until golden. Remove to

paper towel to drain. Add chicken to wok, stir-fry until tender, 5 minutes. Sprinkle with ginger, toss. Add pea pods, toss to coat, fry 1 minute. Stir soy mixture, add to wok. Cook, stirring, until thick. Stir in oranges and nuts. Remove from heat and serve with rice.

## Stuffed Chicken Breasts in *Sauce Suprême*

*Brandy accents the fruit stuffing as well as the sauce. Suggested Menu: Oriental Steamed Rice, Broiled Tomato Slices, Asparagus with Lemon.*

*Serves 4              Cooking time: 35 minutes*

¼ cup seedless raisins
2 dried prunes, finely diced
¼ cup brandy
1 cup herb-seasoned stuffing mix
⅓ cup butter or margarine, melted
¼ cup apples, pared, finely diced
¼ cup toasted almonds, crushed
4 6-ounce skinless, boneless
  chicken breasts
Seasoned Salt (page 17)
1 can condensed cream of chicken
  soup
½ cup milk
2 tablespoons toasted almond slices

Soak raisins and prunes in brandy for 1 hour. Preheat oven to 450°. Combine stuffing mix with 2 tablespoons of the butter and ¼ cup boiling water. Add apples, almonds and drained fruit (reserve brandy), mix well.

Wrap the chicken breasts in plastic and pound to even thickness. Season one side lightly with Seasoned Salt. Place stuffing on seasoned side of each breast; roll, overlapping to seal loosely. Place seam-side down in casserole dish. Brush with remaining melted butter. Bake 5 minutes. *Reduce heat to 325°*, bake 30 minutes longer, basting occasionally.

Combine soup with milk and brandy, stir to blend. Slowly heat through. Spoon sauce over chicken, top with toasted almond slices.

## Stuffed Chicken Breasts Polynesian

*Pineapple provides the Hawaiian touch. Suggested Menu: Oriental Steamed Rice, buttered peas, Almond Float.*

*Serves 4*          *Cooking time: 45 minutes*

- ¼ cup mushrooms, finely chopped
- 2 tablespoons onions, finely chopped
- ½ cup butter or margarine
- ½ cup smoked ham, finely chopped
- ¼ cup walnuts or pecans, ground
- ½ cup crushed pineapple, reserve juice
- ¼ cup oyster sauce
- ¼ cup brown sugar
- 4 8-ounce skinless, boneless chicken breasts
- pineapple juice
- 3 tablespoons soy sauce
- 3 tablespoons sherry
- 3 tablespoons red wine vinegar
- ½ cup tomato ketchup
- ¼ teaspoon ground ginger
- 2 tablespoons cornstarch

Preheat oven to 375°.

Sauté mushrooms and onions in 2 tablespoons of the butter until onions are clear. In mixing bowl, make the stuffing: combine the cooked vegetables, ham, nuts, pineapple, 2 tablespoons of the oyster sauce and 1 teaspoon of the brown sugar; mix well.

Wrap chicken loosely in plastic, pound to an even thickness, and rub with remaining oyster sauce. Divide stuffing evenly on breasts, fold sides and ends to seal, shape into ovals, and place seam-side down in ovenproof skillet with remaining butter and ¼ cup water. Bake 45 minutes, basting frequently.

Add enough pineapple juice to that drained from crushed fruit to make 1 cup and combine with balance of brown sugar and remaining ingredients, except cornstarch, in saucepan. Bring to a boil. Dissolve cornstarch in 2 tablespoons cold water and add to sauce, stirring until thick and clear. Spoon over chicken.

## Chicken "Fondue" with Sweet and Sour Sauce

*Easy and delicious as an item for a fondue party or served as suggested. Suggested Menu: Oriental Steamed Rice, Easy and Grand Caesar Salad, hard rolls, rosé wine.*

*Serves 4*

- 10-ounce jar peach or apricot preserves
- ¼ cup white vinegar
- 2 tablespoons pimentos, chopped
- 4 skinless, boneless chicken breasts
- 4 cups chicken broth
- 1 tablespoon parsley, finely chopped
- 1 teaspoon garlic power
- ½ teaspoon pepper
- eggs (if desired)
- green onions (if desired), finely sliced

Combine preserves, vinegar and pimentos in a mixing bowl, mix very well. Cover and chill at least 1 hour to allow flavors to blend.

Slice chicken breasts into ¼-inch strips. Roll up strips and arrange on a platter, cover and leave at room temperature 30 minutes before serving.

Heat chicken broth in fondue pot; add parsley, garlic powder, and pepper, and stir. Keep broth simmering. Separate preserves mixture into 4 small bowls. Spear chicken rolls with fondue forks, plunge into the simmering broth and cook 15 to 20 seconds. Transfer cooked chicken rolls to a cold fork and swirl in sauce. Meanwhile, the next piece of chicken is already cooking.

The stock may be served as a soup to finish off the meal. Add a little rice, or drizzle in well-beaten eggs for egg drop soup. Serve broth in a small bowl, garnished with finely sliced green onions.

## Turkey Breast, Tarragon

*A delicious and unusual change for family dining. Suggested Menu: New Potatoes in Lemon, Zucchini with Corn.*

*Serves 4*        *Cooking time: 30 minutes*

1½ pounds raw turkey breast
½ cup flour
½ teaspoon Seasoned Salt (page 17)
½ teaspoon pepper
2 tablespoons vegetable oil
¼ cup dry white wine
3 teaspoons fresh tarragon or
   1 teaspoon dried tarragon
¼ cup light cream

Cut turkey into 4 equal portions. Wrap loosely in plastic and pound to an even thickness. (Note: packaged fresh turkey cutlets are available in many supermarkets, and will shorten preparation time.) Combine flour, salt, and pepper in bag, add and shake each portion to coat. Heat oil in skillet and sauté turkey until tender and golden on both sides. Remove to platter. Pour off oil, leaving the crusty bits. Add wine to skillet, stir to deglaze. Bring to a boil and reduce slightly. Add tarragon and cream, reduce heat and stir until semi-thick. Pour over turkey.

## Hickory-Smoked Turkey

*A summertime treat, slow-baked in your covered charcoal cooker along with potatoes and corn — just add a salad.*

*Serves 8 to 10*      *Cooking time: 4½ hours*

10-pound turkey
Seasoned Salt (page 17)
1 large apple, cored, cut in half
1 celery stalk with leaves
1 medium onion, quartered
3 tablespoons salad oil
(hickory chips, dampened)
¼ cup salt
½ cup white vinegar
2 tablespoons pepper
1 teaspoon parsley, chopped
8 to 10 medium potatoes

Rinse turkey and clean cavities, remove excess fat, pat dry. Sprinkle cavities with Seasoned Salt. Insert apple, celery, and onion in large cavity. Skewer and lace shut. Balance turkey on spit or rack, tie wings and drumsticks to body. Brush with 1 tablespoon of the oil. Place in cooker. Have slow coals at rear of firebox, toss damp hickory chips on coals. Place a drip pan under turkey. Roast, hood down, for 1 hour.

Combine salt, vinegar, pepper, and parsley with remaining 2 tablespoons salad oil, stir, and use this mixture to baste turkey. Check coals. Continue roasting for approximately 3½ hours, basting every 30 minutes.

Place Foil-Baked Potatoes (see index) on grill or on coals and bake 2 hours. Roast ears of corn for ½ hour (see index for roasted corn recipe). Drumsticks should twist easily out of joint when turkey is done. Remove from cooker, let stand 15 minutes before carving. Discard stuffing.

## Turkey *alla Parmigiana*

*Serve leftover turkey "Italian style." Suggested Menu: pasta, Easy and Grand Caesar Salad.*

*Serves 4*        *Cooking time: 30 minutes*

3 eggs, well beaten
1 cup grated Parmesan cheese
½ cup fine cracker crumbs
2 cups cooked turkey, finely
   chopped
3 tablespoons butter or margarine
1 tablespoon olive oil
1 garlic clove, minced
¼ cup green pepper, chopped
¼ cup carrot, shredded
½ cup onion, chopped
2 cups tomato sauce
1 teaspoon sugar
½ teaspoon Seasoned Salt (page 17)
¼ teaspoon pepper

¼ teaspoon basil
1 cup mozzarella cheese, shredded

Preheat oven to 350°. Combine eggs, cheese, and crumbs in mixing bowl; stir. Add turkey, mix well, and shape into 8 patties. Melt butter in skillet. Brown patties on both sides and place in casserole dish. Wipe skillet clean, add oil, and heat. Add garlic, peppers, carrots, and onions. Sauté until onions are clear. Add tomato sauce, spices, and ¼ cup water; simmer 5 minutes. Spoon over patties, top with mozzarella cheese, and bake 20 minutes.

## Roast Duckling in Brandied Orange-Raspberry Sauce

*A dish to grace a festive occasion. Suggested Menu: Almond Rice, Maman's Golden Salad, Broccoli with Lemon.*

*Serves 4*               *Cooking time: 3½ hours*

5-pound duckling, ready to cook
2 teaspoons marjoram
½ teaspoon salt
¼ teaspoon pepper
1 small onion, peeled
1 medium apple, cut in half
1 orange, cut in half
2 tablespoons soy sauce
2 cups raspberry preserves
¼ cup brandy
1 tablespoon red wine vinegar

Preheat oven to 325°. Remove wing tips from duck. Clean and rinse cavity, remove all excess fat, rinse duck and pat dry. Sprinkle 1 teaspoon of the marjoram, salt, and pepper in cavity. Place onion, apple, and half the orange in cavity; skewer opening and lace. Skewer neck opening. Rub duck with soy sauce, sprinkle with remaining marjoram. Place breast-side down on rack of pan. Bake 1½ hours, draining off fat as it accumulates. Turn duck and bake 1½ hours longer. When cooked, remove all fat from pan, tip duck slightly to release juices from cavity.

Place duck on cutting board. Remove skewers, discard cavity fruit. Cut duck into 4 serving portions. Sprinkle with salt and place in broiler pan. Set aside 15 minutes. Set oven to broil. Combine preserves, brandy, vinegar, juice and grated rind from remaining orange half, and strained pan juices in saucepan, heat through. Broil duck until skin is crisp. Brush with sauce, broil 1 minute more. Serve with sauce.

# Fish & Seafood

## Applejack Filet of Sole

*Baked in apple cider, topped with a brandied cream sauce. Suggested Menu: Chantilly Potatoes, Onion and Fruit Sauté.*

*Serves 4*      *Cooking time: 20 minutes*

  1 teaspoon butter or margarine
  4 green onions, finely chopped
  1½ pounds or 4 filets of sole
  ¼ teaspoon salt
  pepper
  1 tablespoon lemon juice
  2 tablespoons applejack brandy
  ½ cup apple cider
  2 tablespoons butter or margarine
  2 tablespoons flour
  ¼ cup heavy cream
  ¼ cup Parmesan cheese, freshly
    grated

Preheat oven to 400°. Butter casserole dish with 1 teaspoon butter. Sprinkle green onions on bottom. Arrange fish filets in a single layer. Sprinkle with salt, pepper, lemon juice, and applejack brandy. Heat cider almost to boiling and pour over fish. Cover with foil, bake 12 minutes.

Remove dish from oven and turn oven to broil. Pour off liquid, strain and reserve.

Melt 2 tablespoons butter in saucepan. Add flour and cook until frothy. Add strained liquid and cream. Stir. Heat through, but *do not boil*. Pour sauce over fish, sprinkle with cheese. Pop under broiler until bubbly, 3 to 5 minutes.

## Baked Haddock *au Gratin*

*Down East method, world-famous flavor. Suggested Menu: Noodles and Cashew Toss, Spinach and Grapefruit Sauté.*

*Serves 4*      *Cooking time: 15 minutes*

  1½ pounds haddock filets, skinless,
    boneless
  1 cup buttermilk
  1 cup fresh bread crumbs
  ½ cup grated Parmesan cheese
  ¼ teaspoon thyme
  pinch of basil
  ½ cup butter or margarine, melted
  ½ lemon, cut in 4 wedges

Rinse fish, pat dry. Cut into 4 servings. Soak in buttermilk, 15 to 30 minutes. Preheat oven to 500°. Combine crumbs, cheese, and spices in medium bowl. Mix well. Drain fish, discard milk, and roll in crumbs to coat all sides. Place in 1-quart casserole dish. Slowly pour butter over and around fish. Bake 10 to 15 minutes, or until fish flakes easily. Serve with lemon wedge.

## Baked Salmon Steaks Sebago

*Topped with scallops, smothered in rich dill sauce. Suggested Menu: Lyonnaise Potatoes, Spinach with Lemon.*

*Serves 4*  *Cooking time: 20 minutes*

4 fresh salmon steaks, 1- to 1½-inch thick
¼ pound scallops
1 small onion, thinly sliced
4 thin slices lemon
½ cup dry white wine
3 tablespoons butter or margarine
3 tablespoons flour
1 cup milk
7 ounces Havarti cheese with dill, diced
½ teaspoon salt
¼ teaspoon pepper

Preheat oven to 475°. Rinse steaks, pat dry. Rinse scallops, remove side tendon, and slice ¼-inch thick. Place lightly oiled heavy-duty foil on cookie sheet; place sliced onions on foil, steaks on top of onions, scallops on top of steaks. Top each steak with lemon slice. Pour ¼ cup of the wine over lemon, pinch foil to seal tightly. Bake 15 to 20 minutes.

Melt butter in saucepan. Add flour, cook until frothy. Remove from heat. Add milk all at once, stir well to blend. Return to heat, stir until mixture thickens. Add diced cheese and remaining wine and stir until cheese melts. Add salt and pepper.

When fish is baked, carefully open foil packet to release steam and remove fish to warmed plates. Remove and discard lemon slices. Strain foil juices, add to cream sauce. Pour over fish and serve.

## Baked Stuffed Filet of Sole, Bertrand

*Seafood dressing, a creamy wine-cheese sauce. Suggested Menu: New England "Stuffies," Carrots Vichy.*

*Serves 4*  *Cooking time: 40 minutes*

½ cup butter or margarine, melted
¼ cup onions, finely diced
¼ cup canned mushrooms, finely diced
1 tablespoon parsley, finely chopped
¼ cup crushed milk crackers
4 saltine crackers, crushed
½ cup crushed barbeque potato chips
¼ cup grated Parmesan cheese
8 ounces fresh crabmeat, flaked, or 7½-ounce can crabmeat, drained and flaked
3-ounce can tiny shrimp, drained, chopped
dash each salt and pepper
1 cup thick white sauce (see index)
2 tablespoons dry sherry
4 sole filets, about 1 pound
¼ cup sharp cheddar cheese
paprika

Sauté onions, mushrooms, and parsley in ¼ cup of the butter until onions are clear. Combine crackers, chips, and Parmesan cheese, toss to mix. Remove any cartilage from crabmeat and add with shrimp, cooked vegetables with butter, salt, and pepper to crumb mixture. Mix together. Add just enough melted butter to lightly bind together.

Preheat oven to 350°. Prepare white sauce. Add wine to sauce and blend. Place ½ cup of stuffing in center of each filet. Roll, place seam-side down in lightly buttered casserole dish. Pour sauce over fish, sprinkle each filet with 1 tablespoon cheddar cheese and garnish with paprika. Bake until fish flakes easily, about 25 to 30 minutes.

# Baked Stuffed Jumbo Shrimp

*Long a New England restaurant favorite, equally appealing at home. Suggested Menu: Rice au Gratin, Spinach Elegante.*

*Serves 4          Cooking time: 35 minutes*

¼ cup butter or margarine
2 tablespoons onions, finely chopped
2 tablespoons celery, finely chopped
1 garlic clove, crushed
1 tablespoon parsley, finely chopped
¼ cup crushed milk crackers
4 saltine crackers, crushed
½ cup crushed barbeque flavor
   potato chips
¼ cup grated Parmesan cheese
½ pound fresh crabmeat or
   7½-ounce can crabmeat,
   drained, flaked
3-ounce can tiny shrimp, drained,
   chopped
dash each of salt and pepper
16 jumbo (10 per pound) shrimp,
   in shells
2 tablespoons stick butter or
   margarine

Melt ¼ cup butter in saucepan. Add onions, celery, garlic, and parsley, sauté until onions are clear. Combine crackers, chips, and cheese, toss to mix. Remove any cartilage from crabmeat. Add to crumbs with shrimp, cooked vegetables with butter, salt, and pepper. Mix together. Additional melted butter may be added, if necessary, to lightly bind stuffing.

Preheat oven to 350°. Shell shrimp, leaving tail on. Butterfly shrimp by splitting down the back almost but not all the way through; de-vein. Pack stuffing tightly into slit shrimp. Lay in buttered casserole dish, stuffing side up. Cut stick butter into 8 slices, cut slices in half. Place one piece of butter on each stuffed shrimp. Bake until shrimp are tender, 25 to 30 minutes.

# Braised Stuffed Pickerel

*A succulent way to present the fisherman's catch. Suggested Menu: Rice au Gratin, Broccoli with Fresh Lemon.*

*Serves 4          Cooking time: 45 to 50 minutes*

3- to 4-pound pickerel, dressed
3 slices bacon
½ cup onions, chopped
2 tablespoons celery, finely chopped
1½ cups packaged corn bread
   stuffing mix
¼ cup butter or margarine, melted
1 egg, well beaten
¼ cup ground canned luncheon meat
½ teaspoon pepper
½ teaspoon dried parsley
¼ cup yellow raisins, softened in
   hot water
dry white wine
2 egg yolks, well beaten
juice of 1 lemon

Rinse fish, pat dry. Preheat oven to 350°. Partially cook bacon, set aside. Sauté onions and celery in bacon fat until clear, 3 to 5 minutes. Combine stuffing mix, butter, cooked vegetables, ground meat, and egg. Stir to mix. Add enough boiling water to bind together. Add parsley, pepper, and drained raisins; mix well.

Loosely stuff the fish, skewer closed. Place in baking dish, add wine to cover bottom of dish, top with partially cooked bacon. Bake 45 to 50 minutes. Cover after first 15 minutes, baste frequently.

Remove fish to warmed platter while preparing the sauce. Strain pan juices, skim off excess fat and pour in saucepan. Bring to a near boil, remove from heat. Combine egg yolks and lemon juice and slowly add a little of the pan juice, beating constantly. Add this egg mixture to remaining pan juices. Cover and let stand 5 minutes to thicken. Serve over fish.

# Broiled Scallops in Garlic Butter

*Sweet and tender morsels, New England style. Suggested Menu: Bordeaux Potatoes, Broccoli with Fresh Lemon.*

*Serves 4*       *Cooking time: 15 minutes*

1 cup butter or margarine, softened
1 cup cheese-garlic croutons, crumbled
4 garlic cloves, minced
2 tablespoons onion, finely minced
½ cup parsley, chopped
¼ cup white wine
juice of ½ lemon
½ teaspoon salt
¼ teaspoon pepper
2 tablespoons vegetable oil
2 tablespoons onion, diced
½ pound mushrooms, sliced
1½ pounds bay scallops, fresh
dash each of salt and pepper

Mix butter, crouton crumbs, garlic, onions, parsley, wine, lemon juice, salt, and pepper. Blend completely. Form into a log shape, wrap in waxed paper, and chill until firm, at least 1 hour.

Preheat oven to broil. Heat oil in large skillet over medium heat until haze forms. Add onions, sauté until clear but not brown. Add mushrooms, scallops, salt, and pepper, sauté 2 minutes. Drain off liquid. Arrange scallops and vegetables in lightly buttered dishes. Slice chilled garlic butter and arrange evenly over scallops. Place 3 inches from heat and broil until bubbly, 3 to 5 minutes.

# Clams Steamed in Beer

*Succulent morsels that seem to melt in your mouth. Suggested Menu: Easy and Grand Caesar Salad, Skewers of Baked French Bread and Cheese, beer.*

*Serves 4*       *Cooking time: 15 minutes*

4 quarts fresh clams, in shells
2 tablespoons salt

beer
1 cup butter or margarine, melted
⅛ teaspoon garlic salt

Scrub clam shells thoroughly with brush. Place in kitchen sink and cover with cold water. Add salt, stir to mix. Soak for 2 hours. Drain and rinse.

Pour ¼-inch layer of beer in Dutch oven, add clams, cover. Cook over low heat until shells open, about 15 minutes. Remove clams to large soup plates (discard any with broken or unopened shells). Strain the broth, serve each person a cupful. Combine butter and garlic salt, stir to blend. Pour into individual cups.

To eat: Remove clam from shell, slip off neck skin, dip clams in broth, then butter.

# No-Crust Crabmeat Quiche

*Prepare and serve piping hot in individual ramekins. Suggested Menu: Hashed Brown Potatoes, Nantucket Beets.*

*Serves 4*       *Cooking time: 30 minutes*

1 tablespoon butter or margarine, melted
½ cup coarse dry bread crumbs
½ pound crabmeat
1 cup sharp cheddar cheese, grated
2 tablespoons stick butter or margarine
2 eggs, beaten
2 cups milk
¼ teaspoon Seasoned Salt (page 17)
dash of pepper
1 tablespoon chives, finely snipped

Preheat oven to 350°. Butter bottom and sides of individual baking dishes. Sprinkle 2 tablespoons crumbs on the bottom of each. Layer half the crabmeat over crumbs, cover with half the cheese, repeat layers. Cut butter into 8 slices, place 2 slices atop each dish. Combine eggs, milk, salt, pepper, and chives, blend thoroughly. Pour mixture slowly into ramekins. Bake until a knife tip inserted in center comes out clean, about 30 minutes.

## Filet of Sole Oriental

*Baked-stuffed and covered with a sherry-soy sauce. Suggested Menu: Oriental Steamed Rice, Stir-Fried Broccoli.*

*Serves 4*          *Cooking time: 25 to 30 minutes*

8-ounce can crushed pineapple
1 packet chicken broth with
   seasonings
2 cups herb stuffing mix
½ cup water chestnuts, diced
½ cup butter or margarine, melted
dash of ginger
1½ pounds or 4 filets of sole
2 tablespoons soy sauce
2 tablespoons dry sherry
1 tablespoon white vinegar
1 tablespoon cornstarch
2 teaspoons sugar
2 tablespoons green onions, sliced

Preheat oven to 350°. Drain pineapple and reserve syrup. Add enough hot water to syrup to make ⅔ cup.

Sprinkle packet of chicken broth over herb stuffing mix in mixing bowl. Add diced water chestnuts, drained pineapple, ⅓ cup of the butter, dash of ginger, and the pineapple liquid and blend well.

Rinse fish, pat dry. Spoon 3 tablespoons stuffing onto each filet, roll, and place in greased 8-by-8 baking dish. Brush fish with remaining butter to coat. Add ¼ cup water to remaining stuffing, place in 1½-quart casserole dish, cover, and bake with fish for 20 to 25 minutes.

Bring ¾ cup cold water to rapid boil in saucepan. Combine soy sauce, wine, and vinegar in bowl. Add cornstarch and stir until dissolved; add sugar and a dash of ginger. Add this mixture to boiling water, lower heat, and simmer, stirring, until thick. Remove from heat, add green onions.

Center fish on platter, surround with additional stuffing and rice. Pass the sauce.

## Haddock à l'Orange

*Orange-tomato sauce enhances this sea delicacy. Suggested Menu: baked potato, Green Beans Almondine.*

*Serves 4*          *Cooking time: 30 minutes*

3 tablespoons butter or margarine
½ cup onions, chopped
½ cup orange juice
2 cup canned tomatoes, chopped,
   drained
2 teaspoons orange juice concentrate
½ teaspoon salt
½ teaspoon pepper
½ teaspoon thyme
1½ pounds haddock, cut into
   4 servings
4 thin orange slices

Melt butter in a medium saucepan. Add onions and sauté 1 minute. Add remaining ingredients except the fish and orange slices to the saucepan; stir. Simmer, uncovered 15 minutes.

Preheat oven to 350°. Rinse fish, pat dry, place in shallow 1-quart casserole dish. Cover with sauce. Bake until flaky, about 10 to 15 minutes. Serve covered with sauce and an orange slice twisted atop each portion.

## Haddock Supreme

*Choose any of three simple gourmet sauces to complement poached filets.*

*Serves 4*          *Cooking time: 10 minutes*

1 teaspoon Seasoned Salt (page 17)
1 slice lemon
1 slice onion
1 tablespoon vinegar
2 sprigs parsley
1 bay leaf

6 peppercorns
1½ pounds filet of haddock, cut
    into 4

Pour 2 cups water into skillet. Add all ingredients but fish. Bring to a boil, simmer 5 minutes. Rinse fish. Add to skillet, cover, and simmer until flaky, about 5 minutes. Serve immediately with your choice of sauces.

*Sauce Macadamia:* Melt ½ **cup butter** in saucepan. Add **2 chopped scallions** and 1 **teaspoon each: oregano, rosemary, thyme, sage, marjoram, basil.** Add **1 cup coarsely chopped macadamia nuts.** Sauté lightly. Add **¾ cup dry white wine.** Heat and pour over cooked fish.

*Sauce Monique:* Simmer ½ **cup white seed-less grapes** in water to cover for 3 minutes, drain. Prepare **1 cup Medium White Sauce** (see index). Whip **¼ cup heavy cream,** fold into White Sauce. Fold in ½ **cup tiny cooked shrimp,** grapes, **dash of salt,** and **white pepper.** Pour over cooked fish.

*Sauce Marinara:* Heat **2 tablespoons olive oil** in saucepan. Add **2 cups canned tomatoes,** drained, **1 small garlic clove,** pressed, **¼ teaspoon pepper,** and **1 tea-spoon each: chopped parsley, oregano,** and **salt.** Simmer 30 minutes. Pour over cooked fish.

## Cookout Haddock Penobscot

*Features the flavor of Maine-made cheese. Sugested Menu: Onions in Cinders, Spinach-Mandarin Salad.*

*Serves 4*          *Cooking time: 4 to 8 minutes*

½ **cup butter or margarine, melted**
1 **tablespoon fresh parsley, chopped**

2 **garlic cloves, minced, or**
    ¼ **teaspoon of garlic powder**
**vegetable oil spray**
1½ **pounds fresh haddock filets**
6 **ounces State of Maine brand**
    **Penobscot Cheddar Cheese, sliced**

Combine butter, parsley, and garlic, mix well. Spray inside of wire grilling basket with oil. Rinse fish, pat dry. Cut into 4 serving pieces. Brush one side of each, using half the butter mixture. Cover half of each piece with the cheese slices, fold, and brush outer side of fish with some of the garlic butter. Place in wire basket, secure cover, and grill over medium-hot coals 2 to 4 minutes per side, depending on the thickness of the fish. Baste with remaining butter mixture. Serve hot.

## Halibut *Trois Rivières*

*Cooked the way fishermen along the St. Lawrence serve it. Suggested Menu: Tomatoes Dijon (make ahead), Cheesy-Crouton Salad.*

*Serves 4*          *Cooking time: 20 to 25 minutes*

1½ **pounds fresh halibut**
2 **tablespoons butter or margarine**
2 **medium onions, sliced**
½ **cup flour**
1 **teaspoon garlic salt**
½ **teaspoon pepper**
**vegetable oil spray**

Preheat oven to 350°. Rinse fish, pat dry. Cut into 4 serving pieces. Melt butter in skillet. Add onions and sauté until crisp-tender, not brown. Spoon onto layers of absorbent paper toweling. Combine flour, salt, and pepper in plastic bag. Mix well. Toss fish portions in bag of flour mixture to coat completely, shake off excess. Drain skillet, wipe with paper towel. Spray with non-stick oil. Heat and add fish. Cook on medium heat 3 minutes on each side to brown. Place in shallow baking dish, top with cooked onion slices. Bake until fish flakes easily, about 7 minutes.

## Homard avec Sauce Mornay

*A rich "Newburg" variation using lobster and patty shells. Suggested Menu: Spinach and Grapefruit Sauté.*

Serves 4                     Cooking time: 15 minutes

2 cups Medium White Sauce
  (see index)
1 cup sharp cheddar cheese,
  shredded
2 tablespoons cream sherry
1½ cups cooked lobster meat,
  cut bite-size
4 packaged frozen patty shells,
  baked
paprika

Prepare White Sauce. Add cheese and stir until melted. Add wine and lobster. Heat through. Spoon into cooked shells, sprinkle with paprika.

## Maman's Salmon Pie

*A French-Canadian specialty and family favorite. Suggested Menu: Green Beans in Cream, Jellied Waldorf Salad.*

Serves 4                     Cooking time: 40 minutes

2 cups mashed potatoes
¼ teaspoon salt
dash of pepper
4 tablespoons butter or margarine
1 tablespoon oil
1 cup onions, chopped
16-ounce can salmon, undrained
1 cup Medium White Sauce
  (see index)
pastry for 2-crust, 9-inch pie
  (see index)
cream or milk

Cook potatoes, then mash with 2 tablespoons of the butter, salt, and pepper.

Preheat oven to 400°. Combine remaining butter and oil in skillet. Add onions and sauté until clear but not brown.

Drain liquid from salmon into mixing bowl, set aside. Remove and discard skin and cartilage from salmon. Add salmon to liquid along with onions and White Sauce and mix well. Pour mixture into pastry-lined pie plate. Spread mashed potatoes over mixture. Cut slits in top pastry crust and center over potatoes. Trim and seal. Brush top, *not edges,* with cream or milk. Bake 30 to 40 minutes, until crust is golden.

## Maman's Salmon Sauce in Patty Shells

*Another treasured family recipe. Suggested Menu: Broccoli with Fresh Lemon, Gabrielle's Green Salad.*

Serves 4                     Cooking time: 20 minutes

1 tablespoon butter or margarine
½ cup onions, chopped
2 cups milk
¼ teaspoon Seasoned Salt (page 17)
dash of white pepper
2 tablespoons flour
16-ounce can salmon
3 hard-cooked eggs, sliced
4 frozen patty shells, baked

Melt butter in saucepan. Add onions and sauté until clear but not brown. Add milk, salt, and pepper. Bring to a boil over low heat. Dissolve flour thoroughly in a little cold water. Slowly pour into hot milk. Cook, stirring constantly, until thickened. Drain salmon, discard skin and cartilage. Break into chunks and add to sauce with sliced eggs. Heat through. Spoon into shells.

# Mussels with Linguine

*Maine's newest seafood "star" in a wine sauce over pasta. Suggested Menu: Gabrielle's Green Salad, French Garlic Toast.*

*Serves 4*        *Cooking time: 30 minutes*

4 pounds fresh mussels
⅓ cup butter or margarine
2 tablespoons olive oil
¼ cup onions, finely chopped
2 garlic cloves, finely minced
1 cup dry white wine
2 tablespoons parsley, chopped
2 tablespoons flour
1 teaspoon basil
salt and pepper
16 ounces linguine
grated Parmesan cheese

Scrub mussels to remove sand. Pull off beards. Discard any open shells.

Melt 2 tablespoons of the butter in Dutch oven, add 1 tablespoon oil, and heat through. Add onions and garlic and sauté until onions are clear. Add wine, 1 table-spoon of the parsley, and mussels. Cover and steam until shells open, about 8 to 10 minutes. Discard any mussels that have not opened. Strain and retain juice from mussels, pouring it through several layers of cheese-cloth a few times to remove sand. Remove mussels from shells and set aside.

In a 3-quart saucepan melt remaining butter, add flour, and cook over low heat until frothy. Add strained juice all at once and stir until thick. Add mussels, remaining parsley, basil, salt and pepper to taste. Heat through.

Rinse out Dutch oven, add 4 quarts cold water, remaining olive oil, ½ teaspoon salt and bring to boil. Cook linguine *al dente*, about 5 to 7 minutes. Drain. Top with mussel sauce, sprinkle with cheese, serve.

# Rainbow Trout *Italiano*

*Marinated to enhance flavor. Suggested Menu: Easy and Grand Caesar Salad, Cheese-It Biscuits.*

*Serves 4*        *Marinate 6 hours*
       *Cooking time: 10 to 15 minutes*

4 rainbow trout, cleaned, heads
   removed
bottled Italian dressing
2 tomatoes
¼ teaspoon basil
⅛ teaspoon salt
⅛ teaspoon pepper

Rinse trout and pat dry. Place in casserole dish. Add enough dressing to cover fish. Cover and marinate at least 6 hours.

Preheat oven to broil. Drain trout and reserve marinade. Extend the belly cavity so trout will lay flat, but without cutting through the skin. Place on rack of broiler pan, skin side up. Broil 4 inches from heat source for 3 minutes, turn, baste with marinade, broil an additional 5 to 8 minutes depending on thickness of trout. (If a fork twists easily in the thickest part of the flesh, the fish is cooked.)

Peel tomatoes and coarsely chop. Place in small mixing bowl with 1 tablespoon of the reserved Italian dressing and toss gently. Sprinkle with basil, salt, and pepper. Spoon over cooked trout.

# Rich Man–Poor Man Seafood Thermidor in Shells

*Made with either lobster or cod — both delicious. Suggested Menu: Shoestring Potatoes, French-Style Peas.*

*Serves 4*        *Cooking time: 25 minutes*

*Rich Man:*
1 pound cooked lobster meat

*Poor Man:*
1 pound fresh cod filets

*Both:*

1 small onion, sliced
6 peppercorns
3 sprigs parsley
3 whole cloves
½ cup dry white wine
vinegar
1 cup thick White Sauce (see index)
½ cup Gruyere cheese, grated
3-ounce can tiny shrimp, drained
2 tablespoons parsley, snipped
½ cup soft bread crumbs
2 tablespoons butter or margarine,
  melted
2 tablespoons grated Parmesan
  cheese
dash of paprika

Cut lobster meat or (rinsed and dried) cod into bite-sized chunks.

If using cod, place fish, onion, peppercorns, parsley, cloves, and ¼ cup of the wine in skillet. Add boiling water to cover. For every 2 cups of water added, add 1 tablespoon vinegar (this will keep the fish firm). Cover and simmer until fish flakes easily, 8 to 10 minutes.

Prepare white sauce. Add remaining ¼ cup of wine and cheese to sauce and stir until cheese melts. Add snipped parsley and drained shrimp.

Preheat oven to broil. Drain fish, sprinkle lightly with salt. Fold cooked fish or lobster into sauce, spoon into lobster or coquille shells. Combine crumbs, butter, Parmesan cheese, and dash of paprika, sprinkle atop sauce. Broil until lightly browned, 5 to 8 minutes.


## Soy-Glazed Scallops

*Polynesian flavor with toasted-almond crunch. Suggested Menu: Oriental Steamed Rice, Spinach-Mandarin Salad.*

*Serves 4*　　　　　*Cooking time: 20 minutes*

1½ pounds sea scallops

2 tablespoons soy sauce
1 tablespoon cornstarch
¾ cup unsweetened pineapple juice
2 tablespoons sherry
dash of ground ginger
2 tablespoons peanut oil
1 garlic clove, minced
¼ cup toasted almonds, sliced
1 scallion, finely sliced

Clean and rinse scallops. Remove and discard side tendons, pat dry. Dissolve cornstarch in soy sauce in small bowl. Combine juice, wine, and ginger in saucepan. Slowly bring to a boil. Reduce heat, add blended cornstarch mixture, and stir constantly until thick.

Heat oil in skillet. Add garlic and sauté 1 minute; add scallops. Sauté, turning often, until scallops are hot and cooked through, about 5 to 8 minutes. Drain. Add scallops to sauce, stir to coat. Spoon over rice, cover with sauce. Sprinkle with nuts and scallions.


## Stuffed Whole Maine Lobster

*The king of seafood regally prepared. Suggested Menu: tossed salad, French Garlic Bread.*

*Serves 4*　　　　　*Cooking time: 25 minutes*

4 live lobsters, 1 pound each
¼ cup butter or margarine
2 tablespoons onions, finely chopped
2 tablespoons canned mushrooms,
  chopped
1 garlic clove, pressed
1 tablespoon parsley, finely chopped
¼ cup crushed milk crackers
4 saltine crackers, crushed
½ cup crushed barbeque flavor
  potato chips
¼ cup grated Parmesan cheese
7½-ounce can crabmeat, drained,
  flaked
3-ounce can tiny shrimp, drained,
  chopped
dash each of salt and pepper

Plunge live lobsters headfirst into large pot of boiling salted water, cover. When water returns to boil, simmer for 8 minutes.

Preheat oven to 375°. Sauté onions, mushrooms, garlic, and parsley in butter until onions are clear. Combine crackers, chips, and cheese, toss to mix. Remove and discard cartilage from crabmeat, add to crumbs with shrimp, cooked vegetables with butter, salt, and pepper. Mix well.

Remove lobsters from pan; place on backs on cutting board. With sharp knife, split lengthwise from head down to tail. *Do not cut all the way through.* Spread body open and discard all organs except green liver (add liver to stuffing). Remove black vein from tail. Spoon stuffing into body cavity. Place lobsters, shell-side down, in shallow baking dish. Bake until lightly brown, about 10 minutes. Serve with melted butter.

## Tuna Patricia

*Dress up this pantry staple with nuts and noodles in a creamy sauce. Suggested Menu: Eggplant Parmigiana.*

*Serves 4*        *Cooking time: 40 minutes*

1½ cups egg noodles
¼ cup butter or margarine
¼ cup onions, finely chopped
¼ cup celery, finely chopped
¼ cup flour
2 cups milk
¼ teaspoon salt
¼ teaspoon pepper
¼ teaspoon dry mustard
½ cup canned mushrooms, drained, sliced
7-ounce can tuna, drained, flaked
1 cup salted cashew nuts, chopped
3-ounce can chow-mein noodles

Cook egg noodles according to package directions. Drain, rinse in hot water, and drain again.

Preheat oven to 350°. Sauté onions and celery in butter until onions are clear. Add flour and cook over low heat until frothy. Add milk and whip to blend completely. Add salt, pepper, and mustard. Cook, stirring constantly, until thick. Add mushrooms, tuna, nuts, and drained noodles. Pour into casserole, sprinkle chow mein noodles over top, and bake 30 to 35 minutes.

## White Fish Piquant

*Tangy flavor baked into tender filets. Suggested Menu: New Potatoes in Lemon Sauce, Green Beans in Cream.*

*Serves 4*        *Cooking time: 20 minutes*

1 tablespoon cider vinegar
1 tablespoon Worcestershire sauce
1 tablespoon lemon juice
½ cup butter or margarine, melted
1 teaspoon Dijon mustard
¼ teaspoon Seasoned Salt (page 17)
dash of pepper
½ cup dry bread crumbs, pea sized
1½ pounds white fish filets
    (haddock, sole, etc.)
paprika

Preheat oven to 450°. Combine first 7 ingredients (vinegar to pepper). Mix well. Rinse fish and pat dry. Cut into 4 servings. Lightly butter bottom of casserole dish. Sprinkle crumbs on bottom, top with filets. Pour vinegar mixture over fish. Sprinkle with paprika. Bake, basting twice, until fish is flaky—about 10 minutes per inch of thickness. Spoon crumb base over fish to serve.

# Luncheon & Dinner Salads

## Camille's Vegetable Dinner Salad

*Beautifully arranged vegetables with pineapple and eggs.*

*Serves 4 to 6*          *Cooking time: 12 minutes*

4 eggs
1 small head of lettuce
3 tablespoons onion, finely chopped
3 tablespoons green pepper, finely chopped
16-ounce can Le Sueur peas, drained (very small early peas)
8-ounce can pineapple chunks, drained
1 medium cucumber, sliced
2 tomatoes, each cut into 8 wedges
16-ounce can asparagus spears, carefully opened and drained
Slavic Dressing (see index)

Fill a 2½-quart saucepan with 6 cups of cold water. Bring to a boil. Prick the small end of the eggs with a needle (this will make the shelling easier) and carefully lower them into the rapidly boiling water; immediately lower heat so that water is just under boiling. Cook the eggs 12 minutes, then plunge immediately into cold water. Cool. Shell and slice crosswise in thirds.

Tear the lettuce into bite-size pieces. Rinse, drain, wrap in a clean kitchen towel, and chill.

To assemble: Line a large platter with the torn lettuce. Sprinkle the finely chopped onions and green peppers over the lettuce. Pour the peas, in a mound, in the center of the platter. Arrange the pineapple chunks, egg slices, tomato wedges, and cucumber slices around the platter. Carefully lean the asparagus spears against the mound of peas. Serve with Slavic Dressing.

## Creamy Chicken Salad in Tomato

*A delightful luncheon entrée.*

*Serves 4*

¼ cup seedless raisins
2 cups cooked chicken, diced
½ cup mayonnaise
½ cup dairy sour cream
1 medium apple, cored and diced
½ cup celery hearts, diced
½ cup toasted slivered almonds
3 tablespoons parsley, finely chopped
juice of ½ lemon

½ teaspoon Seasoned Salt (page 17)
¼ teaspoon ground pepper
¼ cup lettuce heart, finely diced
4 large lettuce leaves
4 large firm tomatoes
Herbal Vinaigrette Dressing
  (see index)

Soak raisins in hot water to plump, about ½ hour. Combine chicken, mayonnaise, sour cream, apple, celery, almonds, and drained raisins. Toss to mix. Add parsley, lemon juice, salt, and pepper; toss lightly again. Cover and chill. Rinse, drain, lettuce heart and leaves, wrap in a clean kitchen towel, and chill.

To assemble: Cut a thin slice from stem end of the unpeeled tomatoes. Scoop out centers (save and blend for juice), leaving outer wall. Add diced lettuce heart to chicken salad, toss to mix thoroughly; Carefully fill tomatoes with salad mixture. Place a lettuce leaf on each salad plate, set filled tomato in the center, and splash with Herbal Vinaigrette Dressing.

## Savory Salmon Mousse with Herbal Vinaigrette Dressing

*Serve in a buffet or as a luncheon salad.*

*Serves 6*                       *Chill 6 hours*

16-ounce can salmon
¼ cup vinegar
1 teaspoon Seasoned Salt (page 17)
¼ cup dairy sour cream
1 tablespoon horseradish
1 envelope unflavored gelatin
¼ cup lemon juice
¼ cup cold water
1 teaspoon Dijon mustard
½ cup heavy cream, whipped
1 cucumber, thinly sliced
1 green pepper, cut into strips
1 cup Herbal Vinaigrette Dressing
  (see index)

Drain salmon. Remove all skin and bones,

break into small pieces, and place in a blender with vinegar and salt. Blend at high speed to make a purée. Pour into a large bowl and fold in sour cream and horseradish.

In top pan of double boiler, sprinkle gelatin over lemon juice and cold water. Let stand 5 minutes. Set pan over boiling water and stir with spatula to dissolve gelatin. Stir gelatin into puréed salmon, along with mustard. Fold in whipped cream. Pour into an oiled mold and chill 6 hours or until firm.

Marinate cucumber and green pepper in vinaigrette dressing and refrigerate 2 hours, tossing occasionally.

To assemble: Drain vegetables (reserve dressing) and arrange them on a salad platter. Unmold mousse atop vegetables, serve dressing on the side. To unmold, dip mold in warm water to the depth of the gelatin for 15 seconds.

## Steak and Mushroom Dinner Salad

*A different meal for a hot summer day. Serve with Canadian Potato Salad for a real winner.*

*Serves 6 to 8*          *Marinate 3 to 4 hours*
             *Cooking time: 16 to 20 minutes*

2½-pound New York sirloin steak,
  1½ to 2 inches thick
salt and pepper
1 cup red wine vinegar
¾ cup salad oil
2 teaspoons onion, minced
1 tablespoon Seasoned Salt (page 17)
1½ teaspoon Worcestershire sauce
¾ teaspoon pepper
¾ teaspoon dried tarragon leaves
¾ teaspoon garlic powder
2 medium, firm cucumbers, thinly
  sliced
2 green peppers, thinly sliced
  in rings
1 pound fresh mushrooms, sliced
salad greens
2 tomatoes, each cut into 8 wedges

Set oven rack 6 inches from the heat source. Preheat oven to broil. Slash fat edge of steak and place on a cold broiler pan. Broil, 8 to 10 minutes, until nicely browned. Season with salt and pepper, turn. Broil other side 8 to 10 minutes for medium rare. Cut a slit in the meat; the color inside should be pink to red. Season with salt and pepper. Cool. Remove all fat. Cut steak, against the grain, into ¼-inch slices and chill.

Combine vinegar, oil, onion, and spices in a blender. Blend until smooth and completely mixed. Line bottom of a casserole dish with cold steak slices. Top with sliced cucumbers, green peppers, and mushrooms. Pour marinade over vegetables, cover and chill 3 to 4 hours. Rinse and drain salad greens, wrap in a clean kitchen towel, chill.

To assemble: Line a serving platter with salad greens. Arrange drained steak and vegetables atop greens and surround with tomato wedges.

# Salads &
# Salad Dressings

## Athenian Salad

*Easily assembled for those on a busy schedule.*

*Serves 4*              *Cooking time: 15 minutes*

2 eggs
3 medium tomatoes, cut in wedges
1 teaspoon dried oregano
½ teaspoon Seasoned Salt (page 17)
dash of pepper
1 medium green pepper
salad greens
½ cup Greek olives
½ cup feta (Greek goat cheese) or
   small curd cottage cheese
¼ cup dairy sour cream

(Note: Greek olives are available at specialty stores or in some supermarket deli sections; ripe olives may be substituted, but they don't have the same distinctive flavor.)

Fill a 1½-quart saucepan with cold water. Bring to a boil. Prick the small ends of the eggs with a needle (this will make shelling easier) and carefully lower them into the rapidly boiling water. Immediately lower heat to just under boiling and cook the eggs 10 minutes. Plunge the eggs in cold water the minute they are done; cool. Shell and slice.

Place the tomato wedges in a bowl and sprinkle with the oregano, salt, and pepper. Remove the seeds and membrane from the green pepper and slice thinly. Rinse and drain the salad greens, wrap them in a clean kitchen towel, and chill.

To assemble: Spread the salad greens on a serving platter. Arrange the tomato wedges, olives, green pepper, and egg slices on top of the greens. Crumble the feta cheese over the vegetables and spoon dollops of sour cream over the salad.

## Avocado Sunshine Salad with Orange Mayonnaise

*Looks as good as it tastes.*

*Serves 4 to 6*

½ cup seedless raisins
2 avocados, peeled, seeded
   and sliced
¼ cup lemon juice
1 tablespoon orange rind, freshly
   grated
3 oranges, peeled
lettuce leaves
¾ cup mayonnaise
¼ cup orange juice

dash of paprika

Soak the raisins in hot water to soften. Soak the avocado slices in the lemon juice. Grate the orange rind, then peel and slice the oranges crosswise and remove the seeds. Rinse, drain, and wrap the lettuce leaves in a clean kitchen towel and chill. Combine the mayonnaise, orange juice, orange rind, and paprika. Mix very well.

To assemble: Line a serving bowl with the lettuce leaves. Alternate drained avocado slices and orange slices on the lettuce. Drain the raisins and sprinkle over the fruit. Top with the mayonnaise mixture.


## Banana Split Salad

*As good as the real thing—but not as fattening.*

*Serves 4*

4 large lettuce leaves
2 tart apples
¼ cup lemon juice
3 bananas, peeled
2 oranges, peeled, seeded, sectioned
8-ounce can crushed pineapple, drained
1 recipe Ice Cream Dressing (see index)
½ cup walnuts, coarsely chopped
4 large red cherries

Rinse and drain the lettuce, wrap in a clean kitchen towel, and chill. Core each apple and cut into 8 wedges; place in a mixing bowl with the lemon juice, toss lightly. Cut the bananas into ½-inch slices, add to the apples, and toss.

To assemble: Place a lettuce leaf on each salad plate. Layer the drained apples and banana slices on the lettuce. Add a layer of orange sections and spread the crushed pineapple over the oranges. Top with the ice cream dressing, sprinkle with the nuts, and add a cherry on the top.

## Canadian Potato Salad

*Prepare the day before your cookout to allow the flavors to blend.*

*Serves 6*   *Requires overnight chilling*
*Cooking time: 15 to 20 minutes*

2 pounds potatoes, unpeeled
1 clove garlic, cut in half
1 tablespoon Dijon style mustard
2 tablespoons tarragon vinegar
¼ cup olive oil
1 end slice of bread
¾ cup chicken broth
½ teaspoon Seasoned Salt (page 17)
¼ teaspoon pepper
1 tablespoon chopped chives
¼ cup salad olives, drained
¼ cup black pitted olives, chopped
salad greens
paprika
2 tablespoons sesame seeds, toasted

Cook the potatoes in water to cover until tender. Drain. Let stand until cool enough to handle. Peel and cube.

Rub a wooden salad bowl with half the garlic clove; discard garlic. Combine the mustard and vinegar in the salad bowl and beat with a wire whip; gradually add the olive oil, beating constantly, until well blended.

Crush the remaining half clove of garlic in a press, spread the mashed garlic on the crust side of the bread. Dice the bread and add to the salad bowl, toss gently. Add potatoes and broth, toss again very gently. Season with salt, pepper, and chives. Add the olives and toss once more. Cover and chill (overnight is best).

Rinse and drain the salad greens, wrap them in a clean kitchen towel and chill.

To assemble: Line a salad bowl with the salad greens, spoon the salad into the bowl. Sprinkle with paprika and toasted sesame seeds.

# Cheesy-Crouton Salad

*Serves 4*  *Cooking time: 4 to 5 minutes*

⅓ cup butter, softened
¼ teaspoon paprika
2 tablespoons grated Parmesan
  cheese
⅛ teaspoon garlic powder
3 slices day-old bread
4 cups lettuce, in bite-size pieces
Italian Cheese Dressing (see index)

Preheat oven to broil. Combine the butter, cheese, paprika, and garlic powder. Blend well. Spread on both sides of the bread. Broil both sides of buttered bread until brown and crunchy. Dice into croutons and cool.

Rinse and drain the salad greens, wrap them in a clean kitchen towel and chill.

To assemble: Toss lettuce with cooled croutons and top with Italian Cheese Dressing.

# Cucumber and Onion Slices in Sour Cream

*Especially refreshing with hot-weather meals.*

*Serves 4*

2 medium cucumbers, peeled and
  sliced thin
1 mild onion, peeled and sliced thin
1 tablespoon Seasoned Salt (page 17)
½ cup dairy sour cream or
  plain yogurt
¼ cup tarragon vinegar
1 teaspoon dill seed
dash of hot pepper sauce
3 tablespoons chives, chopped
3 medium radishes, sliced

Place the sliced cucumbers and onions in a bowl with the salt. Cover with ice cold water; weigh contents down with a plate. Let stand 30 to 40 minutes. Drain completely. Combine the sour cream or yogurt, vinegar, hot pepper sauce, and dill seeds. Mix well. Pour over drained vegetables and top with chives and sliced radishes.

# Easy and Grand Caesar Salad

*A classic.*

*Serves 4 to 6*

¼ cup butter or margarine, softened
1 clove garlic, cut in half
3 bread slices
1 small head iceberg lettuce
1 small head romaine lettuce
1 bunch watercress
½ cup Parmesan cheese, freshly
  grated
¼ teaspoon Seasoned Salt (page 17)
dash each of dry mustard and pepper
1 egg
3 tablespoons lemon juice
dash Worcestershire sauce
¼ cup peanut oil
3-ounce chunk of hard salami, cubed
  (optional)
2-ounce can anchovy filets

Press half the garlic clove into a small bowl (discard pulp) and blend with softened butter. Trim the crust off the bread slices and toast. Spread the warm toast with the garlic butter and place on a rack to cool, then cut into cubes. Rinse and drain the salad greens, wrap them in a clean kitchen towel, and chill. Combine the cheese, salt, mustard, and pepper together. Rub the inside of a large wooden salad bowl with the cut side of the remaining garlic clove. Place the garlic clove in the blender bowl with the egg, lemon juice, and Worcestershire sauce and blend 30 seconds. Remove cover, slowly add the oil, and continue to blend until completely smooth.

To assemble: Tear the greens into bite-size pieces, sprinkle with the cheese mixture, toss. Add half the egg-oil mixture, toss. Add the croutons, the anchovies, salami cubes (if desired), and the remaining oil and toss once again.

# Fresh Fruit *à la* Grand Marnier

*Serves 4*                    *Chill overnight*

1 banana, peeled and sliced
¼ to ½ cup lemon juice
¼ to ½ cup sifted confectioners'
  sugar
½ cup fresh pineapple chunks,
  drained
1 apple, cut in wedges
½ pint strawberries, hulled
1 peach, washed and sliced
4 tablespoons walnut pieces
1 orange, peeled and sectioned
1 pear, washed and sliced
1 cup red raspberries
½ cup plus 1 tablespoon
  Grand Marnier
½ cup heavy cream
1 teaspoon sugar
1 teaspoon orange rind, grated

Grate orange rind before peeling the orange.

Prepare in 4 large "on the rocks" glasses with straight sides. Divide and layer the banana slices in the bottom of each glass. Sprinkle generously with lemon juice, then sprinkle lightly with confectioners' sugar. Arrange the remaining fruit and nuts in layers on bananas, sprinkling each layer with lemon juice and confectioners' sugar. Pour Grand Marnier, 2 tablespoons per glass, over the fruit. Cover and chill overnight to blend flavors.

When ready to serve, whip the cream to stiff peaks. Add the sugar and 1 tablespoon Grand Marnier and beat to mix thoroughly. Fold in the orange rind. Mound on chilled fruit.

# Frozen Cheese and Strawberry Salad

*Serves 4*                    *Freezing time: 4 hours*

½ cup fresh strawberries, sliced
  thick
½ cup pineapple chunks, drained
½ cup sugar
1½ teaspoons lemon juice
1 cup creamed cottage cheese
½ cup heavy cream
salad greens
4 whole strawberries, 4 pineapple
  chunks (for garnish)

Sprinkle fruit chunks with the sugar. Mix well. Combine the lemon juice and the cottage cheese in a blender and process until smooth. Whip the cream. Gently fold the fruit into cheese blend; fold in whipped cream. Spread evenly into ice cube tray and freeze several hours. Rinse and drain the salad greens, wrap them in a clean kitchen towel, and chill. Cut the frozen salad into 4 portions. Arrange on chilled salad greens, distributed on 4 plates. Garnish each with a speared pineapple chunk and strawberry.

# Gabrielle's Green Salad

*Beautiful, delicious, and easy to make.*

*Serves 6*

3-ounce package lime gelatin dessert
3-ounce package cream cheese,
  softened
1 cup boiling water
1 envelope whipped topping mix, or
  2 cups sweetened whipped cream
½ cup cold milk
½ teaspoon vanilla
8-ounce can crushed pineapple
¼ cup walnuts, chopped
¼ cup red maraschino cherries,
  chopped

Combine the lime gelatin and the softened cheese. Stir until very well blended. Add boiling water and stir to dissolve. Chill until partially set. Prepare the whipped topping mix with the cold milk and vanilla according to package directions. Fold in the partially set gelatin, add the pineapple with juice, nuts, and chopped cherries. Stir to mix well.

**Salads & Salad Dressings    85**

Pour into a 2-quart mold. Chill until firm.

To unmold: Dip mold in warm water the depth of the salad for 15 seconds. Invert serving plate on top of mold and carefully turn both over. Gently shake the mold, lifting it carefully from firm salad.

## Jellied Waldorf Salad

*Serves 4*

3 medium red apples
1 tablespoon lemon juice
1 cup apple juice
3-ounce package lemon flavored
   gelatin
1/8 teaspoon salt
1/2 cup mayonnaise
1/2 cup heavy cream
1 cup celery, diced
1/2 cup walnuts, chopped
4 large lettuce leaves
1 bunch grapes
ginger ale
sugar

Core apples but do not peel. Cut 1 apple into thin, even slices; dice the other two. Sprinkle apples with the lemon juice to prevent discoloration. Arrange the slices around the bottom of a 5-cup ring mold. Chill.

Heat the apple juice to boiling, dissolve the gelatin in the juice, and add salt. Chill until slightly thickened and blend in mayonnaise.

Whip the cream. Fold the diced apples, celery, nuts, and whipped cream into the juice and mayonnaise mixture. Turn into the chilled mold and refrigerate until firm.

Rinse and drain the lettuce leaves, wrap them in a clean kitchen towel, and chill. Rinse grapes and allow to dry. Separate into small bunches, dip into ginger ale and roll in the sugar; shake off excess and allow to dry.

To assemble: Arrange the lettuce leaves on a serving plate. Unmold the salad by dipping the mold in warm water for 15 seconds and inverting onto the lettuce leaves. Garnish with the frosted grapes.

## Maman's Golden Salad

*Serves 6*

1 tablespoon plain gelatin
1/4 cup cold water
1 cup pineapple juice
1/4 cup white vinegar
1/2 cup orange juice
1/4 cup sugar
dash of salt
1 cup orange sections, chopped
   in small pieces
1 1/2 cups pineapple chunks, diced
1 medium carrot, grated

Soak the gelatin in the cold water for 5 minutes. Heat the pineapple juice, remove from heat, add the gelatin mixture, and dissolve. Add the vinegar, orange juice, sugar, and salt. Chill until partially set. Add the oranges, pineapple, and grated carrots. Stir to blend. Pour into a wet 2-quart mold and chill until firm. To unmold, dip mold in warm water for 15 seconds and invert onto serving dish.

## Cranberry and Fruit Salad

*Perk up a chicken dinner with this tart mixture.*

*Serves 4 to 6*

1 pound whole raw cranberries
1 whole orange
1 pound (about 4 medium) apples,
   peeled and cored
1 cup sugar
2 tablespoons brandy

Grind the cranberries, whole orange (rind included), and apples and stir to mix well. Add half the sugar. Stir. Add brandy and remaining sugar, stir well. Chill several hours before serving. May be spooned into hollowed oranges or on chilled lettuce leaves.

## Spinach-Mandarin Salad with Oriental Dressing

*Serves 4*

4 cups spinach leaves
1 cup cauliflower
8-ounce can Mandarin oranges,
   drained
1 recipe Oriental Dressing
   (see below)

Rinse and drain spinach leaves, wrap them in a clean kitchen towel, and chill.

To assemble: Tear spinach into bite-size pieces and place in a salad bowl. Separate the cauliflower into bite-size pieces and add to the spinach. Toss gently. Add oranges and toss to mix. Top with Oriental Dressing.

## Oriental Dressing

*Tart and refreshing.*

*Makes 1 cup*

1 cup plain yogurt
2 tablespoons orange juice
1 tablespoon orange peel, freshly
   grated
1 teaspoon sesame seeds

Combine all ingredients in a bowl and mix well with a spoon. Chill.

## Cream Cheese and Nectar Dressing

*A honey of a dressing to pour over mixed tropical fruit and pecans.*

*Makes 2 cups*

8-ounce package cream cheese,
   softened
¼ cup honey
juice of ½ lemon
1 cup whipping cream

Place the softened cheese in a small bowl and mash. Blend in the honey and lemon juice and, using a wire whip, beat until smooth. Beat the cream to soft peaks. Fold into the cheese mixture. Spoon over fruit or fresh broccoli.

## Herbal Vinaigrette Dressing

*Outstanding on salad greens or fresh vegetables.*

*Makes 1½ cups*

¼ cup red wine vinegar
1 teaspoon Dijon mustard
2 teaspoons Seasoned Salt (page 17)
½ teaspoon black pepper
1 teaspoon onions, chopped
1 clove garlic, pressed
1 teaspoon parsley, finely chopped
¼ teaspoon Worcestershire sauce
½ teaspoon dried tarragon leaves
½ teaspoon dried chives
1 cup olive oil

In a blender, combine all ingredients but the oil. Turn blender to medium, gradually add the oil, and blend until smooth. Cover and chill. Shake well before using.

## Ice Cream Dressing

*Dresses up fresh or canned fruit.*

*Makes 2 cups*

1 pint vanilla ice cream, softened
¾ cup mayonnaise
2 tablespoons orange or lemon peel,
   grated

Combine all ingredients in a mixing bowl and stir to blend. Pour over well-drained fruit. Prepare just before serving to avoid separation.

## Italian Cheese Dressing

*Makes 2¼ cups*

½ cup salad oil
¼ cup red wine vinegar
½ cup sharp cheese, shredded
2 teaspoons Worcestershire sauce
2 tablespoons parsley, finely snipped
1 teaspoon sugar
½ teaspoon Seasoned Salt (page 17)
½ teaspoon black pepper
dash of garlic salt
dash of paprika

Place all ingredients except the cheese in blender. Turn blender to a medium setting and gradually add the cheese. Blend until the dressing is smooth.

Cover and chill. Shake vigorously before using.

## Lemonade Dressing

*Refreshing!*

*Makes 2½ cups*

2 eggs, beaten
⅓ cup sugar
6-ounce can lemonade concentrate
1 cup heavy cream, whipped

Pour eggs into top portion of a double boiler. Stir in the sugar and the concentrate. Cook over simmering water until thick, stirring constantly. Cool. Fold in the whipped cream. Chill. Use promptly, though this will keep, refrigerated, for a day or two. Some separation may occur.

## Low-Calorie Celery-Seed Dressing

*Makes 1¼ cups*

1 tablespoon cornstarch
1 teaspoon paprika

1 teaspoon celery seeds
1 teaspoon sugar
½ teaspoon onion salt
½ teaspoon dry mustard
½ teaspoon Seasoned Salt (page 17)
1 cup water
¼ cup red wine vinegar

Mix first 7 ingredients together in a saucepan. While stirring, gradually add water and vinegar. Bring to a boil, stirring constantly until mixture thickens and becomes clear. Cool and chill. Shake well before using.

## Maman's Parisian Dressing

*An exceptional French-style dressing.*

*Makes 4½ cups*

10-ounce can condensed
   tomato soup
¾ cup white vinegar
½ cup sugar
1 tablespoon Seasoned Salt (page 17)
1 tablespoon dry mustard
½ teaspoon black pepper
⅛ teaspoon garlic salt
dash of hot pepper sauce
1½ cups salad oil

Combine all ingredients but the oil in blender. Turn blender to medium and gradually add the oil; blend at high speed until smooth. Cover and chill. Shake well before using.

## Roquefort Cheese Dressing

*Rich and creamy.*

*Makes 2 cups*

1 cup Parisian Dressing (see above)
1½ ounces cream cheese, softened
3 ounces Roquefort cheese

Pour Parisian dressing in blender with the

cream cheese and blend until smooth. Crumble the Roquefort cheese into a bowl. Add ¼ cup blended dressing and mix well with a fork. Add remaining dressing. Store covered in refrigerator. Mix again before using.

## Slavic Dressing

*A chunky delight to pour over fresh greens.*

*Makes 1 cup*

- ½ cup Parisian Dressing (see above) or bottled French dressing
- ¼ cup mayonnaise
- 2 tablespoons onions, finely chopped
- 2 tablespoons green pepper, finely chopped
- 3 tablespoons sweet pickles, drained and chopped

Place all ingredients in a blender and blend until smooth. Cover and chill. Shake before using.

# Egg, Cheese &
# Vegetable Dinners

## Eggs Monique

*For Sunday morning brunch or special occasions. Suggested Menu: Fresh Fruit à la Grand Marnier, Sticky Caramel Buns.*

*Serves 8*      *Cooking time: 20 minutes*

8 eggs
dash of Seasoned Salt (page 17)
dash of pepper
¼ cup whipping cream
1 teaspoon Grand Marnier
1 cup Parmesan cheese, freshly
   grated
2 tablespoons butter

Preheat oven to 350°. Separate eggs; drop whites into mixer bowl, leave yolks in half shells and set upright in egg carton. Beat whites to stiff peaks, add salt and pepper. Whip cream, add Grand Marnier, blend well. Fold into egg whites with cheese.

Brush casserole dish with butter. Turn whipped mixture into dish, level off. Make 8 evenly spaced indentations in mixture with buttered back of a tablespoon; slide 1 yolk into each indentation. Sprinkle with salt. Cover with foil tent. Bake 15 minutes, until eggs are set. Uncover and bake until whipped mixture is lightly browned. *Bon Appétit!*

## Eggs *Oscar*, Dijon

*A brunch classic or scrumptious light supper. Suggested Menu: Spring Greens Soup, Fruit Scones.*

*Serves 4*      *Cooking time: 10 to 15 minutes*

1 pound fresh asparagus spears
1 tablespoon vinegar
4 eggs
2 English muffins
6 ounces frozen king crabmeat,
   thawed (or fresh)
4 egg yolks
2 tablespoons Dijon mustard
½ cup butter or margarine, melted

Snap off and discard woody ends of asparagus stalks. Lay in skillet, cover, and cook in 1 inch boiling salted water until tender, 10 to 15 minutes; drain. Bring 4 inches of water to a boil in a Dutch oven, add vinegar, reduce heat to low. Break eggs, one at a time, in small dish and slide into simmering water. Cook 4 minutes. Drain crabmeat. Split muffins; toast and butter them. Combine egg yolks in blender with mustard, process while slowly adding *hot* melted butter. Arrange asparagus spears across muffins; top with crabmeat, then eggs, and sauce. Serve at once on warm plates.

## Eggs *au Fromage*

*A cheese and egg dish for luncheon or Sunday brunch. Suggested Menu: Broiled Tomato Slices.*

*Serves 4*  *Cooking time: 10 minutes*

6 eggs
⅓ cup light cream
¼ teaspoon Seasoned Salt (page 17)
dash of pepper
2 teaspoons chives, snipped
4 ounces cream cheese, diced
2 tablespoons butter

Beat eggs with whip. Add cream, salt, pepper, and chives and mix well. Add cheese and stir lightly. Melt butter in skillet, add egg mixture. Turn heat to low. As mixture sets, lift edges to allow uncooked part to go to bottom. Cook 8 minutes until glossy and moist.

## Maple Sugar Omelet

*A "special occasion" breakfast. Suggested Menu: Minted Grapefruit, toast with Strawberry Butter.*

*Serves 4*  *Cooking time: 18 minutes*

4 eggs
¼ cup maple syrup
½ teaspoon vanilla
¼ teaspoon salt
2 tablespoons butter or margarine
½ cup almonds, coarsely chopped

Preheat oven to 350°. Separate eggs. Beat yolks until foamy. Add 3 tablespoons of the syrup, vanilla, and salt; mix well. Beat whites in chilled bowl to stiff peaks, gently fold in yolk mixture. Melt butter in ovenproof skillet, spread almonds on bottom, pour egg mixture over nuts, and cook over medium-low heat for 8 minutes. Place omelet in oven, bake 10 minutes. Fold and slide onto warm plate. Sprinkle remaining tablespoon of syrup on top and serve.

## Quiche Lorraine with Pistachios

*A quiche with crunch* – delicieux! *Suggested Menu: Banana Split Salad, Dijon Beets.*

*Serves 4*  *Cooking time: 1 hour*

pastry for 1-crust, 9-inch pie
  (see index)
8 slices bacon
2 cups imported Swiss cheese
3 eggs, beaten
1 cup heavy cream
½ cup milk
½ cup pistachios, shelled, chopped
½ teaspoon salt
¼ teaspoon pepper
dash of nutmeg
dash of paprika

Preheat oven to 400°. Prick bottom of pie shell with a fork. Bake 7 minutes. Remove from oven. Reduce oven temperature to 350°. Cook bacon in skillet until crisp; drain and crumble. Sprinkle bacon and 1½ cups of the cheese on bottom of pie shell. Combine eggs, cream, milk, nuts, salt, pepper, and nutmeg in mixing bowl, blend. Pour into shell. Bake 45 to 50 minutes. Remove from oven, top with remaining cheese and sprinkle with paprika. Return to oven to melt cheese. Let cool 10 minutes before cutting.

## Stuffed Cannelloni

*A tasty change of pace from lasagne. Suggested Menu: salad greens with Italian-Cheese Dressing, Garlic Toast.*

*Serves 4*         *Cooking time: 30 minutes*

1 egg, beaten
8 ounces cream cheese, softened
½ cup ricotta cheese
½ cup grated Parmesan cheese
½ cup cooked ham, finely diced
3 whole scallions, finely diced
1 teaspoon parsley, chopped
¼ teaspoon basil
dash pepper
12 cannelloni (large, hollow pasta)
1 tablespoon salt
2 cups Brother Paul's Italian Sauce
   Parmigiana (see index), or
   14-ounce jar spaghetti sauce

Combine first 9 ingredients, egg to pepper; mix well, chill. Pour 6 quarts cold water in Dutch oven, add salt, bring to a boil. Add 6 cannelloni, cook uncovered, 3 minutes, stir to separate. Scoop out and drain. Cook remaining 6 cannelloni, drain well.

Preheat oven to 400°. Heat spaghetti sauce, pour half in casserole dish. Stuff each cannelloni with cheese mix. Arrange in single layer over sauce. Cover evenly with remaining sauce. Bake 25 minutes. Serve with additional grated Parmesan cheese.

## Salters' Stuffed Bread

*Crusty bread with salami-cheese stuffing. Suggested Menu: Potage Canadienne, Easy and Grand Caesar Salad, and a robust Chianti.*

*Makes 1 loaf*      *Rising time: 30 minutes*
                    *Cooking time: 30 minutes*

1 teaspoon dried parsley, crushed
¼ teaspoon dried basil
¼ teaspoon dried oregano

dash of garlic powder
dash of pepper
2½ to 2¾ cups all-purpose flour
1 package active dry yeast
5 tablespoons butter or margarine
1 tablespoon sugar
½ teaspoon salt
1 egg
¾ cup Gruyère cheese, shredded
3 ounces thinly sliced soft salami,
   chopped

Mix herbs together well and set aside. Combine 1 cup of the flour with yeast in mixing bowl and set aside.

Melt 2 tablespoons of the butter in saucepan. Add ¾ cup water, sugar, and salt. Cook over low heat, stirring, until mixture reaches 115° to 120°. Add mixture and egg to flour; beat at low speed for 30 seconds, then at high speed for 3 minutes.

By hand, stir in as much of the remaining flour as you can. Knead 5 minutes, adding more flour if needed, to make a stiff, smooth, elastic dough.

Cover and let rest 10 minutes. Roll out dough on a floured board to make a 9-by-12-inch rectangle. Cut into three 3-by-12-inch strips. Melt remaining butter and brush on each strip. Sprinkle ¼ teaspoon of the herb mix and ⅓ each of the cheese and salami lengthwise down the center of each strip. Bring the long edges of each strip together, enclosing the filling; pinch edges together to seal.

Place the strips side-by-side on a Teflon-coated cookie sheet, seam sides down. Braid strips together, secure ends. Cover and place in oven. Turn oven to 250°; *turn off* heat after 1 minute. Open oven door slightly and let dough rise until nearly doubled in size, about 30 minutes. Remove from oven; heat oven to 375°. Bake 30 minutes or until golden brown. Place loaf on wire rack, brush with butter, and sprinkle with remaining herb mixture and ¼ to ½ teaspoon garlic salt, if desired. Serve warm.

## Ann's Mushroom Pie

*A New Year's tradition. Suggested Menu: Spinach-Mandarin Salad, Cheese and Honey Carrots.*

*Serves 4*      *Cooking time: 45 minutes*

pastry for 2-crust, 9-inch pie
  (see index)
3 tablespoons butter or margarine
1 large onion, thinly sliced
1½ pounds fresh mushrooms, sliced
1 teaspoon Seasoned Salt (page 17)
dash of pepper
½ teaspoon Worcestershire sauce
1 tablespoon lemon juice
½ pound (2 cups) Swiss cheese,
  shredded
1 egg yolk

Preheat oven to 400°. Line bottom of pie plate with half the crust, trim and flute the edge; prick bottom of shell with a fork and bake 7 minutes. Remove from oven. Reduce oven temperature to 375°. Melt butter in skillet, add onions, sauté 2 minutes. Add mushrooms, salt, pepper, Worcestershire sauce, and lemon juice and cook 5 minutes. Strain. Add cheese to mushrooms and mix well. Turn into pastry shell. Arrange remaining pastry, lattice fashion, on top of filling. Beat egg yolk with 1 teaspoon water and brush over pastry. Bake 35 to 40 minutes.

## Fettuccine Armando

*An opulent step up from the familiar Noodles Alfredo. Suggested Menu: Easy and Grand Caesar Salad, Baked French Bread and Cheese.*

*Serves 4*      *Cooking time: 10 minutes*

½ cup butter, softened
1 cup heavy cream
1 cup grated Parmesan cheese
2 tablespoons fresh parsley, finely
  chopped
1 teaspoon fresh basil, finely
  chopped
1 tablespoon butter
1 cup canned whole mushrooms,
  drained
½ cup smoked ham, slivered
1 pound fettuccine
salt
fresh-ground pepper

Cream butter in mixing bowl. Beat in cream, a little at a time, until well combined. Beat in cheese, parsley, and basil. Set aside.

Melt 1 tablespoon butter in saucepan, add ham and mushrooms, heat through. Pour 6 quarts cold water in Dutch oven, add 1 tablespoon salt, bring to a boil. Add fettuccine and boil 10 minutes; stir to separate. Drain very well. Transfer fettuccine to bowl, add cream mix, and toss until coated. Sprinkle lightly with salt and pepper. Stir in drained mushrooms and ham. Serve immediately with additional Parmesan cheese.

## Fresh Vegetable Casserole

*An assortment of crunchy fresh vegetables in a rich cheese sauce. Suggested Menu: lettuce wedge with Slavic Dressing, Bacon-Cheese Biscuits.*

*Serves 4 to 6*      *Cooking time: 45 minutes*

3 medium potatoes, pared and
  quartered
4 cups broccoli clusters
4 cups cauliflowerettes
Seasoned Salt (page 17)
4 tablespoons butter or margarine
3 tablespoons flour
1¾ cups milk
½ teaspoon dry mustard
¼ teaspoon pepper
1½ cups sharp cheddar cheese,
  grated
1 large firm tomato, cut in 8 wedges
paprika

Cook potatoes in boiling salted water until tender, about 20 minutes. Drain, mash, and add 1 tablespoon of the butter, ¼ cup of the milk, ¼ teaspoon salt, dash pepper, and blend. Rinse vegetables, place on steamer rack. Fill Dutch oven with one inch water, insert rack, sprinkle with Seasoned Salt, cover, and cook until just tender. Melt remaining 3 tablespoons butter in saucepan, add flour, cook and stir until frothy. Add 1½ cups milk, stir until thickened. Add mustard, ¼ teaspoon salt, pepper, 1 cup of the cheese; stir until cheese melts. Preheat oven to broil. Arrange clusters of broccoli around the edge of a 10-inch deep-dish pie plate or round casserole dish. Circle inside with cauliflowerettes, repeat process to cover plate bottom. Pour half the sauce over vegetables. Add potatoes in a large mound in center of plate, force tomato wedges into and around potato mound. Pour remaining sauce over potatoes. Sprinkle cheese over, top with paprika, and broil until bubbly.

# Swiss Cheese and Ham Fondue

*Fun for informal entertaining. Try an all-fondue meal: Cheese-Ham Fondue, Chicken "Fondue," Easy and Grand Caesar Salad, Strawberries in Chocolate "Fondue."*

*Serves 4*

1 garlic clove, cut in half
1½ cups dry white wine
1½ pounds natural Swiss cheese, grated
¼ cup Kirsch
1½ tablespoons cornstarch
¼ teaspoon baking soda
dash each of pepper, paprika, and nutmeg
1 loaf French bread or garlic bread, torn bite-size
cooked smoked ham, cubed
celery sticks

Rub inside of fondue pot with cut side of garlic half, discard. Add wine to pot, warm on kitchen stove over medium heat until bubbly. Add cheese by thirds and stir until melted. Press remaining garlic half, add to pot, discarding tougher pulp. Dissolve cornstarch in Kirsch, add to pot when mixture bubbles. Stir constantly until thick. Add soda and spices and transfer to fondue burner. Mix well. Arrange bread cubes, ham, and celery on a platter. Have guests swirl dipper into fondue, figure-eight motion, to coat and to stir fondue.

# Desserts

## Almond Float

*A modern version of the classic Oriental dessert.*

*Serves 4*

2 envelopes unflavored gelatin
1½ cups cold milk
1 tablespoon almond extract
½ cup sugar
1 tangerine, peeled, seeded, sectioned
½ cup raisins

Combine gelatin with ½ cup cold water in large mixing bowl, let stand 5 minutes. Bring 1¼ cups water to a boil in a small saucepan. Add to gelatin and stir until dissolved and mixture is clear. Stir in milk and extract. Pour into 7½-by-12-inch dish. Chill 4 hours, or until firmly set.

Combine the sugar with 2 cups cold water in a small saucepan. Bring to a boil. Cool, then chill. With a sharp knife, make diagonal cuts, 1 inch apart, in almond gelatin mixture. Spoon out the diamond-shaped pieces and arrange them in layers with tangerine sections and raisins in deep dessert dishes. Pour chilled syrup over each and serve.

## Apple Fritters

*Quick and easy.*

*Makes about 1 dozen*　　　　*Cooking time: 3 to 5 minutes*

2 eggs, beaten
½ cup sugar
½ teaspoon salt
¼ teaspoon cinnamon
¼ teaspoon nutmeg
4 teaspoons baking powder
2 cups flour
1 cup milk
1 tablespoon orange liqueur
vegetable oil for frying
3 large cooking apples
confectioners' sugar

Combine eggs, sugar, salt, cinnamon, and nutmeg; mix well. Sift together flour and baking powder. Gradually add to egg mixture, alternating with milk. Stir in liqueur. Heat 2½ inches of oil in an electric skillet to 365–375° (or use a deep skillet with frying thermometer). Pare, core, and cut apples into ½-inch slices. Dip slices in batter and fry until golden. Remove with slotted spoon to paper toweling to drain. Place confectioners' sugar in sifter and sprinkle over fritters before serving. Serve warm.

## Bea's Fresh Blueberry Pie

*A tart glaze accents the flavor of firm, uncooked fruit.*

*Makes 1 pie*          *Cooking time: 25 minutes*

pastry for single-crust, 9-inch pie
  (see index)
4 cups fresh-picked blueberries,
  rinsed
¾ cup sugar
3 tablespoons cornstarch
dash of salt
1 tablespoon lemon juice
whipped cream

Preheat oven to 400°. Prick bottom of pie shell with a fork. Bake 7 minutes. Cool.

Pour 1¼ cups water into a 2-quart saucepan with ½ cup of the berries. Bring to a boil, mash berries, and simmer 5 minutes. Strain, discard blueberry pulp. Return liquid to rinsed saucepan, add sugar, cook and stir until sugar dissolves. Dissolve cornstarch in 4 tablespoons cold water, add to sauce, and simmer, stirring, until thick and clear. Add salt, stir, remove from heat, and cool slightly. Stir in lemon juice and remaining blueberries. Pour into pie shell and chill until set. Top with whipped cream to serve.

Note: This recipe can also be made with fresh strawberries, following the same procedure.

## Biscuits au Citron

*Lemon cookies.*

*Makes 8 to 10 dozen*     *Cooking time: 10 minutes*

*Cookies:*
2 cups walnuts, ground
2 eggs, beaten
1 teaspoon lemon extract
2 cups sugar

2 cups sifted flour
¼ teaspoon salt

*Frosting:*
2 cups confectioners' sugar
1 teaspoon grated lemon rind
lemon juice

Combine all cookie ingredients in a large mixing bowl. Mix thoroughly with your hands until mixture is soft enough to hold together. (Mixture will be dry at first.) Shape into 2 rolls 1½ inches in diameter. Wrap rolls in wax paper and chill for several hours.

Preheat oven to 325°. Mix confectioners' sugar, lemon rind, and enough juice to moisten. Cut cookie dough into ⅛-inch-thick slices and put on greased cookie sheets and bake for 10 minutes. Brush cookies with frosting while still hot.

## Brandied Macaroons

*A rich dessert, adapted and simplified from the version served at the George le Roi restaurant in Paris.*

*Serves 4 to 6*

1½ cups crushed macaroons
½ cup sugar
½ cup half-and-half
dash of salt
1½ cups whipping cream, whipped
½ cup brandy

Combine first 4 ingredients in large mixing bowl, mix well. Fold in whipped cream. Gradually fold in brandy. Spoon into sherbet glasses and freeze. Remove from freezer 15 minutes before serving.

## *Bûche de Noël* (Yule Log)

*A Canadian version of the traditional Christmas cake.*

*Makes 1 cake*       *Cooking time: 15 minutes*

4 eggs
1 cup sugar
¼ cup milk
1½ teaspoons vanilla extract
1 tablespoon butter or margarine
1¼ cups sifted flour
¼ teaspoon salt
1 tablespoon grated orange rind
2 tablespoons sherry
confectioners' sugar
your favorite fruit jelly
chocolate frosting
grated pistachio nuts

Preheat oven to 400°. Beat eggs until frothy. Gradually add sugar, ¼ cup at a time, beating well after each addition. Warm the milk, add vanilla and butter, stir to melt butter. Fold flour and salt into egg mixture. Gradually stir in milk, orange rind, and wine. Pour into a foil-lined jellyroll pan, 1 by 15 by 10 inches. Bake 15 minutes.

Sift confectioners' sugar all over a clean towel. Transfer cake to the towel, roll up from the 10-inch end, and let stand until cold. Unroll carefully and spread with jelly to within ½ inch of the edges. Reroll and spread entire roll with chocolate frosting (see below). Run tines of a fork the length of the cake to create a texture resembling bark. Sprinkle top with nuts.

## Chocolate Frosting for Yule Log

*Makes 1½ cups*

3 squares unsweetened chocolate
3 tablespoons butter or margarine
4 cups confectioners' sugar
⅛ teaspoon salt
¼ cup milk
3 tablespoons coffee brandy

1 teaspoon vanilla

Melt chocolate in a 1½-quart saucepan. Add butter and stir until melted. Mix sugar, salt, milk, brandy, and vanilla. Add to chocolate mixture and blend well. Let stand, stirring occasionally, until it reaches spreading consistency.

## Cherries Jubilee

*A spectacular ending for a special dinner.*

*Serves 4*       *Cooking time: 15 minutes*

1-pound can pitted bing cherries
port wine (about ½ cup)
1½ tablespoons cornstarch
¼ cup toasted, slivered almonds
juice of half a lemon
1 teaspoon grated lemon rind
1 teaspoon grated orange rind
2 tablespoons orange liqueur
¼ cup brandy
1 pint vanilla ice cream

Drain cherries and combine liquid and port to make 1 cup. (Reserve cherries.) Stir mixture slowly into cornstarch in a saucepan and blend well. Add almonds, lemon juice, and fruit rinds. Cook and stir until thick. Stir in orange liqueur and cherries. *Remove from heat.*

Warm brandy. Scoop ice cream into 4 serving dishes. Pour brandy over cherry mixture, ignite, and spoon flaming cherry mixture over ice cream. Do the flaming by candlelight for a special effect.

Note: This dish is traditionally prepared in a chafing dish, right at the table. Even if you prefer to cook the sauce in the kitchen, bring the cherries into the dining room before igniting, so your guests can enjoy the show.

## Cherry Chew Squares

*Makes 6 dozen*        *Cooking time: 45 minutes*

4 egg whites at room temperature
¼ teaspoon salt
1¾ cup sugar
2 cups walnuts, chopped
2 cups red maraschino cherries,
  chopped
⅔ cup butter or margarine, melted
1½ teaspoons vanilla
1¾ cup sifted flour

Preheat oven to 350°. Line a 9-by-13-inch baking pan with buttered wax paper. Beat egg whites with salt until foamy. Gradually add sugar and beat until stiff peaks form. Combine nuts, cherries, butter, and vanilla, mix well. Fold into egg whites alternately with the flour. Spread into baking pan and bake 45 minutes. Cool and cut into squares.

## Chewy Peanut Butter Chocolate Bars

*Makes 2½ dozen*        *Cooking time: 35 minutes*

¼ cup butter or margarine, melted
1 cup graham cracker crumbs
1 cup shredded coconut
6-ounce package peanut butter chips
6-ounce package semi-sweet
  chocolate chips
1 cup walnuts, chopped
12-ounce can evaporated milk

Preheat oven to 350°. Combine butter and cracker crumbs in a mixing bowl, stir to mix. Spread evenly on the bottom of a 13-by-9-inch baking pan, pack down. Sprinkle with a layer of coconut, a layer of peanut butter chips, a layer of chocolate chips, a layer of walnuts. Press lightly. Carefully pour the milk over all. Bake 35 minutes. Cool and cut in bars.

## Chocolate Caramels

*A delicious gift or family treat.*

*Makes 1½ pounds,*        *Cooking time:*
*about 50 pieces*        *¾ to 1 hour*

1 cup sugar
½ cup brown sugar, firmly packed
½ cup light corn syrup
½ cup heavy cream
1 cup milk
¼ cup butter or margarine
4 squares (4 ounces) unsweetened
  chocolate
½ cup walnuts, chopped
1 teaspoon vanilla

Lightly butter a Teflon-coated 9-by-5-inch loaf pan. Combine all ingredients but walnuts and vanilla in a heavy, medium saucepan. Cook and stir over low heat until the sugars melt. Increase heat to medium and cook, uncovered, to 248° on a candy thermometer or until a little mixture in cold water forms a ball as firm as caramels. Remove from heat, add nuts and vanilla quickly. Pour into prepared pan, cool. Score and cut. Wrap each piece in waxed paper.

*Variations:* Substitute 2 tablespoons instant coffee for the chocolate to make coffee caramels. One-quarter cup raisins and/or ½ cup well-drained, chopped cherries can also be added to coffee caramels.

## Dawn's Hawaiian Holiday Pie

*An impressive dessert.*

*Makes 1 9-by-13-inch pie*        *Cooking time:*
*5 minutes*

2 cups graham cracker crumbs
¼ cup sugar
6 tablespoons butter or margarine,
  melted
2 cups confectioners' sugar
2 eggs
½ cup butter or margarine, softened

1 teaspoon vanilla
4 bananas
2½ cups crushed pineapple, drained
2 10-ounce packages strawberries,
  thawed, drained
whipped cream or prepared
  whipped topping
1 cup toasted almonds, sliced
maraschino cherries

Preheat oven to 350°. Mix first 3 ingredients together and press into 9-by-13-inch pan. Bake 5 minutes. Cool.

Mix together sugar, eggs, butter, and vanilla and beat until fluffy, 10 to 15 minutes. Spread over graham cracker crumbs. Chill for 20 minutes. Place sliced bananas, pineapple, and strawberries, in layers, on top of egg mixture. To serve: top pie with whipped cream or prepared topping, sprinkle with nuts and cherries.


## Dessert Crêpes

*Try one of these or use your favorite fruit to create your own filling.*

*Batter for 20 to 24 crêpes*　　　*Cooking time: 25 to 30 minutes*

4 eggs
1 cup flour
½ cup milk
1 teaspoon salt
2 tablespoons butter or margarine,
  melted
2 tablespoons brandy

Combine all ingredients with ½ cup water in blender. Process to blend completely. Chill for at least 2 hours, preferably overnight.

Heat a 6-inch skillet, add 1 teaspoon butter, heat. Add 2 tablespoons batter, and tilt skillet to spread batter. Brown, turn to brown other side. Repeat, adding more butter as needed. Stack and keep warm.

*Peppermint-Patty Crêpes:* Combine **1 cup** Hershey chocolate syrup with ¼ cup green crême de menthe in a medium mixing bowl. Mix well, using a wire whip. Add 1½ cups whipped cream and whip to blend.

Place **3 small scoops of vanilla ice cream** in center of each crepe, and overlap edges over ice cream. Spoon sauce over crêpe, top with **almond slices**. Serve 2 crêpes per person.

*Strawberry Crêpes:* Thaw a **10-ounce package of frozen strawberries**. Drain berries. To juice add **cranberry juice** to make 1½ cups. Combine ¼ **cup sugar, 2 tablespoons cornstarch,** and a **dash of salt** in a 2-quart saucepan. Slowly stir in juice. Cook and stir until bubbly. Add strawberries, **1 tablespoon orange liqueur, 1 teaspoon lemon juice.** Keep warm.

Place **3 small scoops of chocolate ice cream** in each crêpe, fold. Top with strawberry sauce and **whipped cream.** Serve 2 per person.


## Faa-Foons

*When we were young children, Maman would make these treats as a special reward for good behavior, and always on Mardi Gras.*

*Makes approximately*　　　*Cooking time: 30 cakes*　　　*15 to 20 minutes*

3 eggs, well beaten
2 cups milk
4 cups flour, sifted
⅓ cup sugar
½ teaspoon salt
1 tablespoon baking powder
2 drops almond flavoring
vegetable oil for deep frying
confectioners' sugar

Combine beaten eggs and milk, mix well. Gradually beat in flour, sugar, salt, almond flavoring, and baking powder. Beat until very smooth. Heat oil to 375°. Hold the end of a funnel closed and fill with batter. Allow batter to stream into the hot oil, using a swirling motion, starting in the center and spiraling outward. Fry 2 to 3 minutes, turning to brown both sides. Drain on paper toweling and sprinkle with confectioners' sugar.

# Fast and Easy Ice Cream Pies

*Makes 1 9-inch pie*

*Basic Chocolate Crumb Shell:* Combine **2 cups chocolate wafer crumbs, ⅓ cup butter or margarine,** and **2 tablespoons coffee liqueur.** Mix well. Press into 9-inch pie plate; freeze.

*Chocolate-Cherry Mint Pie:* Soften **1 quart vanilla ice cream.** Stir in **1½ ounces each of chocolate mint liqueur and cherry brandy.** Blend well. Mix in **½ cup well drained, diced red maraschino cherries.** Pour into frozen crumb shell and freeze overnight. Garnish with **chocolate curls** and **cherry halves.** Cut pie with hot knife. Serve on chilled plate.

*Mud Pie:* Soften **1 quart coffee ice cream.** Spread in frozen crumb shell and freeze until firm. Top with **1½ cups chocolate fudge sauce** spread evenly over surface, and freeze overnight. Slice pie with hot knife. Serve on chilled plate, topped with **whipped cream** and **toasted slivered almonds.**

*Banana Split Pie:* Soften **1 pint strawberry ice cream.** Add **½ cup crumbled soft macaroons.** Mix well, spread in frozen crumb shell, and freeze. Soften **1 pint vanilla ice cream.** Add **1 tablespoon cream sherry.** Mix well, and spread over frozen strawberry ice cream. Freeze. Soften **1 pint chocolate ice cream,** add **¼ cup sliced toasted almonds.** Spread over frozen vanilla ice cream; freeze overnight. Slice pie with hot knife, and serve on chilled plates, topped with **whipped cream, sliced bananas,** and **pineapple ice cream topping.**

# Five Elegant, Easy Desserts Made with Ice Cream

*Ice cream in pretty glasses topped with fruit, liqueur, or sauce.*

*Orangey Orange:* Place a scoop of **orange sherbet** in a glass. Arrange **6 mandarin orange sections** around base of sherbet. Pour **1 ounce of orange liqueur** over all. Top with **mint leaf.**

*Strawberries Belle-Isle:* Soften **1 pint vanilla ice cream.** Whip **1 cup heavy cream** to soft peaks. Fold into softened ice cream. Stir in **⅓ cup orange liqueur.** Spoon over **2 quarts hulled fresh strawberries.**

*Peaches and Cream:* Blend **2 large scoops vanilla ice cream** with **¾ ounce light crème de cacao** and **¾ ounce orange liqueur** until smooth. Alternate layers of ice cream mixture and **sliced peaches** in tall, stemmed 13-ounce wine glasses, starting and ending with ice cream. Serve with a **twist of orange peel.**

*Chocolate or Coffee with Cinnamon and Fudge:* Soften **chocolate** or **coffee ice cream,** add **ground cinnamon** to taste. Pour **chocolate fudge sauce** in parfait glass, then alternate layers of ice cream and sauce. Top with **whipped cream.** Sprinkle with cinnamon.

*Coffee Sundae:* Place a scoop of **vanilla ice cream** in dessert dish. Pour **coffee liqueur** liberally over ice cream. Sprinkle top with **ground instant coffee.**

## Frozen Chocolate Chip Cheesecake

*An elegant make-ahead party dessert.*

*Makes 1 8-inch cake*      *Freeze overnight*
                   *Cooking time: 8 minutes*

2 cups graham cracker crumbs
¼ cup sugar
6 tablespoons butter or margarine, melted
8-ounce and 3-ounce package cream cheese, softened
1 quart chocolate ice cream, softened
2 tablespoons Amaretto liqueur (optional)
½ cup chopped semisweet chocolate pieces
whipped cream

Preheat oven to 375°. Combine first 3 ingredients, mix well. Press on bottom and 1¾ inches up the side of an 8-inch spring-form pan. Bake 8 minutes. Cool. Chill.

Beat cheese in large mixer bowl with mixer until fluffy. Gradually add ice cream and Amaretto, beating until smooth. Fold in chocolate chips. Pour into crust. Cover and freeze overnight. Let stand half an hour before serving. Top with whipped cream and more chocolate chips.

## Galette des Rois

*Known as twelfth-cake, traditionally eaten during Epiphany.*

*Makes 2 9-inch cakes*      *Cooking time:*
                      *40 to 45 minutes*

1 cup butter or margarine, softened
2 cups sugar
5 eggs, separated, whites kept cold
3 cups sifted flour
1 teaspoon baking powder
½ teaspoon salt
1 teaspoon baking soda
½ cup fresh orange juice
grated rind of one orange
¼ cup brandy
1 teaspoon vanilla
2 tablespoons blanched, slivered almonds
1 cup whipping cream
2 tablespoon confectioners' sugar
1 tablespoon orange liqueur

Preheat oven to 350°. Grease 2 9-inch round cake pans. Cream the butter and gradually add 1 cup sugar and the egg yolks, one at a time, beating well after each addition. Combine 1½ cups sifted flour with baking powder and salt, add to creamed mixture and mix well. Combine baking soda, orange juice and rind, brandy, and vanilla, mix well. Add to creamed mixture with the remaining sifted flour, mix well. Whip egg whites until firm, gradually beat in remaining sugar. Gently fold into batter. Pour batter into prepared cake pans. Sprinkle with almonds. Bake 40 to 45 minutes. Cool on rack.

Whip cream until stiff, adding confectioners' sugar 1 tablespoon at a time. Add liqueur and beat in gently. Serve with the cakes.

## Hot Orange Pudding

*A fitting finale to an Oriental dinner.*

*Serves 4*      *Cooking time: 15 to 20 minutes*

½ cup tapioca
1 large orange
¼ cup sugar
½ cup tiny marshmallows

Soak tapioca in ½ cup cold water for 4 hours. Grate orange to yield 1 tablespoon rind. Peel orange, remove white membrane, and cut pulp into small pieces. Mix sugar with 2 cups cold water in a 2-quart saucepan, bring to a boil, and stir until sugar is dissolved. Drain tapioca and pour slowly into boiling liquid, stirring constantly over medium heat until thick—about 5 minutes.

Stir in orange and rind, return to boil. Remove from heat, stir in marshmallows, and pour into individual dessert dishes. Serve hot.

## Hurry-Up Elegant Glazed Cake

*A simple, eye-catching cake for entertaining.*

*Makes 8 to 10 servings*         *Cooking time: 5 to 7 minutes*

8- or 9-inch, round yellow cake layer (purchase, or make ahead of time)
4 or 5 tablespoons orange liqueur
10-ounce jar strawberry preserves
3 kiwi fruit, pared and sliced
¼ cup toasted almond slices
8 to 10 whole strawberries, hulled
½ cup heavy cream, whipped
1 tablespoon sugar
¼ teaspoon almond extract

Prick surface of cake with a fork. Slowly spoon on the orange liqueur, allowing it to run into the holes. Let stand 30 minutes. Heat preserves, strain. Brush top and sides of cake with some of the strained glaze. Arrange the kiwi slices on the cake top. Spoon remaining glaze over the fruit. Arrange the whole strawberries around the kiwi slices. Press the almonds on sides of cake. Fold the sugar and almond extract into the whipped cream, and serve with the cake.

## Individual Grand Marnier Soufflés

*France's great liqueur flavors these delicate creations.*

*Serves 6*         *Cooking time: 10 minutes*

6 teaspoons butter or margarine, softened
sugar
5 egg yolks
½ cup plus 1 tablespoon sugar
¼ cup orange juice

3 tablespoons Grand Marnier liqueur
2 teaspoons orange rind, finely grated
7 egg whites
1 tablespoon sugar
1 tablespoon fresh lemon juice
confectioners' sugar

Grease six 4-inch round soufflé dishes with 1 teaspoon butter each. Dust each with sugar, shake out excess.

Preheat oven to 450°. Combine egg yolks, ½ cup sugar, juice, liqueur, and orange rind in a large mixing bowl. Use a wire whip to blend.

In a separate bowl, beat egg whites to soft peaks, add 1 tablespoon sugar, and continue beating to stiff peaks, gradually adding juice. Carefully but quickly fold into yolk mixture. Spoon into soufflé dishes and bake 10 minutes. Remove from oven, sprinkle with confectioners' sugar, and serve *immediately*.

## Instant Strawberry Ice

*Only minutes to make, refreshingly light.*

*Serves 4*

10-ounce package frozen strawberries, softened
2 tablespoons orange juice concentrate
1 cup ice cubes, coarsely crushed

Break up the frozen strawberries and place in a blender bowl. Blend until smooth, about 1 minute. Add the concentrate, blend one more minute. Add the ice cubes through the cover hole, one at a time, and blend until smooth and consistency of sherbet. Store in freezer until serving time.

# Lemon *Sorbet*

*A cooling dessert or palate refresher between courses.*

*Makes 1 quart          Cooking time: 15 minutes*

2 cups sugar
6-ounce can frozen lemonade
  concentrate
1 tablespoon frozen orange juice
  concentrate
1 cup fresh lemon juice
rind of 1 lemon, grated
1 teaspoon Kirsch brandy
2 egg whites

Combine sugar with 1 cup water in a 3-quart saucepan. Slowly bring to a boil, stirring constantly until sugar is dissolved. Simmer 3 minutes. Cool, cover, and chill.

Add concentrates, juice, rind, and Kirsch to cold syrup and blend well. Cover and freeze until almost solid. Stir once after one hour in freezer.

Spoon into ice cream machine or food processor with steel knife attachment and process until smooth. Beat egg whites to soft peaks, add to processor, and blend. Freeze until mixture thickens to sherbet consistency.

# Mariette's Fresh Strawberry Pie

*Lemon-lime soft drink adds sparkle.*

*Makes 1 9-inch pie          Cooking time: 7 minutes*

pastry for single-crust, 9-inch pie
  (see index)
12-ounce can Sprite beverage
3-ounce package strawberry gelatin
½ cup sugar
3 tablespoons cornstarch
1 quart fresh strawberries, hulled
whipped cream
¼ teaspoon grated lemon rind

Preheat oven to 400°. Prick bottom of pie

shell with fork. Bake 7 minutes. Cool. Combine first 4 ingredients in a 2-quart saucepan. Bring to a boil and stir until thick and clear. Cool slightly. Slice strawberries thickly, add to cooled syrup, and pour into pie shell. Chill until set. Spread top with whipped cream, sprinkle with grated lemon rind.

# Marinated Strawberries and Kiwi

*An elegant yet simple dessert.*

*Serves 6*

1 quart fresh strawberries, rinsed,
  hulled, sliced
2 kiwi fruit, pared, sliced
½ cup plus 1 tablespoon orange
  liqueur
¼ cup plus 2 tablespoons sugar
¾ cup whipping cream
½ teaspoon vanilla
1 tablespoon grated orange rind

Combine strawberry and kiwi slices with ½ cup liqueur and ¼ cup sugar in large mixing bowl. Stir gently. Cover and chill 2 to 3 hours. Whip cream with 1 tablespoon liqueur, 2 tablespoons sugar, vanilla, and orange rind until soft peaks form. Spoon berries and liquid into sherbet glasses, top with cream mixture.

# Mint Surprise Cookies

*Makes 4½ dozen          Cooking time:*
*10 to 12 minutes*

1 cup butter or margarine
1 cup sugar
½ cup brown sugar, firmly packed
2 eggs
1 teaspoon vanilla
3 cups flour
1 teaspoon baking soda
½ teaspoon salt

9-ounce package solid chocolate
mint candy wafers
54 walnut or pecan halves

Cream butter and sugars until light. Beat in eggs, 2 tablespoons of water, and vanilla. Sift dry ingredients together, blend into creamed mixture. Cover and chill 2 hours.

Preheat oven to 375°. Enclose a mint wafer in each tablespoon of cookie dough. Place on greased cookie sheets, 2 inches apart. Top each with a nut half and bake 10 to 12 minutes.

## Mocha-Ricotta Custard

*A no-cook dessert — fast, easy, and deliciously different.*

*Serves 4*

½ pound ricotta cheese
½ cup grated milk chocolate
¼ cup walnuts, chopped
6 tablespoons prepared whipped
  topping or whipped cream
1 tablespoon coffee brandy
4 medium stemmed cherries

Pour cheese into blender and process until creamy. Add all but 2 teaspoons chocolate and process 30 seconds. Add nuts, 2 tablespoons of topping or whipped cream, and brandy. Turn blender on/off just to blend. Pour into pretty sherbet or wine glasses. Chill until set. Top each serving with 1 tablespoon topping, ½ teaspoon grated chocolate, and a cherry.

## Petits Pôts de Chocolat

*A quick version of this rich chocolate mousse.*

*Serves 6*        *Cooking time: 8 to 10 minutes*

1½ cups milk
2 cups semi-sweet chocolate chips

2 eggs
¼ cup sugar
1 tablespoon orange liqueur
pinch of salt
1 cup prepared whipped topping or
  sweetened whipped cream
1 tablespoon chopped pistachio nuts

Heat milk in saucepan to boiling point. Meanwhile combine chips, eggs, sugar, liqueur, and salt in blender, add hot milk, and blend at low speed for 1 minute until smooth. Pour into 6 5-ounce custard cups. Chill 2 hours. Spoon a dollop of topping onto each cup and sprinkle each with ½ teaspoon nuts.

## Pineapple Snow

*Airy and delicious. Serve in pretty sherbet glasses.*

*Serves 4*

1 envelope unflavored gelatin
½ cup sugar
⅛ teaspoon salt
6-ounce can frozen pineapple juice
  concentrate
3 egg whites
½ cup heavy cream
2 tablespoons confectioners' sugar
1 tablespoon orange liqueur

Combine gelatin, sugar, and salt with ¾ cup water in top of double boiler. Stir and place over boiling water until sugar is dissolved. Remove from heat. Add frozen juice, mix well. Chill until mixture begins to thicken.

Beat egg whites until stiff but not dry; fold in pineapple mixture. Pour into serving dishes, chill. To serve: whip cream until stiff peaks form. Add confectioners' sugar, 1 tablespoon at a time, beating gently; gradually add liqueur. Top each serving with a generous mound of flavored cream.

## Raspberry Filled Cookies

*Makes about 2 dozen    Cooking time: 10 minutes*

½ cup shortening
½ cup sugar
½ cup brown sugar, firmly packed
2 eggs
1 teaspoon vanilla
2 cups flour
¼ teaspoon salt
½ teaspoon baking soda
¾ cup raspberry preserves

Cream shortening and sugars until light. Add one egg at a time with vanilla and beat well. Sift dry ingredients together and blend into creamed mixture. Chill 2 hours.

Preheat oven to 400°. Roll out cookie dough ⅛-inch thick on a lightly floured surface. Cut with floured cookie cutter. Place one teaspoon of preserves in the center of a cookie and cover with another, pressing the edges together with the tines of a fork. Make a tiny slit in the center of the cookies to allow steam to escape. Place on a greased cookie sheet and bake 10 minutes or until golden brown.

## Rita's Cinnamon Apple Roll

*Spicy apple pie flavor encased in tender pastry.*

*Serves 6 to 8              Cooking time: 1 hour*

1½ cups plus 1 tablespoon sugar
2 cups flour
4 teaspoons baking powder
½ teaspoon salt
4 tablespoons solid shortening
⅔ cup milk
2 tablespoons butter or margarine, softened
3 cups apples, pared, chopped
½ cup walnuts, chopped
¼ cup sugar
1 teaspoon cinnamon

Combine 1½ cups sugar with 2 cups water in a small saucepan. Bring to a boil, simmer 10 minutes.

Preheat oven to 400°. Grease a 9-inch round cake pan. Sift together flour, baking powder, 1 tablespoon of the sugar, and salt in large mixing bowl. Blend in shortening with a pastry blender. Add milk and stir to make a soft dough. Turn out on floured pastry board. Roll out to ¼-inch thick rectangle. Spread with butter, cover with apples and nuts. Combine ¼ cup sugar and cinnamon, sprinkle over apples. Roll up lengthwise, jelly-roll style. Cut into 1-inch thick slices and place slices cut-side up in pan.

Pour sugar syrup over top. Bake 20 minutes, lower oven temperature to 350° and bake about 30 minutes longer, until golden brown.

## Rita's Perfect Pastry Crust

*Light and flaky, resists tearing. Make ahead and chill or freeze.*

*Makes five 2-crust pies*

1 egg, well beaten
1 tablespoon vinegar
5 level cups unsifted flour, spooned into measure
2 teaspoons salt
¾ pound solid shortening
flour

Add egg and vinegar to 1 cup *very cold* water. Whip to blend. Refrigerate 30 minutes.

In a large bowl, mix flour, salt, and shortening with pastry blender until the pieces are the size of small peas. Make a well in the center. Add cold liquid all at once. Stir with a spoon. Roll dough on floured board. Make all your pies the same day or freeze remaining pastry for later use.

## Strawberries in Chocolate Fondue

*A delightful company dessert.*

*Serves 4*

8 1-ounce squares semisweet
  chocolate
15-ounce can sweetened condensed
  milk
½ cup light cream
¼ cup orange liqueur
1 quart fresh strawberries, rinsed

Heat first 3 ingredients in a fondue pot on the stove, stirring until chocolate melts. Stir in liqueur and place over fondue burner. Thin with milk if necessary. Let guests dip strawberries in chocolate. Bananas, marshmallows, or cubes of angel food cake make great dippers also.

## T-Bea's Rice Pudding

*Substitute skim milk and Egg-Beaters for low-cholesterol diets.*

*Serves 4          Cooking time: 15 minutes*

⅓ cup rice
3 cups milk, scalded
¾ cup sugar
1½ tablespoons cornstarch
2 eggs, well beaten
1 teaspoon vanilla
cinnamon

Combine rice with ⅓ cup cold water in a small saucepan, cover. Bring to a boil, reduce heat to low, and cook for 15 minutes. Turn heat off. Leave saucepan on burner *(do not lift cover)*, for an additional 10 minutes. Scald milk; add sugar and cornstarch. Stir until mixture coats a wooden spoon. Add a little of the hot milk mixture to beaten eggs, then add eggs to milk, stirring constantly. Strain into a 1½-quart glass casserole dish. Add hot cooked rice and vanilla, stir to blend. Sprinkle top with cinnamon. (This pudding will thicken as it cools.)

## White Russian Pie

*Serves 8          Cooking time: 5 to 7 minutes*

2 cups chocolate wafer crumbs
⅓ cup butter or margarine
½ cup coffee liqueur
1 envelope unflavored gelatin
⅓ cup sugar
3 eggs, separated
¼ cup vodka
2 cups heavy cream, whipped
chocolate curls

Preheat oven to 350°. Combine crumbs, butter, and 3 tablespoons of the coffee liqueur in medium mixing bowl; mix well. Press into a 9-inch pie plate. Bake 5 minutes. Cool.

Mix gelatin with ¼ cup of the sugar in 2-quart saucepan. Beat egg yolks with ½ cup water, add to gelatin, and let stand one minute. Stir over low heat until gelatin dissolves, about 5 minutes. Stir in vodka and remaining liqueur. Pour into a bowl and chill, stirring frequently, until mixture mounds when dropped from spoon.

Beat egg whites in a chilled bowl to form soft peaks, gradually add remaining sugar, beat until stiff. In another bowl, whip cream. Fold whites and 1 cup whipped cream into chilled mixture; turn into crust. Chill until firm, 5 hours. Top with additional cup of whipped cream and chocolate curls.

To make chocolate curls: shave off thin curls of sweet cooking chocolate with a vegetable parer or sharp knife. Curls will hold together better if chocolate is at room temperature, not chilled.

# Vegetables

## Asparagus *au Gratin*

*A hearty casserole with ham.*

*Serves 4*          *Cooking time: 40 minutes*

2 pounds asparagus, fresh
Seasoned Salt (page 17)
1 cup Medium White Sauce
  (see index)
1 cup cooked ham, finely diced
¼ teaspoon pepper
2 hard cooked eggs, sliced
½ cup Gruyère cheese, grated
¼ cup fresh bread crumbs
2 tablespoons butter or margarine,
  melted

Rinse asparagus stalks and snap off woody base. Bias-cut asparagus into 1½-inch pieces. Place on a collapsible steamer rack. Pour one inch of water in Dutch oven, add rack of asparagus, sprinkle with Seasoned Salt. Cover and steam until barely tender, about 5 to 7 minutes. Reserve ¼ cup cooking liquid.

Meanwhile, make White Sauce. When sauce thickens add ham, pepper, and reserved liquid. Stir well.

Preheat oven to 400°. Arrange asparagus in a 1½-quart casserole dish. Top with egg slices. Pour sauce over asparagus and eggs. Combine cheese with crumbs and sprinkle over sauce. Drizzle melted butter evenly over crumbs. Bake 20 minutes.

## Beets, Two Ways

*Children will love Nantucket beets; Dijon beets are super with ham.*

*Serves 4*          *Cooking time: 35 minutes*

1½ pounds small to medium fresh
  beets or 2 1-pound cans small
  whole beets

Cut off all but one inch of stems on fresh beets. Scrub and rinse. Cook, covered, in boiling water until tender, about 35 to 60 minutes, depending on size. Drain, cool slightly, slip off skins.

If using canned beets, heat them and drain.

Serve with one of the following sauces.

*Nantucket Beets*          *Cooking time: 40 minutes*

1 tablespoon cornstarch
1 tablespoon sugar
dash of salt

1 cup cranberry-grape juice
1 tablespoon grated orange peel

Combine cornstarch, sugar, and salt in medium saucepan. Stir in juice. Bring to a boil and stir until thick. Add orange peel. Slice cooked beets and add to sauce. Heat through.

*Dijon Beets*          *Cooking time: 40 minutes*

3 tablespoons butter
2 tablespoons Dijon mustard
1 tablespoon honey
1 teaspoon Worcestershire sauce
¼ teaspoon salt

Cut the cooked beets in half, or quarters if large. Combine butter, mustard, honey, Worcestershire sauce, and salt in small saucepan. Bring to a boil. Spoon over hot beets.

## Broccoli, Three Ways

*With fresh lemon, stir-fried, or in cheese custard.*

*Serves 4*          *Cooking time: 6 to 8 minutes*

*Basic recipe for all but stir-fried*
1½ pounds fresh broccoli
Seasoned Salt (page 17)

Cut off and discard tough lower stems, leaving 4-inch stems attached to heads. Rinse thoroughly. Split the stems in half and place on collapsible steamer rack. Pour 1 inch of water into a Dutch oven. Add rack with broccoli, sprinkle with Seasoned Salt. Cover and steam until barely tender, about 6 to 8 minutes. Remove from heat and prepare one of the following ways.

*Fresh Lemon Broccoli:* Cut 1 lemon into 4 wedges. Squeeze juice from 1 wedge over each serving.

*Cheese-Custard Broccoli*          *Cooking time: 36 to 38 minutes*

3 eggs
¾ cup milk
1½ cups shredded sharp cheddar cheese
½ teaspoon Seasoned Salt (page 17)
¼ teaspoon pepper

Preheat oven to 350°. Beat eggs. Add milk, cheese, and seasonings. Mix well. Chop cooked broccoli and place in a shallow casserole dish. Pour egg mixture over vegetable. Set casserole in a larger pan containing 1 inch of hot water. Bake 30 minutes or until firm.

*Stir-Fried Broccoli*          *Cooking time: 10 minutes*

1½ pounds fresh broccoli
2 tablespoons peanut oil
1 teaspoon salt
½ teaspoon sugar
¼ cup chicken broth
1 teaspoon cornstarch
1 tablespoon cold water

Cut stems off *uncooked* broccoli. Slice stems diagonally and break up heads into florets.

Heat oil in wok or large skillet. Add sliced stems, stir-fry 1 minute. Add florets, stir-fry one minute more. Sprinkle with salt and sugar. Add chicken broth. Cover and cook until tender, about 2 minutes. Dissolve cornstarch in cold water, add to wok, and stir until thickened.

## Broccoli in Foil

*Serves 3 to 4*

10-ounce package frozen broccoli (fresh broccoli may be used; see note below)
¼ teaspoon Seasoned Salt (page 17)
dash of pepper
1 tablespoon lemon juice
2 teaspoons butter or margarine

Place frozen broccoli on a large square of double-thickness aluminum foil. Season with salt and pepper. Sprinkle with lemon juice. Top with butter. Bring edges of foil up, and leaving a little space for expansion of steam, seal tightly with a double fold. Heat over hot coals about 40 minutes, turning frequently.

Note: when using fresh broccoli, rinse broccoli and place dripping wet on the foil. Proceed as above, cutting cooking time to 10 minutes.

## Carrots, Four Ways

*Serves 4*                    *Cooking time: 10 minutes*

1½ pounds carrots
¼ teaspoon Seasoned Salt (page 17)

Peel carrots, slice ½ inch thick. Place on a collapsible steamer rack. Pour one inch water in a Dutch oven. Add rack of carrots, sprinkle with salt. Cover and steam until tender, about 10 minutes. Remove from heat and prepare in one of the following ways.

*Vichy Carrots*              *Cooking time: 15 minutes*

2 tablespoons butter or margarine
½ teaspoon sugar
cooked carrots
1 tablespoon parsley, finely chopped

Melt butter in a skillet, add sugar and stir to melt. Add cooked carrots and parsley, stir to coat.

*Orange-Glazed Carrots*           *Cooking time:*
                                   *20 minutes*

½ cup orange juice
¼ cup maple syrup
2 tablespoons orange marmalade
cooked carrots

Combine juice, syrup, and marmalade in a medium saucepan. Bring to a boil, stirring constantly. Add cooked carrots, stir gently, and let stand 5 minutes before serving.

*Lyonnaise Carrots*        *Cooking time: 45 minutes*

1 medium onion, sliced
¼ cup butter or margarine
1 tablespoon flour
¼ teaspoon Seasoned Salt (page 17)
dash of pepper
¾ cup chicken broth
cooked carrots
pinch of sugar

Cover and cook onions in butter 15 minutes. Stir in flour, salt, and pepper. Stir and cook 2 minutes. Add broth and bring to a boil. Add cooked carrots and sugar. Simmer, uncovered, 5 minutes.

*Cheese and Honey Carrots*          *Cooking time:*
                                    *15 to 20 minutes*

1½ pounds carrots
¼ cup honey
1 cup sharp cheddar cheese,
    shredded

Peel and cut each carrot into 8 sticks. Cook as in basic recipe until barely tender, about 6 to 7 minutes.

Preheat oven to 400°. Dip sticks in honey, place in a lightly buttered casserole dish. Sprinkle cheese on top. Bake 10 minutes.

## Cauliflower, Two Ways

*Serves 4*            *Cooking time: 5 to 7 minutes*

Separate 1 medium cauliflower into florets. Rinse and place into a collapsible steamer rack. Pour 1 inch of water into a Dutch oven. Add rack with cauliflower, sprinkle with Seasoned Salt (page 17). Cover and steam until tender, about 5 to 7 minutes. Remove from heat and prepare in one of the following ways.

*Sesame Cauliflower*                *Cooking time:*
                                    *15 to 17 minutes*

1 cup dairy sour cream
1 cup shredded Monterey Jack
    cheese

Vegetables  109

4 teaspoons toasted sesame seeds

Preheat oven to 350°. Place half of cooked cauliflower in a 1½-quart casserole. Spread with half the sour cream; sprinkle with half the cheese and sesame seeds. Repeat layers. Bake 10 minutes.

*Cauliflower Mornay*        *Cooking time: 30 minutes*

1 cup Medium White Sauce
  (see index)
1 cup fresh grated Parmesan cheese
melted butter

Preheat oven to broil. Prepare White Sauce, adding the grated cheese. Stir over low heat until cheese melts. Arrange cooked cauliflower in 1½-quart casserole, drizzle with melted butter. Cover with the sauce and broil until bubbly.

# Bacon-Fried Corn

*A great side dish with fried chicken.*

*Serves 4*              *Cooking time: 25 minutes*

2 slices bacon
1-pound can whole kernel corn
1 teaspoon sugar
1 teaspoon salt
dash of pepper

Sauté bacon slices in a medium-sized skillet over low heat until crisp. Remove from pan, cool, and crumble. Set aside.
Drain corn, reserving 2 tablespoons liquid. Add drained corn to bacon fat and sauté, stirring constantly to coat corn. Heat through. Add sugar and salt to reserved liquid, mix well, and add to corn. Add a dash of pepper and mix well. Heat through and serve topped with crumbled bacon.

# Roasted Corn

*Fresh corn on the cob barbeque.*

*Serves 4*              *Cooking time: 20 minutes*

¾ cup butter or margarine, softened
½ cup cheddar cheese spread,
  softened
½ teaspoon garlic salt
1½ tablespoons bacon bits
1 dozen ears fresh corn

Combine first 4 ingredients. Turn corn husks back but do not detach. Strip off silk. Spread 1 tablespoon of butter-cheese mixture evenly on each ear of corn. Lay husks back. Wrap loosely in foil and place over hot coals, turning frequently until tender, about 20 minutes. Serve with additional butter.

# Eggplant Parmigiana

*A delicious "continental style" casserole.*

*Serves 4*              *Cooking time: 45 minutes*

1 medium eggplant
¼ teaspoon Seasoned Salt (page 17)
⅛ teaspoon pepper
1 cup dry bread crumbs
2 eggs, beaten
½ cup olive oil
1½ cups Brother Paul's Italian
  Sauce Parmigiana (see index) or
  14-ounce jar prepared spaghetti
  sauce
½ pound mozzarella cheese, sliced
1 teaspoon dried basil
¼ cup fresh Parmesan cheese,
  grated

Wash eggplant. Cut in half lengthwise, then into ¼-inch slices. Do not peel. Season with salt and pepper. Dip in crumbs, then eggs, and again in crumbs. Chill for half an hour. Heat oil in large skillet. Fry slices on both sides until golden. Drain on paper toweling.

Preheat oven to 350°. Pour half the sauce in a large, shallow, buttered casserole dish. Arrange a layer of eggplant over the sauce, top with a layer of mozzarella cheese, sprinkle with some basil and Parmesan cheese. Add more sauce and repeat layers until casserole dish is full. Bake 30 minutes.

## Ratatouille in Toasted Bread Cups

*A delightful vegetable combination in a crunchy cup.*

*Serves 4*            *Cooking time: 45 to 50 minutes*

4 large bulkie rolls
1 medium eggplant, cubed
⅓ cup olive oil
2 medium onions, finely chopped
3 garlic cloves, minced
1 large sweet red pepper, chopped
3 small zucchini, sliced
4 medium tomatoes, chopped
1 teaspoon dried basil
1 teaspoon parsley, chopped
1½ teaspoons Seasoned Salt
  (page 17)
½ teaspoon sugar
¼ teaspoon pepper
1 teaspoon fennel seed (optional)
Parmesan cheese, freshly grated

Set oven to broil. Cut tops off the rolls and scoop out center, making a shell. Toast very well under broiler, turn and toast the bottoms. Cool, shape foil around bread to form cups. (Foil prevents filling juices from leaking through bottom.)

Trim ends from the eggplant, slice and cube. Place in a bowl of cold salted water, weigh down with a plate, and soak for 15 minutes.

Heat oil in a large skillet. Add the onions, garlic, and red pepper. Sauté until wilted. Add rinsed and drained eggplant and sliced zucchini and sauté, covered, for 10 minutes. Add tomatoes and spices. Cover and cook for an additional 10 minutes to blend the flavors. Remove cover and cook down until the mixture has thickened.

Fill bread cups with ratatouille, sprinkle with seeds and Parmesan cheese, and serve.

## Fresh Green Vegetables with Lemon

*Low in calories, high in flavor.*

*Serves 4*            *Cooking time: 3 to 10 minutes*

1½ pounds fresh asparagus,
  broccoli, Brussels sprouts, or
  spinach
½ teaspoon Seasoned Salt (page 17)
1 lemon, cut in 4 wedges

Rinse the vegetables thoroughly. Separate or cut into bite-sized pieces. Place on a collapsible steamer rack. Pour one inch of water in a Dutch oven. Add rack of vegetables and sprinkle generously with Seasoned Salt, cover, and steam until crisp and tender. Squeeze one lemon wedge over each serving.

## Fresh Vegetable Stir-Fry

*Add your own favorites for variety.*

*Serves 4*            *Cooking time: 10 to 12 minutes*

1 cup broccoli florets
1 cup celery, bias cut
Seasoned Salt (page 17)
¼ cup chicken broth
3 tablespoons soy sauce
1 tablespoon cornstarch
2 tablespoons peanut oil
1 garlic clove, minced
dash of ground ginger
1 cup Chinese pea pods, fresh
  or frozen
1 carrot, peeled, cut in thin strips
1 cup fresh mushrooms, sliced
½ cup broken walnuts
1 tomato, cut into 8 wedges

Place broccoli and celery on a collapsible steamer rack. Pour one inch water into a Dutch oven. Add rack of vegetables, sprinkle with salt. Cover and steam until crisp and barely tender, about 3 minutes. Blend chicken broth with soy sauce and cornstarch, set aside.

Heat oil in wok or large skillet over medium high heat; sauté garlic with dash of ginger for ½ minute. Add remaining vegetables except the tomato and steamed vegetables. Stir-fry 2 to 3 minutes. Add the walnuts. Push vegetables up along the sides of wok, where they will stay warm but not get overcooked. Pour well-stirred broth mixture in center, cook until mixture thickens. Slide vegetables into the liquid, add the tomato and steamed vegetables, stir. Cover and cook 2 minutes.

## Fresh Vegetables with Onion Butter

*Serves 4*          *Cooking time varies according to vegetables selected*

¼ cup butter or margarine, softened
¼ teaspoon dry mustard
¼ teaspoon pepper
1½ teaspoons Worcestershire sauce
2 tablespoons onions, minced
2 tablespoons parsley, finely
   chopped
1½ pounds of fresh vegetables—
   use asparagus, broccoli, brussels
   sprouts, carrots, cauliflower,
   green beans, summer squash,
   spinach, turnip, or any
   combination thereof
Seasoned Salt (page 17)

Combine softened butter, mustard, and pepper. Using a wire whip or an electric mixer, blend in Worcestershire sauce, and whip until light and fluffy. Stir in onions and parsley.

Rinse vegetables. Separate or cut into bite-sized pieces. Place vegetables on a collapsible steamer rack. Pour one inch of water in a Dutch oven. Add rack of vegetables, sprinkle generously with Seasoned Salt. Cover and steam until a fork easily pierces the thickest part of the vegetable. Spoon cooked vegetables into a serving dish, dot with onion butter, toss.

Note: Leftover butter will keep, tightly covered, in the refrigerator for several weeks.

## Green Beans, Three Ways

*Serves 4*          *Cooking time: 20 minutes*

1 pound fresh green beans,
   French-cut, or 1-pound can
   French-style green beans

Cook fresh beans in a small amount of boiling salted water until just tender, about 20 minutes. Drain.

If using canned beans, heat through and drain.

Serve in one of the following ways.

*Green Beans in Cream:* To hot drained beans add **1 cup Thick White Sauce** (see index). Mix well.

*Green Beans with Cheddar Cheese:* Combine **½ cup shredded sharp cheddar cheese** with **1 cup Medium White Sauce** (see index). Stir in hot green beans. Sprinkle with **crumbled bacon.**

*Green Beans Almondine*

½ cup slivered almonds
¼ cup butter
2 teaspoons lemon juice
dash of salt

Cook almonds in butter until golden. Add lemon juice, salt, and hot green beans. Stir well.

# Fresh Kale

*A forgotten green vegetable that's very rich in vitamins and flavor.*

*Serves 4          Cooking time: 10 to 15 minutes*

1½ pounds fresh kale
½ teaspoon salt
½ teaspoon Seasoned Salt (page 17)
¼ teaspoon pepper
1 tablespoon butter
2 tablespoons cooked, crumbled bacon

Rinse kale thoroughly. Remove the tough stems and midribs. Chop leaves into 2-inch pieces. Pour 1 inch of boiling water in a Dutch oven. Stir in the ½ teaspoon of plain salt, add the kale and simmer for 10 to 15 minutes, until just tender. Drain. Season with Seasoned Salt and pepper. Toss with the butter. Sprinkle with bacon bits.

# Onions, Two Ways

*Serves 4          Cooking time: 20 to 25 minutes*

Peel 1 pound small onions and cook, covered, in a small amount of boiling salted water until tender, about 20 to 25 minutes. Drain and prepare in one of the following ways.

*Onion and Fruit Sauté          Cooking time: 25 to 30 minutes*

2 slices bacon
4 medium red apples
½ cup seedless yellow raisins

Cook bacon in a large skillet until crisp. Set aside to cool; crumble. Add cooked onions to bacon fat, sauté gently.

Wash and core apples and cut each into 8 wedges. Add apple wedges and raisins to onions. Cover and cook over low heat until apples are tender, about 5 minutes. Drain and spoon into serving dish. Sprinkle with bacon crumbs.

*Onions in Cheese Sauce with Peanuts*

1 cup Medium White Sauce (see index)
1 cup grated sharp cheddar cheese or 8-ounce jar smokey cheddar spread
¼ cup finely chopped salted peanuts

Combine White Sauce and cheese. Cook over low heat, stirring, until cheese melts. Add cooked onions, stir to coat evenly. Sprinkle with chopped peanuts.

# Onions in Cinders

*An easy cookout favorite.*

*Serves 4          Cooking time: 1 hour*

4 large, sweet onions, unpeeled
¾ cup Italian Cheese Dressing (see index)

Have dressing at room temperature. Cut 4 pieces of foil, 12 by 24 inches, fold in two. Place one *unpeeled* whole onion in the center of each piece, seal loosely. Place on grill over medium-hot coals, or in 375° oven, and bake 1 hour, turning frequently. A fork will penetrate the onions easily when done. Carefully unwrap *(watch out for the steam)*, slip off peels, and top with cheese dressing to serve.

# Parsnips in Pineapple Glaze

*A touch of orange liqueur sparks this vegetable.*

*Serves 4          Cooking time: 25 minutes*

8 medium parsnips
Seasoned Salt (page 17)
8-ounce can crushed pineapple
½ cup orange juice
1 teaspoon grated orange peel
2 tablespoons brown sugar
2 tablespoons butter or margarine
2 tablespoons orange liqueur

Pare parsnips, cut in half, and slit lengthwise. Place on a collapsible steamer rack. Pour one inch water into a Dutch oven. Add rack of parsnips, generously sprinkle with Seasoned Salt. Cover and steam until tender, about 10 minutes. Meanwhile, combine pineapple, orange juice, orange peel, sugar, and butter in a saucepan. Heat through. Stir in liqueur.

Preheat oven to 350°. Place cooked parsnips in a 1½-quart casserole dish. Pour pineapple mixture over parsnips. Bake 15 minutes, basting frequently.

## Peas, French Style

*Mixed with tiny onions and glazed — lettuce is the secret.*

*Serves 4*          *Cooking time: 17 minutes*

3 tablespoons butter or margarine
1 dozen tiny pearl onions, peeled
1 cup Bibb or Boston lettuce,
   shredded
2 cups fresh peas, shelled, or
   10-ounce package frozen peas
½ teaspoon Seasoned Salt (page 17)
dash of pepper
½ teaspoon sugar
1 teaspoon cornstarch
¼ cup chicken broth, hot

Melt butter in Dutch oven. Add onions and lettuce, stir well. Add peas, salt, pepper, sugar. Stir. Cover and steam over low heat 10 minutes. Dissolve cornstarch in hot broth. Add to vegetables, stir and simmer until peas are tender, about 5 minutes.

## Baked Potatoes, Three Ways — Plain and Fancy

*Serves 4*          *Cooking time: 45 to 50 minutes*

4 large baking potatoes
salad oil
Seasoned Salt (page 17)

8 teaspoons butter or margarine, or
4 tablespoons dairy sour cream

Preheat oven to 425°. Scrub potatoes, prick with a fork to allow steam to escape, wipe dry. Rub with oil. Place potatoes on a cookie sheet. Bake until tender when pressed, about 45 to 50 minutes. Remove from oven. Make cross-cuts on one side of each potato. Fluff the cut area lightly with a fork. Sprinkle with salt, fluff again. Add 2 teaspoons butter or 1 tablespoon sour cream to each. Serve.

*Hand Warmers:* Make cross-cuts on one end of each baked potato. Insert a 1-ounce stick (½-by-½-by-2-inch) of **cheddar cheese** in the opening. Wrap bottom half of potato with a napkin.

*Yummy Puppies:* While potatoes are baking, prepare this topping.

2 slices of bacon, chopped
½ cup onions, chopped
1 cup canned tomatoes, crushed
1 cup canned whole kernel corn,
   drained
¼ teaspoon basil
¼ teaspoon pepper
¼ teaspoon Seasoned Salt (page 17)
1 cup sharp cheddar cheese, grated

Sauté bacon and onions until onions are clear. Drain off fat. Add tomatoes with juice, corn, and spices. Bring to a boil. Lower heat, add cheese, and stir until melted. Spoon mixture atop potatoes. (Omit the butter or sour cream from basic recipe.)

## Baked Stuffed Potatoes, Four Ways

*Serves 4*          *Cooking time: 50 to 55 minutes*

4 large baking potatoes
salad oil
2 tablespoons butter or margarine
½ teaspoon Seasoned Salt (page 17)

dash of pepper
1 egg yolk
¼ cup half-and-half, warm

Preheat oven to 425°. Scrub potatoes. Prick with fork to allow steam to escape. Wipe dry. Rub with oil. Place potatoes on a cookie sheet, bake until tender when pressed, about 45 to 50 minutes. Remove from oven immediately when done. Cut a lengthwise slice from top of each potato. Scoop out insides, reserve shells. Combine potato, butter, salt, and pepper. Whip until fluffy. Add egg yolk and continue mixing while adding half-and-half. Spoon mixture into shells. Return to oven to heat through, about 5 minutes.

*New England "Stuffies":* To basic recipe add: ½ cup sharp cheddar cheese, grated, ¼ teaspoon dry mustard, 1 tablespoon chives, chopped. Mix well. Stuff shells. Broil to brown.

*Bleu Cheese Bakers:* To basic recipe add: ¼ cup bleu cheese, crumbled, ¼ cup dairy sour cream. Mix well. Stuff shells. Sprinkle with paprika. Broil to brown.

*Roman Style:* To basic recipe add: 1 cup spinach, cooked, well drained and puréed, and ¼ teaspoon dried basil. Mix well. Stuff shells. Sprinkle generously with grated Romano cheese. Broil to brown.

## Boiled Potatoes, Four Ways

*Choose one of the four distinctive combinations.*

*Serves 4          Cooking time: 15 to 25 minutes*

Cook 4 medium or 1 dozen small new potatoes in boiling salted water until tender, about 15 to 25 minutes. Drain. Serve with one of the sauces below.

*New Potatoes in Lemon Sauce      Cooking time: 15 to 25 minutes*

¼ cup butter or margarine, melted
1 tablespoon fresh lemon juice

dash of nutmeg
dash of pepper
1 teaspoon grated lemon peel
1 teaspoon chives, chopped

Combine butter, juice, nutmeg, and pepper and stir well. Pour over cooked potatoes, turn to coat evenly. Sprinkle with lemon rind and snipped chives.

*Potatoes au Gratin      Cooking time: 35 minutes*

1 cup Medium White Sauce (see index)
1 cup sharp cheddar cheese, shredded
1 garlic clove, pressed
¼ cup fresh bread crumbs
¼ cup Parmesan cheese
¼ teaspoon paprika

Preheat oven to 400°. Combine White Sauce, sharp cheddar cheese, and garlic. Stir over low heat until the cheese is melted. Combine bread crumbs, Parmesan cheese, and paprika, mix well. Peel and slice cooked new potatoes. Layer in a buttered 1½-quart casserole dish. Top with cheese sauce. Sprinkle Parmesan-crumb-paprika mixture over top and bake 10 minutes. Broil to brown.

*Lyonnaise Potatoes      Cooking time: 45 minutes*

½ cup onions, chopped
¼ cup butter or margarine, melted
½ teaspoon Seasoned Salt (page 17)
¼ teaspoon pepper
¼ cup chicken broth
2 tablespoons parsley, minced

Sauté onions in butter until golden. Peel and dice cooked potatoes. Add to skillet with remaining ingredients except parsley. Cover and cook over low heat until bottom is nicely browned. Fold like an omelet and top with minced parsley.

*Pommes Dijon      Cooking time: 40 minutes*

1 cup Medium White Sauce (see index)

1 tablespoon Dijon mustard
½ cup watercress, chopped

Combine White Sauce and mustard. As sauce starts to boil add the cooked, peeled potatoes, stir well. Remove from heat, add watercress just before serving.

## Cookout Potatoes

*Great for a barbeque, or cook in your oven for a taste of summer.*

*Serves 4          Cooking time: 25 to 35 minutes*

    4 medium potatoes
    ¼ cup butter or margarine
    ½ cup bacon bits
    ½ teaspoon garlic salt
    ¼ teaspoon pepper

Scrub potatoes, but do not peel. Cut into ¼-inch slices. Brush bottom of a large, shallow aluminum pan with butter. Spread potatoes, top evenly with remaining butter and bacon bits. Sprinkle with garlic salt and pepper. Cover with foil and bake over hot coals for 25 minutes, or until tender, or cook in a 400° oven until tender, about 35 minutes.

## Foil-Baked Potatoes

Choose firm, medium-sized **baking potatoes** (or **yams** or **sweet potatoes**). Scrub clean, then brush with **salad oil.** Wrap each potato in a square of foil, overlapping the ends. Bake 40 to 60 minutes on the grill (about twice as long if hood is down) or right on top of the coals. Turn potatoes occasionally (unless hood is down). When potatoes are tender, make a slit with a fork on the top of each potato and push ends to fluff. (Protect hands with paper towels or potholder when potatoes are hot-off-the-coals.) Season with **Seasoned Salt** and **pepper** and serve. Pass **butter, chopped green onions, sour cream,** or **crisp bacon bits.**

## Hashed Brown Potatoes

*A great way to use leftover boiled or baked potatoes.*

*Serves 4          Cooking time: 15 to 20 minutes*

    3 cups cooked cold potatoes,
        diced or shredded
    2 tablespoons onions, shredded
    3 tablespoons flour
    ¼ cup milk
    ½ teaspoon Seasoned Salt (page 17)
    ¼ teaspoon pepper
    1 teaspoon parsley, finely chopped
    3 tablespoons salad oil

Combine all ingredients except oil and mix well. Heat 2 tablespoons of the oil in a large skillet. Add potato mixture and pack into a large pancake. Cook over medium heat until brown and crusty on the bottom. Shake pan to prevent mixture from sticking. Slide onto a plate. Wipe skillet clean with paper towels. Add and heat remaining tablespoon of oil. Return pancake to skillet, brown side up. Cook to brown other side. Cut into wedges and serve.

## Potatoes *Bordeaux*

*Using precooked frozen potatoes makes this side dish a snap.*

*Serves 4          Cooking time: 7 to 8 minutes*

    1½ tablespoons olive oil
    1 garlic clove, sliced
    1½ cups tomatoes, peeled, diced
        (4 medium) or 1½ cups canned
        tomatoes, drained, chopped
    ½ teaspoon thyme
    1½ teaspoons salt
    dash of cayenne pepper
    10-ounce package frozen sliced
        fried potatoes

Heat olive oil in large skillet, sauté garlic until brown. Remove garlic and discard. Add tomatoes, thyme, salt, and cayenne pepper to oil. Simmer 2 to 3 minutes. Add frozen potatoes. Cook covered, over medium heat, until thoroughly heated – no longer than 3 minutes. Serve immediately.

## Quick-Bake Potatoes, Four Ways

*Basic Recipe for 4*                    *Cooking time:*
                                        *25 to 30 minutes*

½ cup Parmesan cheese, grated
¼ cup fresh bread crumbs
1 teaspoon Seasoned Salt (page 17)
¼ teaspoon pepper
4 large baking potatoes
½ cup butter or margarine, melted

Preheat oven to 425°. Combine cheese, crumbs and spices, mix well. Scrub potatoes, cut lengthwise into halves. Dry cut surface well on towels. Dip cut potato surface into melted butter, then into cheese mix. Arrange, cut side down, on a well-greased cookie sheet. Bake until tender, 25 to 30 minutes.

*Chili and Cheese Bakes:* Replace bread crumbs with **1 tablespoon chili powder.**

*Onion Bake:* Replace Parmesan cheese, crumbs, and spices with **dry onion soup mix.**

*Cheddar-Garlic Bake:* Replace Parmesan cheese and crumbs with **crushed cheddar-garlic croutons.**

## Shoestring Potatoes

*Serves 4*          *Cooking time: 7 to 10 minutes*

4 medium potatoes
oil for frying
Seasoned Salt (page 17)

Wash and peel potatoes. Slice into long "matchstick" size. Soak in ice water to crisp,

at least 30 minutes. Drain, pat dry.

Heat oil in a deep fryer with a basket, or a large skillet with oil 2 inches deep. Heat to 350° or until oil smokes lightly. Place a handful of potato sticks into basket, slowly dip into fat. Shake basket to prevent sticking. Remove potatoes when nicely browned, spread on a double thickness of paper toweling, sprinkle to taste with salt. Keep warm until all potatoes are cooked.

## Whipped Potatoes, Four Ways – Plain and Fancy

*Serves 4*          *Cooking time: 25 minutes*

6 medium potatoes, peeled,
    quartered
½ teaspoon Seasoned Salt (page 17)
½ cup hot milk
¼ cup butter or margarine, melted
¼ teaspoon salt
dash of pepper

Cook potatoes in boiling water with Seasoned Salt until tender, about 25 minutes. Drain. Whip with hot milk and melted butter. Season with salt and pepper. Whip until completely blended. Serve as is or try one of the following recipes.

*Chantilly Potatoes*     *Cooking time: 35 minutes*

½ pint heavy cream
½ cup Parmesan cheese, grated

Preheat oven to 400°. Spread whipped potatoes in a buttered 1½-quart casserole dish. Whip cream and spread evenly over potatoes. Sprinkle with cheese and bake until golden brown.

*Potatoes Almondine*     *Cooking time: 40 minutes*

1 egg, beaten
2 tablespoons butter or margarine
¼ cup almonds, slivered

Reduce amount of milk in basic whipped potato recipe to ¼ cup. Preheat oven to 400°. Add egg to whipped potatoes and stir.

Melt butter in a small skillet and sauté almonds for 2 minutes. Drop potatoes by spoonfuls, about 12, onto a greased cookie sheet. Top with sautéed almonds and bake until golden brown, about 15 minutes.

*Cheese-Chive Potatoes*　　　*Cooking time: 40 minutes*

3 ounces cream cheese, softened
¼ cup chives, chopped
2 tablespoons butter or margarine, diced

Preheat oven to 400°. Combine whipped potatoes and cream cheese, blend. Stir in chives. Spread into a well-buttered 1½-quart casserole dish. Sprinkle with diced butter and bake until golden brown, about 15 minutes.

## Spinach Elegante

*Serves 4*　　　*Cooking time: 25 minutes*

2 slices bacon
¼ pound fresh mushrooms, sliced
1 pound fresh spinach, or
　2 10-ounce packages frozen chopped spinach
Seasoned Salt (page 17)
1 cup sharp cheddar cheese, grated
dried crushed thyme leaves
pepper

Sauté bacon slices until crisp. Cool and crumble. Drain all but 1 tablespoon bacon fat from skillet. Add mushrooms and sauté lightly, about 5 minutes. Spoon onto layers of paper toweling to drain.

Rinse fresh spinach, place in a Dutch oven, sprinkle with salt, cover. Turn heat to high. As soon as steaming begins, turn heat off. Leave pot on burner for 3 minutes. Drain thoroughly. Chop spinach coarsely.

Set oven to broil. Butter a 1½-quart casserole dish; spoon in half the spinach, half the crumbled bacon, half the mushrooms, and half the cheese. Sprinkle lightly with thyme and pepper. Repeat layers. Broil until cheese bubbles and browns.

## Spinach and Grapefruit Sauté

*Serves 4*　　　*Cooking time: 6 minutes*

2 grapefruit
1 pound fresh spinach
Seasoned Salt (page 17)
2 tablespoons butter or margarine

Cut grapefruit in half. Using a grapefruit knife, remove fruit sections and place in a strainer. (Save juice for a tart drink.)

Rinse spinach. Place in a Dutch oven, sprinkle with salt, cover. Turn heat to high; as soon as steaming begins, turn heat off. Leave pot on burner for 3 minutes. Drain very well.

Melt butter in medium saucepan. Add drained grapefruit sections, gently sauté 3 minutes. Add to drained spinach, toss gently.

## Stuffed Pumpkin

*The pumpkin is the container for fresh fruits and nuts.*

*Serves 6 to 8*　　　*Cooking time: 1½ to 2 hours*

1 cup fresh cranberries
¼ cup sugar
12-inch pumpkin
4 apples, unpeeled and cubed
2 oranges, peeled, seeded, chopped
1 cup walnuts
1 cup raisins
½ cup maple syrup
¼ teaspoon cinnamon
¼ teaspoon nutmeg

Preheat oven to 400°. Chop cranberries and mix with sugar, set aside.

Scrub the pumpkin thoroughly. Leave the stem on for a handle. Carve out a notched 6-inch circle from the top to serve as a cover. Scrape out seeds and save for roasting.

Scrape, remove and discard stringy interior.

Combine remaining ingredients in a large mixing bowl, add cranberry mixture, and stir to blend. Spoon into pumpkin shell. Top with carved pumpkin cover. Place in a deep-dish pie plate and bake until a fork easily penetrates pumpkin. Do not overcook. Remove cover and serve directly from the pumpkin.

To roast pumpkin seeds: Separate, rinse clean, and spread seeds out on a paper towel to absorb moisture. Place on a lightly buttered cookie sheet, sprinkle with Seasoned Salt (page 00) and bake 2 to 3 minutes at 400°. Cool and enjoy.

## Blue Hubbard Squash and Marmalade Purée

*Serves 4*       *Cooking time: 10 minutes*

4 cups (approximately 1½ lbs.)
   blue hubbard squash
Seasoned Salt (page 17)
¼ cup butter or margarine, melted
¼ cup orange marmalade
¼ cup walnut pieces

Pare the squash and cut into cubes. Place squash on collapsible steamer rack. Pour 1 inch water in Dutch oven. Add rack of squash, sprinkle generously with Seasoned Salt and pepper. Cover and steam until tender, about 10 minutes. Spoon into blender, blend until smooth. Gradually add remaining ingredients. Adjust seasonings.

## Acorn Squash Bake with Fruit

*Adds a festive touch to any meal.*

*Serves 4*       *Cooking time: 1 hour*

2 medium acorn squash
½ cup dried pitted prunes, diced
2 cups apples, chopped
1 medium orange, peeled, diced
½ cup brown sugar

¼ cup butter or margarine, melted
½ teaspoon Seasoned Salt (page 17)

Preheat oven to 350°. Cut squash in half crosswise, remove seeds and stringy membrane. Place cut side down in a casserole dish. Bake 30 minutes.

Pour boiling water over prunes, soak 5 minutes. Drain. Combine prunes, apples, oranges, sugar, and melted butter. Stir to mix.

Remove squash from oven, turn, sprinkle with salt, fill cavities with fruit mixture. Return to oven and bake another 30 minutes.

## Fried Pattypan Squash

*A different way to cook this tasty squash.*

*Serves 4*       *Cooking time: 4 to 5 minutes*

2 3- to 4-inch pattypan squash
3 tablespoons butter or margarine,
   melted
Parmesan cheese, grated
salt
pepper

Wash and dry squash. Trim off the stem ends and slice into ¼-inch slices. Heat griddle to medium high. Brush butter on griddle. Place squash on griddle and cook 2 minutes. Turn, lightly season with salt and pepper. Sprinkle tops with Parmesan cheese. Cook until just tender.

## Sweet Potatoes à la Sugar Shack

*Maple syrup coats these sweet morsels.*

*Serves 4*       *Cooking time: 50 minutes*

4 medium sweet potatoes
salt
½ cup maple syrup
¼ cup butter or margarine
1 teaspoon lemon juice
½ cup seedless raisins
2 tablespoons chopped walnuts

Scrub potatoes. Boil in water to cover until just tender, about 35 minutes. Drain, cool slightly. Peel potatoes and cut in half lengthwise. Sprinkle with salt.

Combine syrup and butter in a large skillet. Slowly bring to a boil. Add juice, stir. Add raisins and potatoes, turn to coat. Cook over low heat about 15 minutes, turning potatoes occasionally. Sprinkle with nuts to serve.

For variation, add cooked, drained **small onions** to syrup mixture with potatoes.


## Broiled Tomato Slices

*With cheese topping — cook along with steak.*

*Serves 4*          *Cooking time: 3 to 4 minutes*

4 large ripe tomatoes
Seasoned Salt (page 17)
pepper
¼ cup soft bread crumbs
½ cup sharp cheddar cheese,
   shredded
3 tablespoons butter or margarine,
   melted
¼ teaspoon garlic powder
2 tablespoons parsley, finely
   chopped

Cut tomatoes in ½-inch-thick slices. Sprinkle lightly with salt and pepper. Combine remaining ingredients. Sprinkle generously over slices. Lay in shallow broiler pan and broil until bubbly.


## Tomatoes Dijon

*An unusual and tasty combination.*

*Serves 4*          *Cooking time: 55 minutes*

2 tablespoons butter or margarine
1 cup celery, diced
½ cup onions, chopped
2 tablespoons flour
2-pound can tomatoes
1 tablespoon sugar

1 teaspoon Seasoned Salt (page 17)
¼ teaspoon pepper
2 teaspoons Dijon mustard
3 slices of toast, buttered

Preheat oven to 350°. Melt butter. Add celery and onions and sauté until barely tender. Sprinkle flour over cooked vegetables and stir to blend. Add tomatoes, spices, and mustard. Stir well.

Cut toast in small cubes, add half to vegetables. Stir. Pour vegetable mixture in a 1½-quart casserole dish. Bake 30 minutes. Top with remaining toast cubes and bake for another 15 minutes.


## Tomato and Onion Simmer

*Serve over cooked potatoes or thick French toast.*

*Serves 4*          *Cooking time: 15 minutes*

2 tablespoons butter or margarine
½ cup onions, finely chopped
2-pound can tomatoes
1 tablespoon parsley
1 teaspoon Seasoned Salt (page 17)
¼ teaspoon pepper
¼ teaspoon dried thyme
2 tablespoons cornstarch
¼ cup cold water

Melt butter in a large saucepan. Add onions and sauté until clear. Add tomatoes and spices, heat through. Dissolve cornstarch in water. Add to simmering tomato mixture and stir constantly until thick.


## Zucchini with Anisette

*Flamed, with a taste of licorice.*

*Serves 4*          *Cooking time: 5 to 7 minutes*

6 small zucchini
⅓ cup olive oil
1 garlic clove, crushed
1 ounce Anisette liqueur

Wash zucchini, remove ends. Cut length-wise into 3 strips. Sauté zucchini in oil and garlic until tender but still crisp. Remove from heat. Add anisette and flame, using long matches.

## Zucchini with Corn

*Serves 4*          *Cooking time: 10 to 15 minutes*

4 small zucchini
Seasoned Salt (page 17)
2 tablespoons butter or margarine
½ cup onions, chopped
¼ cup green peppers, chopped

16-ounce can whole kernel corn, drained
¼ teaspoon dried dill

Wash zucchini, remove both ends, and cut into ¼-inch slices. Place on a collapsible steamer rack. Pour 1 inch of water in a Dutch oven. Add rack of zucchini. Sprinkle with salt, cover, and steam until crisp-tender, about 5 minutes. Meanwhile, melt butter in a medium skillet. Add onions and green peppers and sauté until tender. Add drained corn and toss, heat through. Add cooked drained zucchini and dill, toss carefully, serve.

# Biscuits & Breads, Noodles & Rice

## Maman's Bacon and Cheese Biscuits

*Makes 12 biscuits*     *Cooking time: 10 minutes*

2 cups biscuit mix
⅔ cup milk
½ cup sharp cheddar cheese,
   shredded
¼ cup cooked bacon bits
sesame seeds

Preheat oven to 450°. Combine biscuit mix and milk, blend well, then beat vigorously for 30 seconds. Mix in cheese and bacon. Drop by spoonfuls onto ungreased cookie sheet. Sprinkle tops with seeds. Bake 10 minutes.

(Cheese, bacon, and sesame seeds can also be added in the same manner to homemade biscuit dough.)

## Cheese-It Biscuits

*Cheese and tomato make these special and colorful.*

*Makes 18 to 20*     *Cooking time: 10 to 12 minutes*

2¼ cups biscuit mix

¾ cup sharp cheddar cheese,
   shredded
½ cup tomato juice
butter or margarine, melted
celery seeds

Preheat oven to 450°. Combine biscuit mix and cheese in a large mixing bowl. Add juice and mix. Turn onto cloth-covered pastry board, well dusted with biscuit mix. Gently roll to coat. Shape into ball, knead 12 times. Roll out to ½-inch thick and cut with 2-inch cutter dipped in biscuit mix. Place on ungreased cookie sheet, brush with butter; sprinkle with seeds. Bake 10 to 12 minutes.

(Cheese, tomato juice, and celery seeds can also be added in the same manner to a standard biscuit recipe.)

## Corn Bread

*Hearty accompaniment for soup or stew.*

*Makes 9 to 12 squares*     *Cooking time: 20 to 25 minutes*

1 cup flour, sifted
4 teaspoons baking powder
3 tablespoons sugar

¾ teaspoon salt
1 cup cornmeal
2 eggs, beaten
½ cup milk
½ cup half-and-half
¼ cup butter or margarine, melted

Preheat oven to 425°. Grease an 8 x 8 x 2-inch pan. Sift together flour, baking powder, sugar, and salt in large mixing bowl. Mix in cornmeal. Add eggs, milk, half-and-half, and butter; whip until blended, 1 minute. *Do not overmix.* Pour into pan and bake 20 to 25 minutes. Cut into squares and serve hot.

## Sticky Caramel Buns

*This quick treat uses packaged biscuits — gooey but good.*

*Makes 16*          *Cooking time: 20 minutes*

2 tablespoons butter or margarine
½ cup brown sugar
2 tablespoons light corn syrup
2 tablespoons maple syrup
½ cup pecan halves
2 packages refrigerator biscuits

Preheat oven to 425°. Melt butter in bottom of 9-by-1½-inch round pan. Add brown sugar and syrups. Heat in oven to dissolve sugar. Arrange nuts on bottom in the butter-sugar mixture. Place biscuits atop nuts in a single layer. Bake 15 minutes. Let stand 5 minutes, then invert on serving platter. Serve warm.

## Brandied Banana Bread

*An old favorite with a little spirit.*

*Makes 1 loaf*          *Cooking time: 1 hour*

½ cup butter or margarine, softened
⅔ cup honey
3 eggs, beaten
1 cup mashed ripe banana

⅓ cup milk
3 tablespoons coffee brandy
2 cups whole wheat flour
1 teaspoon salt
2 teaspoons baking powder
1 teaspoon baking soda
1 cup seedless raisins
¼ cup dried apricots, finely chopped

Preheat oven to 350°. Butter and flour an 8½ x 4½ x 2½-inch loaf pan. Combine butter and honey in mixer bowl, beat until light and fluffy. Beat in eggs, bananas, milk, and brandy. Sift together flour, salt, baking powder, and soda and gradually add to banana mixture. Stir in raisins and apricots. Pour into pan. Bake 1 hour. Cool and remove from pan. Slice and serve.

## French Garlic Toast or Bread

*Perfect with a fine wine as a snack, or a versatile addition to many meals.*

*Makes 1 loaf*

½ cup butter or margarine, softened
2 garlic cloves, crushed
dash of Seasoned Salt (page 17)
1 loaf French or Vienna bread

Cream butter, add garlic and salt.

*For Toast*          *Cooking time: 5 to 7 minutes*

Slice bread into inch-thick slices. Toast *one side only.* Spread untoasted side thickly with butter, then grill until the bread becomes beautifully crisp.

*For Bread*          *Cooking time: 30 minutes*

Preheat oven to 350°. Slice bread on the bias, cutting to *but not through* bottom crust. Spread butter on one side of each slice. Wrap in foil. Bake 30 minutes.

## Fruit Scones

*A classic teatime treat, simple and speedy.*

*Makes 12 to 16*      *Cooking time: 15 minutes*

 2 cups flour, sifted
 2 tablespoons sugar
 3 teaspoons baking powder
 ½ teaspoon salt
 6 tablespoons butter or margarine
 1 egg, beaten
 ½ cup milk
 ¼ cup seedless raisins
 ¼ cup dried apricots, finely diced
 1 egg, slightly beaten for brushing

Preheat oven to 425°. Sift dry ingredients together. Cut in butter with pastry blender until mixture resembles coarse crumbs. Add egg and milk, stir with fork. Add fruit and stir until mixture follows fork around the bowl. Turn onto floured pastry board and knead gently 12 times. Cut dough in half. Shape each half into a ball. Gently roll out to ½-inch thick, 6 inches around. Cut into 6 or 8 pie-shaped wedges. Place wedges on ungreased cookie sheet, sides *not* touching. Brush tops with slightly beaten egg. Bake to golden brown, about 15 minutes. Serve with apricot preserves or whipped butter.

## Stuffed French Bread

*A great cookout accompaniment – roasted on the grill.*

*Makes 1 loaf*      *Cooking time: 15 to 18 minutes*

 ¼ cup butter or margarine, softened
 2 tablespoons dill or chervil, finely
    chopped
 ¼ teaspoon Seasoned Salt (page 17)
 ¼ teaspoon pepper
 1 teaspoon lemon juice
 1 loaf French bread
 6 ounces imported Swiss cheese,
    sliced

Cream butter, add seasonings and juice, blend well. Slice bread into ¾-inch-thick slices, cutting to *but not through* bottom crust. Fill every other space between the slices with cheese slices and spread with butter mixture. Wrap in foil and grill 15 minutes. Open foil under a broiler and toast 2 to 3 minutes for a crusty top if desired. Slice through unfilled openings and serve.

## Salty's No Sugar-No Salt Bran Muffins

*Here's to good health!*

*Makes 12 muffins*      *Cooking time: 25 minutes*

 1¼ cups flour
 1¼ tablespoons baking powder
 1 cup All Bran cereal
 1 cup milk
 2 eggs
 3 tablespoons vegetable oil
 2 medium apples, cored, pared,
    and diced
 1 cup dates, pitted, coarsely chopped

Preheat oven to 400°. Lightly grease a 12-muffin pan. Combine the flour and baking powder, stir to mix, set aside. In a large mixing bowl combine the bran and milk, stir to blend, let stand 2 minutes or until the cereal is softened. Add eggs and oil. Beat with an electric mixer, medium speed, for 2 minutes or until well blended. Stir in apples and dates, mix well. Fold in flour mixture, stirring only to combine. Divide batter evenly into the muffin cups. Bake for 25 minutes or until lightly browned.

## Yorkshire Pudding

*A must with prime rib.*

*Serves 4*      *Cooking time: 25 minutes*

 2 eggs
 1 cup milk

1 cup flour
½ teaspoon salt
2 tablespoons butter or margarine,
  melted
beef drippings

Preheat oven to 450°. Break eggs into a large mixing bowl, beat well. Stir in milk. Add flour and salt, beat until smooth. Beat in butter. Pour ¼ cup beef drippings into a 9-inch square baking pan. Add batter. Bake 10 minutes. Reduce oven temperature to 350°, bake 15 minutes longer. Pudding should be puffy and golden brown. Cut in squares and serve with roast.

## Noodle and Cashew Toss

*Crunchy, nutty egg noodles.*

*Serves 4*          *Cooking time: 18 minutes*

8 ounces egg noodles
1 teaspoon Seasoned Salt (page 17)
1 tablespoon salad oil
½ cup butter or margarine
½ cup salted cashew nuts, coarsely
  broken
¼ cup grated Parmesan cheese

Fill a large Dutch oven to within 2 inches of top with cold water. Add Seasoned Salt and oil, cover, bring to a boil. Add noodles. Cook, uncovered, in rapidly boiling water until *al dente*. (Check package directions for cooking time.) Drain immediately, rinse in hot water, drain. Meanwhile, melt butter in small skillet. Add nuts and brown lightly. Add to drained noodles, toss to mix. Add cheese and toss.

## Noodle Omelet

*Fast, easy, and versatile.*

*Serves 4*          *Cooking time: 25 minutes*

1 teaspoon Seasoned Salt (page 17)

1 tablespoon salad oil
12 ounces egg noodles
½ cup butter or margarine, melted
8 slices bacon, diced
3 egg yolks, beaten
dash of salt
dash of pepper
¼ cup Parmesan cheese, freshly
  grated

Fill a large Dutch oven to within 2 inches of top with cold water. Add salt and salad oil. Cover and bring to a boil. Add noodles. Cook uncovered in rapidly boiling water, *al dente*. (Check package directions for cooking time.) Drain, rinse in hot water, drain. Toss with melted butter to coat. Sauté bacon in skillet until crisp. Drain. Reserve 1 tablespoon bacon fat in pan. Add buttered noodles, cooked bacon, egg yolks, salt, and pepper. Cook until eggs are set, about 1 minute. Top with cheese.

## Spinach Noodles
## with Cream Cheese Sauce

*Easy, and so good you'll serve them often.*

*Serves 4*          *Cooking time: 25 minutes*

3 tablespoons butter or margarine
2 tablespoons parsley flakes
1 teaspoon dried basil
½ teaspoon pepper
1¼ teaspoon Seasoned Salt (page 17)
8 ounces cream cheese, softened
1 tablespoon salad oil
8 ounces spinach egg noodles
¼ cup butter or margarine
1 garlic clove, minced
½ cup grated Parmesan cheese

Melt butter in top half of double boiler over simmering water. Add parsley, basil, pepper, and ¼ teaspoon of the Seasoned Salt. Add cream cheese. Cover. When cheese is melted, stir to blend, add ½ cup boiling water, and blend completely. Keep warm.

Fill a large Dutch oven to within 2 inches of top with cold water. Add 1 teaspoon of the Seasoned Salt and oil. Cover and bring to a boil. Add noodles and cook, uncovered, in rapidly boiling water until *al dente*. (Check package directions for cooking time.) Drain, rinse in hot water, drain. Cook garlic in butter 2 minutes, add noodles, and toss. Add Parmesan cheese, toss. Top with cream cheese sauce.

## Almond Rice

*Nuts add crunch. Bake right along with a roast.*

*Serves 4*                    *Cooking time: 1¼ hours*

2 teaspoons Seasoned Salt (page 17)
1 cup long grain rice
⅓ cup butter or margarine
dash of garlic salt
1¼ cups chicken broth
1 tablespoon parsley, chopped
½ cup almonds, slivered, toasted

Combine salt and 2 cups water; bring to a boil and pour over rice. Let stand half an hour. Drain. Rinse with cold water and drain well. Melt butter in skillet. Add rice and cook until butter is absorbed, stirring frequently.

Meanwhile, preheat oven to 350°. Pour rice into 1-quart casserole dish, sprinkle with garlic salt. Pour broth over rice. Cover and bake 45 minutes. Add parsley and toss. Sprinkle with almonds, and bake uncovered for 10 minutes at 350°.

## Rice *au Gratin*

*Great with chops.*

*Serves 4*                    *Cooking time: 50 minutes*

2 cups cooked rice
¼ cup onions, finely chopped
¼ cup green peppers, finely chopped
2 tablespoons pimentos, finely chopped

1 cup Medium White Sauce (see index)
1 teaspoon mayonnaise
1½ cups sharp cheddar cheese, grated
⅓ cup milk
½ teaspoon salt
dash of pepper

Preheat oven to 350°. Combine rice, onions, green peppers, and pimentos in large mixing bowl. Add white sauce, mayonnaise, 1 cup of the cheese, milk, and seasonings. Mix well. Pour into greased 1½-quart casserole dish. Sprinkle remaining cheese on top. Bake 35 minutes.

## Oriental Steamed Rice

*Serves 4*                    *Cooking time: 25 minutes*

1 cup rice
1 cup cold water
¼ teaspoon Seasoned Salt (page 17)

Rinse rice, strain, repeat. Add to small saucepan with water and salt. Stir, cover, bring to a boil over high heat. Reduce to lowest setting, cook 15 minutes. Turn heat off and leave on burner 10 minutes. *Do not peek during cooking process.* Excellent with any Oriental entrée.

## Bacon-Fried Rice

*Serves 4*                    *Cooking time: 30 minutes*

8 slices bacon
2 eggs, well beaten
2 tablespoons plus 1 teaspoon peanut oil
¼ cup onions, coarsely chopped
½ cup frozen peas, thawed
3 cups cooked cold rice
¼ cup mushroom soy sauce
½ teaspoon Seasoned Salt (page 17)
1 tablespoon butter or margarine
¼ cup scallions, sliced diagonally

Fry bacon in a medium skillet until crisp. Cool, break into ½-inch pieces. Discard all but 1 teaspoon bacon fat. Add beaten eggs to skillet. Cook until set, turn, and cook until dry. Remove from pan, cool, dice. Add 1 teaspoon peanut oil to skillet, add onions, and sauté until clear; add peas. Remove from heat. Add diced eggs and toss to coat, set aside. Heat 2 tablespoons peanut oil in a wok or large skillet. Add cooked rice, separate well. Stir-fry 10 minutes. Add soy sauce, salt, and butter, mix well. Add cooked vegetables and eggs, toss, heat through. Top with scallions and serve.

## Carrot Rice

*Adds color and flavor to any entrée.*

*Serves 4*                    *Cooking time: 25 minutes*

1 cup rice
⅓ cup raw carrots, coarsely
    shredded
1 chicken bouillon cube

Rinse rice in cold water twice, drain, and place in a small saucepan with 1 cup cold water, the carrots, and the bouillon cube. Cover and bring to a boil over high heat; reduce heat to lowest setting and cook 15 minutes. Turn heat off and leave pan on burner for an additional 10 minutes. *Do not peek during cooking process.* Fluff rice with a fork before serving.

## Rice and Cheese Squares

*A different and tasty substitute for potatoes.*

*Serves 6 to 8*                    *Cooking time: 1 hour*

1½ cups rice
2 chicken bouillon cubes
1 small onion, coarsely chopped
1½ cups milk
3 eggs
1½ teaspoons Worcestershire sauce
1 teaspoon Seasoned Salt (page 17)
¾ cup fresh parsley, finely chopped
1¼ cups sharp cheddar cheese,
    grated

Rinse rice in cold water twice, drain, and place in a medium saucepan with 1½ cups cold water and the bouillon cubes; stir and cover. Turn heat to high and bring to a boil, then reduce heat to lowest setting and cook 15 minutes. Turn heat off and leave pan on burner an additional 10 minutes. *Do not remove cover during cooking process.*

Preheat oven to 325°. In a blender bowl combine the onion, milk, eggs, sauce, and salt; process until smooth, add parsley, and blend 10 seconds more. Combine cooked rice and cheese, add blender mixture, and pour into a greased 10x6x2-inch baking dish. Bake for 35 to 40 minutes, or until set. Cut into squares and serve.

# Butters & Sauces

## Strawberry Butter

*Delicious on toast or waffles, and makes a good welcoming gift.*

*Makes 2½ cups*

10 ounces frozen strawberries,
   thawed
1 cup butter or margarine, softened
1¼ cup confectioners' sugar, sifted

Combine all ingredients in a blender. Process at high speed until smooth (this will take a while). Pack into pretty half-pint jars for gift giving. Keeps refrigerated for one month, but probably will be gone much sooner than that!

## Tomato Butter

*Try this on biscuits fresh from the oven.*

*Makes 1 cup                    Cooking time: 1 hour*

1 pound ripe tomatoes
¾ cup brown sugar, firmly packed
¼ teaspoon ground cloves
¼ teaspoon ground cinnamon
dash of allspice

dash of Seasoned Salt (page 17)

Dip tomatoes in boiling water to loosen skin; peel, stem, and quarter. Put in saucepan, cover, and cook until mushy. Measure 1½ cups. Pour into blender bowl and process until smooth. Return to saucepan, add remaining ingredients, and bring to a boil. Reduce heat and simmer, uncovered, until thick (about 45 minutes), stirring frequently.

## Herb Butter

*A great food enhancer.*

*Makes ¾ cup*

1 slice of bacon
½ cup butter or margarine, softened
3 tablespoons onions, minced
2 garlic cloves, pressed
2 tablespoons parsley, minced
1 tablespoon lemon juice
1 teaspoon basil
¼ teaspoon thyme
½ teaspoon salt
⅛ teaspoon pepper

Cook bacon until crisp. Cool and crumble.

With an electric mixer, cream the butter till fluffy. Add onion, garlic, and parsley and continue beating, adding the lemon juice a little at a time. Add spices and bacon and mix until completely blended.

## White Sauce, Canadian Style

*Thin Sauce (1 cup)*

1 tablespoon butter or margarine
1 tablespoon flour
¼ teaspoon Seasoned Salt (page 17)
¼ teaspoon dry mustard
dash of white pepper
1 cup milk

*Medium Sauce (1 cup)*

2 tablespoons butter or margarine
2 tablespoons flour
¼ teaspoon Seasoned Salt (page 17)
¼ teaspoon dry mustard
dash of white pepper
1 cup milk

*Thick Sauce (1 cup)*

3 tablespoons butter or margarine
¼ cup flour
¼ teaspoon Seasoned Salt (page 17)
¼ teaspoon dry mustard
dash of white pepper
1 cup milk

Melt butter in a saucepan. Add flour and cook over low heat until frothy. Remove from heat. Add milk and stir to blend completely. Add spices. Return to heat and cook, stirring constantly, until sauce thickens and bubbles.

## Camille Fournier's Imitation Maple Syrup

*This sirop d'erable was one of grand-maman's treasured secrets.*

*Makes 2 quarts          Cooking time: 15 minutes*

4½ cups sugar
¾ cup brown sugar, firmly packed
⅓ cup light corn syrup
¾ teaspoon Crescent brand
   Mapleine flavoring

Note: Two things are important to the success of this recipe: An accurate candy thermometer, and Crescent brand Mapleine flavoring.

Combine sugars, syrup with 4¾ cups of water in a heavy 3-quart saucepan. Cook over low heat, stirring constantly, until sugars dissolve. Increase heat to medium and boil until thermometer registers 216°, about 10 minutes. Remove from heat, add Mapleine flavoring, stir to blend. Cool, pour into glass containers, seal, and keep under refrigeration.

# Fruit

## Maple-Baked Apples

*A wonderful addition to lamb or pork dishes.*

*Serves 4*          *Cooking time: 30 to 40 minutes*

4 large baking apples
½ cup seedless raisins
¾ cup maple syrup
1 teaspoon lemon juice
1 teaspoon lemon peel, grated

Preheat oven to 375°. Wash apples. Pare top half and remove core. Place in a shallow 1½-quart casserole dish. Fill cavities with raisins. Combine syrup, juice, and lemon peel. Stir well. Pour into cavities and over apples. Bake until tender, 30 to 40 minutes.

## Bananas, Three Ways

*Each a great side dish.*

### Baked Bananas

*Serves 4*          *Cooking time: 15 minutes*

Preheat oven to 350°. Peel **4 bananas.** Center each on a foot-square piece of foil. Roll in **2 tablespoons lemon juice.** Brush with **melted butter.** Sprinkle with Sea-soned Salt (page 17) and **paprika.** Seal tightly to retain steam. Bake 15 minutes. Serve in foil.

### Broiled Bananas

*Serves 4*          *Cooking time: 8 minutes*

Set oven to broil. Cut **4 bananas** in half crosswise. Brush with **melted butter** and roll in ¾ **cup fresh bread crumbs** or ¾ **cup crushed toasted almonds.** Set on broiler pan, 6 inches from heat. Broil 5 minutes. Turn over carefully and broil until golden, about 3 minutes.

### Banana Fritters

*Makes 16 to 18*          *Cooking time: 12 minutes*

1½ cups flour, sifted
1½ teaspoons baking powder
½ teaspoon salt
3 tablespoons sugar
2 eggs
2 tablespoons milk
¼ cup banana liqueur or brandy
1 ripe banana, mashed
solid vegetable shortening for frying

Sift first 4 ingredients. Using an electric mixer, medium speed, add eggs one at a time, then milk, liqueur, and mashed banana, mixing after each. Heat shortening to 375°. Form fritters with a tablespoon. Fry 6 at a time until fork inserted comes out clean, about 4 minutes. Drain on paper towels.

## Minted Grapefruit

*A special breakfast treat or accompaniment for fish.*

*Serves 4*               *Cooking time: 3 to 4 minutes*

2 grapefruit
4 teaspoons green crème de menthe

Set oven to broil. Cut grapefruit in half, remove seeds. Cut around sections to loosen pulp. Pour 1 teaspoon crème de menthe on each half, broil to warm.

## Baked Stuffed Oranges

*An unusual complement to a fish dish.*

*Serves 4*               *Cooking time: 35 minutes*

4 medium oranges, thick-skinned
½ cup dates, chopped
¼ cup flaked coconut
2 tablespoons orange liqueur
dash of bitters
4 large marshmallows
4 pecan halves

Preheat oven to 325°. Cut tops off oranges. Scoop out inside pulp with a grapefruit knife. Cut zigzag edges around shell openings; set aside. Chop fruit pulp. Add dates, coconut, liqueur, and bitters and mix well. Stuff orange shells with mixture. Place in 1½-quart casserole dish. Add ½ cup water around oranges. Bake 30 minutes. Remove from oven. Turn oven to broil. Place one marshmallow and a pecan half atop each orange. Broil until marshmallows are golden and bubbly.

## Spiced Hot Peaches

*A tart contrast to a creamy casserole.*

*Serves 4*               *Cooking time: 25 minutes*

2 1-pound cans peach halves
¼ cup sugar
3 tablespoons white vinegar
3-inch stick of cinnamon
¼ teaspoon whole cloves

Drain peaches, reserving syrup. Combine syrup, sugar, vinegar, and spices in a 3-quart saucepan. Stir until sugar dissolves. Bring to a boil, reduce heat, and simmer 5 minutes. Add peach halves and simmer 15 minutes, carefully turn halves occasionally.

## Broiled Pineapple Slices

*Ideal with ham steak, or marinated beef.*

*Serves 4*               *Cooking time: 6 minutes*

8-ounce can sliced pineapple
¼ cup orange liqueur
2 tablespoons butter or margarine, melted
2 teaspoons brown sugar

Drain pineapple slices. Add liqueur and soak 2 hours. Drain. Cover and refrigerate liqueur to use again (see note). Preheat oven to broil. Brush pineapple slices with melted butter, sprinkle with sugar. Place on broiler pan, 6 inches from heat, cook for 6 minutes. Do not turn.

Note: Add **3 tablespoons of soy sauce, ½ teaspoon ground ginger, ½ teaspoon sugar,** and **¼ teaspoon garlic powder** to pineapple juice and orange liqueur and use as a marinade for **1½ to 2 pounds beef sirloin,** cut into 1-inch cubes. Marinate 1 hour, drain, skewer, and broil over hot coals or in oven.

# Beverages

## Monique's Orange Tea Mix

*A deliciously relaxing mix and a great gift idea. This version is less spicy than some!*

*Makes 2 cups*

- ¾ cup iced tea mix with lemon and sugar
- 1½ cups orange breakfast drink powder
- ½ teaspoon ground cinnamon
- ¼ teaspoon ground allspice
- ¼ teaspoon ground cloves

Combine all ingredients, mix well. Keep in tightly covered container. To serve, combine 1 heaping tablespoon with 1 cup boiling water, stir.

## Tony Buyo

*A tasty drink for children.*

*Makes 2 cups*

- 1 frozen banana
- 2 tablespoons lemon juice
- 1 cup natural apple juice
- ½ cup cranberry juice

- 1 tablespoon raisins
- 1 tablespoon chopped walnuts (optional)

Brush peeled banana with lemon juice, wrap in plastic and freeze 1 hour. Combine all ingredients in a blender. Process until smooth. Pour into chilled glasses. Here's to your good health!

## Minted Iced Tea

*Perfect refresher for a hot summer day.*

*Makes 2 quarts*

- 12 tea bags
- ¼ cup fresh mint leaves
- 1 quart water
- 6 ounces frozen orange juice concentrate
- juice of 2 lemons
- 1 cup sugar
- mint leaves
- lemon twists

Combine tea and mint with water in a 3-quart saucepan, cover. Bring to a boil, remove from heat. Steep for half an hour.

Squeeze and remove tea bags. Add concentrate, lemon juice, and sugar. Stir to melt. Strain. If necessary, add more water to make 2 quarts. Chill. Serve in chilled glasses over ice, adding a mint leaf and lemon twist to each glass.

## Big Dave

*Gourmet breakfast in a glass.*

*Serves 4*

6-ounce package frozen
   strawberries, partially thawed
1 cup orange juice
2 eggs
2 tablespoons powdered milk
2 scoops vanilla ice cream

Break up strawberries and place in blender with remaining ingredients. Process until smooth. Pour into glasses and start your day with a smile.

## Café Cointreau

*Serves 4*

½ cup whipping cream
4 ounces plus 1 tablespoon
   Cointreau
sugar for dipping
1 quart freshly brewed hot coffee

Whip cream in a chilled bowl until soft peaks form. Add 1 tablespoon Cointreau. Whip to blend. Warm remaining Cointreau. Moisten outside edges of 4 brandy snifters or 10-ounce glasses with warmed Cointreau; dip into sugar to frost moistened edges. Add 1 ounce Cointreau to each glass. Tilt glasses slightly and ignite contents. As flames subside, add hot coffee. Top with whipped cream.

## Café Royale

*A flaming finale to a perfect dinner.*

*Serves 6 to 8*

½ to ¾ cup orange liqueur
fresh-brewed coffee
6 to 8 sugar cubes

Float 1 tablespoon liqueur on top of each demitasse of fresh hot coffee. Warm ¼ cup liqueur. Place a sugar cube in a large soup spoon. Fill spoon with warmed liqueur, ignite, and lower flaming cube and liqueur into coffee.

## Claire's Slumber Milk

*A tasteful send-off to "The Land of Nod."*

*Serves 4 sleepyheads*

3 cups milk
4 tablespoons honey
½ cup dark Jamaican rum

Combine milk and honey in a 2-quart saucepan, stir to mix. Heat to very hot but *do not boil*. Pour into 4 warmed mugs. Lace each with 2 tablespoons rum. Sip as hot as possible before going to sleep.

## Flaming Coffee Ice Cream Sipper

*A delicious after-dinner coffee.*

*Serves 4*

½ cup orange liqueur
4 cups hot coffee
4 small scoops vanilla ice cream

Pour 1 tablespoon liqueur into each of 4 coffee cups. Add hot coffee to within 1 inch of rim. Top each with a scoop of ice cream. Warm remaining liqueur in small saucepan. *Remove from heat.* Ignite, and spoon flaming liquid into coffee.

## John's Amazing "Hot Apple Pie"

*Dessert in a glass.*

*Serves 4*

1 quart fresh apple cider
4 whole cloves
6 ounces Tuaca, or other orange
    liqueur
¼ cup whipping cream, whipped
4 cinnamon sticks

Pour cider in a 3-quart saucepan, add cloves and bring to a boil. Pour 1½ ounces Tuaca into each of 4 12-ounce wine glasses. Strain cider into glasses. Top each with whipped cream. Use cinnamon sticks as stirrers.

## Lapa Lapa

*A relaxing after-dinner treat.*

*1 serving*

cracked ice
1½ ounces coffee brandy
½ ounce crème de banana liqueur
2 tablespoons cream
freeze-dried coffee

Combine first 4 ingredients in blender. Process until thick and smooth. Pour, unstrained, into "on the rocks" glass. Dust with dried coffee.

# Index

Acorn Squash Bake with Fruit, 119
Almond Float, 95
Almond Rice, 126
Almondine, Green Beans, 112
Almondine, Whipped Potatoes, 117
Ann's Mushroom Pie, 93
Appetizers, 19–27
  Apricot Steak Bites, 19
  Baked Clams, 19
  Barbecued Chicken Wings, 20
  *Beignets au Fromage*, 22
  *Champignon Farci de Noix*, 25
  Cheese-Onion Tidbits, 20
  Christmas Wreath of Vegetables, 20
  Clams Gourmet, 21
  *Creton*, 21
  Flamed Hickory-Smoked Mussels, 21–22
  Frogs' Legs Nuggets with Hot Pepper Sauce, 22
  Gourmet Avocado Dip, 19
  Mini Seafood Quiche, 24
  Miniature Crab Puffs, 23
  *Moules Marinière*, 24
  Parmesan Mousse, 23
  *Pâté de Trois Foies*, 25
  Porky Melons, 24
  Potted Cheese, 24
  Rita's Mystery Canapés, 26
  *Saucisson en Croûte*, 26
  Shrimp in Beer Batter, 25
  Skewers of Baked French Bread and Cheese, 26
  Smoked Oyster Spread, 26
  Tangy Cheddar Spread, 25
Apple Fritters, 95
Apple "Pie," John's Amazing Hot, 134
Apple Roll, Rita's Cinnamon, 105

Apples
  Maple-Baked, 130
  Acorn Squash Bake with Fruit, 119
  Cranberry and Fruit Salad, 86
  Onion and Fruit Sauté, 113
Applejack Filet of Sole, 69
Apricot-Almond Glazed Pork, 46
Apricot Sauce, Chicken Breasts in, 58
Apricot Steak Bites, 19
Asparagus *au Gratin*, 107
Athenian Salad, 82
Avocado Dip, Gourmet, 19
Avocado Sunshine Salad with Orange Mayonnaise, 82

Bacon-Fried Corn, 110
Bacon-Fried Rice, 126
Baked Chicken Breast, Yvette, 57
Baked Clams, 19
Baked Haddock *au Gratin*, 69
Baked Potatoes, Three Ways, 114
Baked Salmon Steaks Sebago, 70
Baked Sirloin Steak, 36
Baked Stuffed Filet of Sole, Bertrand, 70
Baked Stuffed Jumbo Shrimp, 71
Baked Stuffed Oranges, 131
Baked Stuffed Pork Chops, 47
Baked Stuffed Potatoes, Four Ways, 114
Banana Fritters, 130
Banana Split Ice Cream Pie, 100
Banana Split Salad, 83
Bananas
  Baked, 130
  Broiled, 130
Barbecued Chicken Wings, 20
Barbecued Spareribs, 47

Bean casserole (*Cassoulet*), 52
Beans, Baked (Maman's "Canadian Style"), 49
Beans, Green, 112
  Almondine, 112
  with Cheddar Cheese, 112
  in Cream, 112
Bea's Fresh Blueberry Pie, 96
Beef, 36–45
  Apricot Steak Bites, 19
  *Boeuf Poitou,* 38
  ground,
    Brother Paul's "Italian Sauce Parmigiana"
      with Meatballs, 38
    Chili by Rhum, 39
    *Pain de Boeuf Fromager,* 40
    *Pâté Chinois,* 40
    Rich Man-Poor Man Steak *au Poivre,* 41
    Steak Tartare *en Croûte,* 44
  in Oyster Sauce, 36
  *Ragout de Boeuf,* 41
  Rib Roast, Standing, *au Jus,* 43
  Rib Roast, Teriyaki, 45
  Steak
    Steak and Mushroom Dinner Salad, 80
    Baked Sirloin, 36
    Béarnaise, Sirloin, 43
    Delmonico, Roquefort, 39
    Diane, 43
    Flamed Tenderloin, Dijon, 39
    Marinated London Broil Cookout, 40
    Onion-Buttered Sirloin, 43
    Rich Man-Poor Man Steak *au Poivre,* 41
    Savory London Broil, 42
    Sirloin Steak Kebabs, 131
    Steak Roast Wrap with Vegetables, 44
    Teriyaki Sirloin, 43
  Stew *Maison,* 37
  Stock, Basic, 31
  Stroganoff, 37
  Wok Pepper Steak, 45
Beets
  Dijon, 108
  Nantucket, 107
*Beignets au Fromage* (deep-fried cheese fritters), 22
Beverages, 132–34
  Café Cointreau, 133
  Café Royale, 133
  Claire's Slumber Milk, 133
  Flaming Coffee Ice Cream Sipper, 133
  John's Amazine "Hot Apple Pie," 134
  Lapa Lapa, 134
Beverages, non-alcoholic
  Big Dave, 133
  Minted Iced Tea, 132
  Monique's Orange Tea Mix, 132
  Tony Buyo, 132
Big Dave, 133

Biscuits
  Cheese-It, 122
  Maman's Bacon and Cheese, 122
*Biscuits au Citron* (lemon cookies), 96
Bleu Cheese Bakers (potatoes), 114
Blue Hubbard Squash and Marmalade Purée, 119
Blueberry, Bea's Fresh Pie, 96
Blueberry Soup, Cold Maine, 29
*Boeuf Poitou* (Bean-Pot Beef with Vegetables), 38
Boiled Potatoes. 115
Braised Stuffed Pickerel, 71
Bran Muffins, Salty's No Sugar-No Salt, 124
Brandied Banana Bread, 123
Brandied Macaroons, 96
Brandied Orange-Raspberry Sauce, Roast Duckling in, 68
Brandied Pumpkin Soup, 28
Brandied Raspberry Sauce, Broiled Ham Slice in, 47
Bread, 122–124
  Brandied Banana, 123
  Corn, 122
  Cups, Toasted, 111
  French Garlic Toast or Bread, 123
  French Bread, Stuffed, 124
  Rita's Mystery Canapés, 26
  Salters' Stuffed Bread, 92
  Skewers of Baked French Bread and Cheese, 26
Broccoli
  Cheese Custard, 108
  in Foil, 108
  with Fresh Lemon, 108
  Stir-Fried, 108
Broiled Ham Slice in Brandied Raspberry Sauce, 47
Broiled Pineapple Slices, 131
Broiled Scallops in Garlic Butter, 72
Broiled Tomato Slices, 120
Brother Paul's "Italian Sauce Parmigiana" with Meatballs, 38
*Bûche de Noël* (Yule Log), 97
Buns, Sticky Caramel, 123
Butter
  Herb, 128
  Onion, Fresh Vegetables with, 112
  Strawberry, 128
  Tomato, 128

Café Cointreau, 133
Café Royale, 133
Cake
  Hurry-Up Elegant, Glazed, 102
  *Bûche de Noël,* 97
  *Galette des Rois,* 101

Cakes, fried (Faa-Foons), 99
Camille Fournier's Imitation Maple Syrup, 129
Camille's Vegetable Dinner Salad, 79
Canadian Cheese Soup with *Grands-Pères*
  (dumplings), 28
Canadian Potato Salad, 83
Candy (Chocolate Caramels), 98
Caramel Buns, Sticky, 123
Carrot Rice, 127
Carrot Soup, Cream of, 30
Carrots
  Cheese and Honey, 109
  Lyonnaise, 109
  Orange-Glazed, 109
  Vichy, 109
Casseroles
  Asparagus *au Gratin*, 107
  *Boeuf Poitou*, 38
  *Cassoulet,* 52
  Chicken Divan, 59
  Fresh Vegetable, 93
  *Pâté Chinois*, 40
  Pork in Apple Cider, 46
  Stuffed Cannelloni, 92
  Tuna Patricia, 78
*Cassoulet* (meat and bean casserole), 52
Cauliflower
  Mornay, 110
  Sesame, 109
  Soup, Cream of, 30
Champagne Ham, 48
*Champignon Farci de Noix* (walnut-stuffed
  mushrooms), 25
Chantilly Potatoes, 25
Charcoal-Grilled Chicken with Peach Glaze, 58
Chawan-Mushi (shrimp custard soup), 29
Cheddar-Garlic Baked Potatoes, 117
Cheese
  and Honey Carrots, 109
  and Rice Squares, 127
  Ann's Mushroom Pie, 93
  Canadian Cheese Soup with *Grands-Pères*, 28
  Custard Broccoli, 108
  Eggs *au Fromage*, 91
  Fresh Vegetable Casserole, 93
  Fried (*Beignets au Fromage*), 22
  Frozen Cheese and Strawberry Salad, 85
  Mini Seafood Quiche, 24
  Mocha-Ricotta Custard, 104
  No-Crust Crabmeat Quiche, 72
  Parmessan Mousse, 23
  Potted Cheese, 24
  Quiche Lorraine with Pistachios, 91
  Swiss Cheese and Ham Fondue, 94
  Tangy Cheddar Spread, 25
Cheesecake, Frozen Chocolate Chip, 101
Cheese-Chive Potatoes, 118
Cheese-It Biscuits, 122

Cheese-Onion Tidbits, 20
Cheesy-Crouton Salad, 84
Cherries Jubilee, 97
Cherry Chew Squares, 98
Cherry and Fruit Soup, 29
Chewy Peanut Butter-Chocolate Bars, 98
Chicken, 57–66
  Barbecued Wings, 20
  Breast Baked, Yvette, 57
  Breasts in Apricot Sauce, 58
  Breasts Stuffed, Polynesian, 66
  Breasts Stuffed, in Sauce Suprême, 65
  *Cacciatora all Romana*, 60
  Cantonese with Soft-Fried Noodles, 60
  Charcoal-Grilled with Peach Glaze, 58
  *Coq au Vin*, 61
  *Cordon Rouge*, 59
  Creamy Salad in Tomato, 79
  Divan, 59
  Drumsticks Parmesan, 62
  "Fondue" with Sweet and Sour Sauce, 66
  Fricassée, 55
  Lemon-Herb in a Roman Pot, 61
  Olé Molé Chocolate Chicken, 62
  à la Pommery, 58
  *Poulet à l'Ail Chablis*, 62
  *Poulet Suisse*, 63
  *Ragoût de Poule aux Boulettes,* 57
  Roast, with Fruit and Nut Stuffing, 63
  Sesame, with Cumberland Sauce, 64
  Soy-Sauced Bake, 64
  Stir-Fried and Cashews, 65
Chili and Cheese Bakes (potatoes), 117
Chili by Rhum, 39
Chocolate
  Caramels, 98
  Cherry Mint Ice Cream Pie, 100
  Chewy Peanut Butter Bars, 98
  Chicken (Olé Molé), 62
  with Cinnamon and Fudge Sundae, 100
  Crumb Pie Shell, 100
  Curls (for White Russian Pie), 106
  Fondue, Strawberries in, 106
  Frosting for Yule Log, 97
  Frozen Chocolate-Chip Cheesecake, 101
  *Petits Pôts de Chocolat*, 104
*Choucroute Garni* (sauerkraut and pork), 48
Christmas Wreath of Vegetables, 20
Cider (John's Amazing "Hot Apple Pie"), 134
Claire's Slumber Milk, 133
Clam Chowder, New England, 33
Clams
  Baked, 19
  Gourmet, 21
  Steamed in Beer, 72
Cod, Rich Man-Poor Man Seafood Thermidor
  in Shells, 76
Coffee
  Flaming Ice Cream Sipper, 133

*Coffee, cont.*
  Sundae, 100
  Sundae with Cinnamon and Fudge, 100
  Café Cointreau, 133
  Café Royale, 133
Cold Maine Blueberry Soup, 29
Cookies
  Lemon (*Biscuits au Citron*), 96
  Mint Surprise, 103
  Raspberry Filled, 105
Cookout Haddock Penobscot, 74
Cookout Potatoes, 116
*Coq au Vin* (chicken in wine), 61
Corn
  Bacon-Fried, 110
  Bread, 122
  Roasted, 110
  Soup, Oriental Style, 30
  with Zucchini, 121
Country-Style Pork Ribs in Tangy Sauce, 51
Crabmeat
  No-Crust Quiche, 72
  Miniature Puffs, 23
Cranberry and Fruit Salad, 86
Cream Cheese and Nectar Dressing, 87
Cream of Carrot Soup, 30
Cream of Cauliflower Soup, 30
Creamy Chicken Salad in Tomato, 79
Creamy Haddock Stew, 31
Crêpes, Dessert, 99
*Creton*, 21
Cucumber and Onion Slices in Sour Cream, 84
Custard, Mocha-Ricotta, 104

Dawn's Hawaiian Holiday Pie, 98
Delmonico Steaks, Roquefort, 39
Dessert *Crêpes*
  Peppermint Patty, 99
  Strawberry, 99
Desserts, 95–106
  Almond Float, 95
  Applie Fritters, 95
  Bea's Fresh Blueberry Pie, 96
  *Biscuits au Citron*, 96
  Brandied Macaroons, 96
  *Bûche de Noël* (Yule Log), 97
  Cherries Jubilee, 97
  Cherry Chew Squares, 98
  Chewy Peanut Butter-Chocolate Bars, 98
  Chocolate Caramels, 98
  Chocolate Frosting, 97
  Crêpes, 99
  Dawn's Hawaiian Holiday Pie, 98
  Faa-Foons, 99
  Fast and Easy Ice Cream Pies, 100
  Frozen Chocolate Chip Cheesecake, 101
  *Galette des Rois*, 101
  Hot Orange Pudding, 101

Hurry-Up Elegant Glazed Cake, 102
Ice Cream Parfaits and Sundaes, 100
Individual Grand Marnier Soufflés, 102
Instant Strawberry Ice, 102
Lemon *Sorbet*, 103
Mariette's Fresh Strawbery Pie, 103
Marinated Strawberries and Kiwi, 103
Mint Surprise Cookies, 103
Mocha-Ricotta Custard, 104
*Petits Pôts de Chocolat*, 104
Pineapple Snow, 104
Raspberry Filled Cookies, 105
Rita's Cinnamon Apple Roll, 105
Rita's Perfect Pastry Crust, 105
Strawberries in Chocolate Fondue, 106
T-Bea's Rice Pudding, 106
White Russian Pie, 106
Dijon Beets 108
Drumsticks Parmesan, 62
Duckling, Roast, in Brandied Orange-
  Raspberry Sauce, 68
Dumplings, *Grands-Pères* (Canadian Cheese
  Soup with), 28

Easy and Grand Caesar Salad, 84
Eggplant
  Parmigiana, 110
  Ratatouille in Toasted Bread Cups, 111
Eggs
  *au Fromage*, 91
  Maple Sugar Omelet, 91
  Mini Seafood Quiche, 24
  Monique, 90
  *Oscar*, Dijon, 90
  Parmesan Mousse, 23
  Quiche Lorraine with Pistachios, 91
Epiphany Cake (*Galette des Rois*), 101

Faa-Foons (fried cakes), 99
Fast and Easy Ice Cream Pies, 100
Fettucine Armando, 93
Filet of Sole Oriental, 73
Fish and Seafood, 69–78. *See also* individual
  listings
  Mini Seafood Quiche, 24
  White Fish Piquant, 78
Flamed Hickory-Smoked Mussels, 21
Flamed Tenderloin Steak, Dijon, 39
Flaming Coffee Ice Cream Sipper, 133
Foil-Baked Potatoes, 116
Fondue
  Chicken with Sweet and Sour Sauce, 66
  Chocolate, Strawberries in, 106
  Swiss Cheese and Ham, 94
French Bread
  Stuffed, 124
  Garlic Toast or Bread, 123

French Onion Soup *au Gratin*, 31
Fresh Fruit *à la* Grand Marnier, 85
Fresh Vegetable Casserole, 93
Fresh Vegetable Stir-Fry, 111
Fresh Vegetables with Onion Butter, 112
Fried Pattypan Squash, 119
Frogs' Legs Nuggets with Hot Pepper Sauce, 22
Frozen Cheese and Strawberry Salad, 85
Frozen Chocolate Chip Cheesecake, 101
Fruit, 130–131. *See also* individual listings
    Cherry and Fruit Soup, 29
    Cranberry and Fruit Salad, 86
    Fresh, à la Grand Marnier, 85
    and Nut Stuffing, Roast Chicken with, 63
    Scones, 124
    Tony Buyo (beverage), 132

Gabrielle's Green Salad, 85
*Galette des Rois* (Epiphany or Twelfth Cake), 101
Gazpacho Monique (vegetable soup), 32
Gourmet Avocado Dip, 19
Grapefruit
    and Spinach Sauté, 118
    Minted, 131
Green Beans. *See* Beans, Green

Haddock
    à l'Orange, 73
    Baked, *au Gratin*, 69
    Cookout, Penobscot, 74
    Stew, Creamy, 31
    Suprême, 74
Halibut *Trois Rivières*, 74
Ham
    Broiled Slice in Brandied Raspberry Sauce, 47
    Champagne, 48
    Swiss Cheese and Ham Fondue, 94
Hand Warmers (potatoes), 114
Hashed Brown Potatoes, 116
Herb Butter, 128
Herbal Vinaigrette Dressing, 87
Hickory-Smoked Turkey, 67
*Homard avec Sauce Mornay* (lobster), 75
Hot Orange Pudding, 101
Hubbard Squash Soup, 32
Hurry-Up Elegant Glazed Cake, 102

Ice Cream
    Desserts, 100
    Dressing, 87
    Pies, 100
    Sipper, Flaming Coffee, 133
Individual Grand Marnier Soufflés, 102

Instant Strawberry Ice, 102
Italian Cheese Dressing, 88

Jellied Waldorf Salad, 86
John's Amazing "Hot Apple Pie," 134

Kale, Fresh, 113
Kiwi and Strawberries, Marinated, 103

Lamb, 52–55
    *Cassoulet*, 52
    Mint-Barbecued Leg of, 54
    *Ragoût d'Agneau aux Petits Pois*, 53
    Rich Man-Poor Man Chops "Roquefort," 53
    *Rôti d'Agneau Provencal*, 53
    *Tarte d'Agneau*, 54
Lapa Lapa, 134
Leftovers, dishes using
    beef, *Ragoût de Boeuf*, 41
    Chicken, Creamy salad in Tomato, 79
    Chicken Fricassée, 55
    lamb, *Ragoût d'Agneau aux Petits Pois*, 55
    Pork Chow Mein, 51
    Turkey *alla Parmigiana*, 67
    Veal Fricassée, 55
Lemon Cookies (*Biscuits au Citron*), 96
Lemon Sauce for new potatoes, 115
Lemon *Sorbet*, 103
Lemon-Flavored Mayonnaise, 21
Lemon-Herb Chicken in a Roman Pot, 61
Lemonade Dressing, 88
Liver
    Calf's, and Fruit Flambé, 41
    Sautéed, with Bacon Rolls and Broiled Bananas, 42
    *Pâté de Trois Foies*, 25
Lobster
    *Homard avec Sauce Mornay*, 75
    Rich Man-Poor Man Seafood Thermidor in Shells, 76
    Stew *à la Canadienne*, 33
    Stuffed Whole Maine, 77
Low-Calorie Celery-Seed Dressing, 88
Lyonnaise Carrots, 109
Lyonnaise Potatoes, 115

Macadamia, Sauce, 74
Maine Shrimp Stew, 33
Maman's Bacon and Cheese Biscuits, 122
Maman's "Canadian Style" Baked Beans, 49
Maman's Golden Salad, 86
Maman's Parisian Dressing, 88
Maman's Salmon Pie, 75
Maman's Salmon Sauce, 75
Maman's Special *Tourtiere*, 50

Maple-Baked Apples, 130
Maple Sugar Omelet, 91
Maple Syrup, Camille Fournier's Imitation, 129
Mariette's Fresh Strawberry Pie, 103
Marinara, Sauce, 74
Marinated London Broil Cookout, 40
Marinated Steak Kebabs, 131
Marinated Strawberries and Kiwi, 103
Mini Seafood Quiche, 24
Miniature Crab Puffs, 23
Mint-Barbecued Leg of Lamb, 54
Mint Surprise Cookies, 103
Minted Grapefruit, 131
Minted Iced Tea, 132
Mocha-Richotta Custard, 104
Monique's Orange Tea Mix, 132
Moose Steak with Mushroom Sauce, 56
*Moules Mariniére* (mussels), 24
Mousse
  Parmesan, 23
  chocolate *(Petits Pôts de Chocolat)*, 104
  Savory Salmon with Herbal Vinaigrette Dressing, 80
Mud Pie, 100
Muffins, Salty's No Sugar-No Salt Bran, 124
Mushroom Pie, Ann's, 93
Mushrooms, walnut stuffed *(Champignon Farci de Noix)*, 25
Mussels
  Flamed Hickory-Smoked, 21
  with Linguine, 76
  *Moules Mariniére,* 24

Nantucket Beets, 107
New England Clam Chowder, 33
New England "Stuffies" (potatoes), 114
New Potatoes in Lemon Sauce, 115
No-Crust Crabmeat Quiche, 72
Noodle and Cashew Toss, 125
Noodle Omelet, 125
Noodles
  Soft-Fried, 60
  Spinach, with Cream Cheese Sauce, 125

Olé Molé Chocolate Chicken, 62
Omelet
  Noodle, 125
  Maple Sugar, 91
Onion and Cucumber Slices in Sour Cream, 84
Onion and Fruit Sauté, 113
Onion Soup, French, *au Gratin*, 31
Onion Butter, Fresh Vegetables with, 112
Onion-Buttered Sirloin Steak, 43
Onions in Cheese Sauce with Peanuts, 113
Onions in Cinders, 113

Orange
  Hot Pudding, 101
  Mayonnaise, Avocado Sunshine Salad with, 82
  Tea Mix, Monique's, 132
Orange-Glazed Carrots, 109
Oranges, Baked Stuffed, 131
Orangey-Orange Parfait, 100
Oriental dishes
  Almond Float, 95
  Bacon-Fried Rice, 126
  Beef in Oyster Sauce, 36
  Chawan-Mushi, 29
  Chicken Cantonese with Soft-Fried Noodles, 60
  Chicken "Fondue" with Sweet and Sour Sauce, 66
  Corn Soup, Oriental Style, 30
  Egg Drop Soup, *see* Chicken "Fondue," 66
  Filet of Sole Oriental, 73
  Fresh Vegetable Stir-Fry, 111
  Hot Orange Pudding, 101
  Oriental Dressing, 87
  Oriental Steamed Rice, 126
  Pork Chow Mein, 51
  Soy-Glazed Scallops, 77
  Soy-Sauced Chicken Bake, 64
  Spring Greens Soup, 34
  Stir-Fried Broccoli, 108
  Stir-Fried Chicken and Cashews, 65
  Stuffed Chicken Breasts Polynesian, 66
  Sweet and Sour Pork, 52
  Teriyaki Rib Roast of Beef, 45
  Teriyaki Sirloin Steak, 43
  Wok Pepper Steak, 45
Oyster Spread, Smoked, 26

*Pain de Boeuf Fromager* (meatloaf), 40
Parmesan Mousse, 23
Parmesan Drumsticks, 62
Parsnips in Pineapple Glaze, 113
Pasta
  Fettucine Armando, 93
  Mussels with Linguine, 76
  Stuffed Cannelloni, 92
Pastry
  Rita's Perfect Crust, 105
  Rita's Cinnamon Apple Roll, 105
*Pâté*
  *Chinois,* 40
  *Creton,* 21
  *de Trois Foies,* 25
Peach Glaze, Chicken Broiled with, 58
Peaches and Cream Sundae, 100
Peaches, Spiced Hot, 131
Pea Soup *(Potage Canadienne)*, 34
Peas, French Style, 114

Peppermint-Patty Crêpes, 99
*Petits Pôts de Chocolat*, 104
Pickerel, Braised Stuffed, 71
Pie
  Ann's Mushrom, 93
  Banana Split, 100
  Bea's Fresh Blueberry, 96
  Chocolate Cherry Mint, 100
  Chocolate-Crumb Pie Shell, 100
  Dawn's Hawaiian Holiday, 98
  Ice Cream, 100
  Maman's Salmon, 75
  Maman's Special *Tourtiere* (pork pie), 50
  Mariette's Fresh Strawberry, 103
  Mud, 100
  Rita's Perfect Pastry Crust, 105
  *Tarte d'Agneau* (lamb pie), 54
  White Russian, 106
Pineapple
  Snow, 104
  Broiled Slices, 131
  Glaze, Parsnips in, 113
*Pommes Dijon* (potatoes), 115
Pork, 46–53
  in Apple Cider, 46
  Apricot-Almond Glazed, 46
  Barbecued Spareribs, 47
  *Cassoulet*, 52
  Chops
    *alla Parmigiana* on Toasted Garlic Bread, 50
    Baked Stuffed, 47
    in a Jiffy, 50
  *Choucroute Garni*, 48
  Chow Mein, 51
  Country-Style Ribs in Tangy Sauce, 51
  ground
    *Creton*, 21
    Maman's Special *Tourtiere*, 50
    *Ragoût de Poule aux Boulettes*, 57
  Loin Roast Lyonnaise, 49
  Rich Man-Poor Man Chops "Roquefort," 53
  Sweet and Sour, 52
Porky Melons, 24
*Potage Canadienne* (pea soup), 34
Potatoes, 114–118
  Baked, Three Ways, 114
    Hand Warmers, 114
    Yummy Puppies, 114
  Baked Stuffed, Four Ways, 114
    Bleu Cheese Bakers, 114
    New England "Stuffies," 114
    Roman Style, 114
  Boiled, 115
    *au Gratin*, 115
    in Lemon Sauce, 115
    Lyonnaise, 115
    *Pommes Dijon*, 115
  *Bordeaux,* 116

Canadian Potato Salad, 83
Cookout, 116
Foil-Baked, 116
Hashed Brown, 116
Quick-Bake, 117
  Cheddar-Garlic Bake, 117
  Chili and Cheese Bakes, 117
  Onion Bake, 117
Shoestring, 117
*Vichyssoise de Québec*, 35
Whipped, 117
  Almondine, 117
  Chantilly, 117
  Cheese-Chive, 118
Potatoes, Sweet, à la Sugar Shack, 119
Potted Cheese, 24
*Poulet à l'Ail Chablis* (garlic chicken), 62
*Poulet Suisse* (chicken in cheese fondue), 63
Pudding
  Hot Orange, 101
  T-Bea's Rice, 106
  Yorkshire, 124
Pumpkin, Stuffed, 118
Pumpkin Soup, Brandied, 28

Quiche Lorraine with Pistachios, 91
Quiche, Mini Seafood, 24
Quick-Bake Potatoes, Four Ways, 117

*Ragoût d'Agneau aux Petits Pois* (lamb stew with peas), 55
*Ragoût de Boeuf* (beef stew), 41
*Ragoût de Poule aux Boulettes* (chicken stew with pork meatballs), 57
Rainbow Trout *Italiano*, 76
Raspberry-Filled Cookies, 105
Ratatouille in Toasted Bread Cups, 111
Rice
  Almond, 126
  Bacon-Fried, 126
  Carrot, 127
  and Cheese Squares, 127
  *au Gratin*, 126
  Oriental Steamed, 126
  Pudding, T-Bea's, 106
Rich Man-Poor Man Chops "Roquefort," 53
Rich Man-Poor Man Seafood Thermidor in Shells, 76
Rich Man-Poor Man Steak *au Poivre*, 41
Rita's Cinnamon Apple Roll, 105
Rita's Mystery Canapes, 26
Rita's Perfect Pastry Crust, 105
Roast Chicken with Fruit and Nut Stuffing, 63
Roast Duckling in Brandied Orange-Raspberry Sauce, 68
Roasted Corn, 110

Roman Style Potatoes, 114
Roquefort Cheese Dressing, 88
*Rôti d'Agneau Provencal* (roast lamb), 53
*Rôti de Porc aux Patates Brunes* (Roast Pork,
    Canadian Style), 51

Salad Dressings, 87–89
    Cream Cheese and Nectar, 87
    Herbal Vinaigrette, 87
    Ice Cream, 87
    Italian Cheese, 88
    Lemonade, 88
    Low-Calorie Celery-Seed, 88
    Maman's Parisian, 88
    Mayonnaise, Lemon-Flavored, 21
    Mayonnaise, Orange, 82
    Oriental, 87
    Roquefort Cheese, 88
    Slavic, 89
Salads, 79–87
    Athenian, 82
    Avocado Sunshine, with Orange
        Mayonnaise, 82
    Banana Split, 83
    Camille's Vegetable Dinner Salad, 79
    Canadian Potato, 83
    Cheesy-Crouton, 84
    Cranberry and Fruit, 86
    Creamy Chicken in Tomato, 79
    Cucumber and Onion Slices in Sour Cream,
        84
    Easy and Grand Caesar Salad, 84
    Fresh Fruit à la Grand Marnier, 85
    Frozen Cheese and Strawberry, 85
    Gabrielle's Green Salad, 85
    Jellied Waldorf Salad, 86
    Maman's Golden Salad, 86
    Savory Salmon Mousse with Herbal
        Vinaigrette Dressing, 80
    Spinach-Mandarin Salad with Oriental
        Dressing, 87
    Steak and Mushroom Dinner Salad, 80
Salmon
    Baked Steaks Sebago, 70
    Pie, Maman's, 75
    Sauce in Patty Shells, Maman's, 75
    Savory Mousse, 80
Salters' Stuffed Bread, 92
Salty's No Sugar-No Salt Bran Muffins, 124
Sauce
    Apricot, 58
    Apricot-Almond Glaze, 46
    Béarnaise, 43
    Brandied Orange-Raspberry, 68
    Brandied Raspberry, 47
    Brother Paul's "Italian Sauce Parmigiana,"
        38

Cumberland, 64
Hot Pepper, 22
Lemon, for new potatoes, 115
Macadamia, 74
Marinara, 74
Monique, 74
Mornay, 75
Peach Glaze, 58
Pineapple Glaze, 113
Pommery, 58
Suprême, 65
Sweet and Sour, 66
white, Canadian Style (Thin, Medium,
    Thick), 129
*Saucisson en Croûte* (sausage in pastry), 26
Sausage
    *Cassoulet*, 52
    *Saucisson en Croûte*, 26
Sautéed Calf's Liver with Bacon Rolls and
    Broiled Bananas, 42
Savory London Broil Steak, 42
Savory Salmon Mousse with Herbal
    Vinaigrette Dressing, 80
Scallops
    Broiled in Garlic Butter, 72
    Soy-Glazed, 77
Scones, Fruit, 124
Seasoned Salt, 17
Sesame Chicken with Cumberland Sauce, 64
Sherbet
    Lemon, 103
    Instant Strawberry Ice, 102
Shoestring Potatoes, 117
Shrimp
    in Beer Batter, 25
    Baked Stuffed Jumbo, 71
    Stew, Maine, 33
Sirloin Steak, Three Ways, 43
    Béarnaise, 43
    Onion-Buttered, 43
    Teriyaki, 43
Skewers of Baked French Bread and Cheese, 26
Slavic Dressing, 89
Slumber Milk, Claire's, 133
Smoked Oyster Spread, 26
Sole
    Applejack Filet of, 69
    Baked Stuffed Filet of, 70
    Filet of, Oriental, 73
Soufflés, Individual Grand Marnier, 102
Soups 28–35
    Beef
        Basic Stock, 31
        *Ragoût de Boeuf*, 41
        Stew *Maison,* 37
    Blueberry, Cold Maine, 29
    Carrot, Cream of, 30
    Cauliflower, Cream of, 30

Cheese, Canadian with *Grands-Pères,* 28
Cherry and fruit, 29
chicken, *(Ragoût de Poule aux Boulettes),* 57
Clam Chowder, New England, 33
Corn, Oriental Style, 30
egg drop. *See* Chicken "Fondue," 66
Haddock, Creamy Stew, 31
lamb *(Ragoût d'Agneau aux Petits Pois),* 55
Lobster Stew *à la Canadienne,* 33
Onion, French *au Gratin,* 31
pea *(Potage Canadienne),* 34
potato and leek *(Vichyssoise de Québec),* 35
Pumpkin, Brandied, 28
shrimp custard *(Chawan-Mushi),* 29
Shrimp Stew, Maine, 33
Squash, Hubbard, 32
Swiss Chard, 34
Tomato-Cheese, 35
vegetable
    Gazpacho Monique, 32
    Spring Greens, 34
Zucchini Cream, 35
Soy-Glazed Scallops, 77
Soy-Sauced Chicken Bake, 64
Spiced Hot Peaches, 131
Spinach
    Elegante, 118
    and Grapefruit Sauté, 118
    Mandarin Salad with Oriental Dressing, 87
    Noodles with Cream Sauce, 125
Spring Greens Soup, 34
Squash
    Acorn Bake with Fruit, 119
    Blue Hubbard and Marmalade Purée, 119
    Hubbard, Soup, 32
    Pattypan, Fried, 119
Standing Rib Roast of Beef, *au Jus,* 43
Steak Diane, 43
Steak and Mushroom Dinner Salad, 80
Steak Roast Wrap with Vegetables, 44
Steak Tartare *en Croûte,* 44
Sticky Caramel Buns, 123
Stir-Fried Broccoli, 108
Stir-Fried Chicken and Cashews, 65
Strawberries
    Belle-Isle, 100
    in Chocolate Fondue, 106
    Marinated, and Kiwi, 103
Strawberry
    Butter, 128
    Crêpes, 99
    Mariette's Fresh pie, 103
    Salad, Frozen Cheese and, 85
    shake (Big Dave), 133
Stuffed Cannelloni, 92
Stuffed Chicken Breasts Polynesian in Sauce
    Suprême, 65
Stuffed French Bread, 124

Stuffed Pumpkin, 118
Stuffed Whole Maine Lobster, 77
Stuffing, Fruit and Nut, 63
Sweet Potatoes à la Sugar Shack, 119
Sweet and Sour Pork, 52
Swiss Chard Soup, 34
Swiss Cheese and Ham Fondue, 94

Tangy Cheddar Spread, 25
*Tarte d'Agneau* (lamb pie), 54
T-Bea's Rice Pudding, 106
Tea
    Minted Iced, 132
    Monique's Orange Mix, 132
Teriyaki Rib Roast of Beef, 45
Teriyaki Sirloin Steak, 43
Tomato
    Broiled Slices, 120
    Butter, 128
    Cheese Soup, 35
    and Onion Simmer, 120
Tomatoes *Dijon,* 120
Tony Buyo, 132
Trout, Rainbow *Italiano,* 76
Tuna Patricia, 78
Turkey
    *alla Parmigiana,* 67
    Breast Tarragon, 67
    Hickory-Smoked, 67
Twelfth Cake *(Galette des Rois),* 101

Veal
    Fricassée, 55
    Jeannine, 56
Vegetables, 107–121. *See also*
    individual listings.
    Camille's Dinner Salad, 79
    Christmas Wreath of, 20
    Fresh, Casserole, 93
    Fresh Green, with lemon, 111
    Fresh, with Onion Butter, 112
    Fresh, Stir-Fry, 111
    Gazpacho Monique (chilled soup), 32
    Ratatouille in Toasted Bread Cups, 111
Vichy Carrots, 109
*Vichyssoise de Québec* (potato-leek soup), 35

Walnut-Stuffed Mushrooms *(Champignon Farci de Noix),* 25
Watermelon rind preserves (Porky Melons), 24
Whipped Potatoes, Four Ways, 117
White Fish Piquant, 78
White Russian Pie, 106
White Sauce, Canadian Style (Thin, Medium, Thick), 129

Wok Pepper Steak, 45

Yorkshire Pudding, 124
Yule Log *(Bûche de Noël),* 97
Yummy Puppies (potatoes), 114

Zucchini
  with Anisette, 120
  with Corn, 121
  Cream Soup, 35